Behavior, Social Problems, and Change

Behavior, Social Problems, and Change

A Social Learning Approach

John H. Kunkel

Prentice-Hall, Inc.
Englewood Cliffs, New Jersey

Library of Congress Cataloging in Publication Data

KUNKEL, JOHN H.
   Behavior, social problems, and change.

   (Prentice-Hall social learning series)
   Bibliography: p.
   Includes index.
   1. Sociology—Methodology.   2. Social psychology.
3. Social problems.   4. Social change.   I. Title.
[DNLM: 1. Social behavior.   2. Social problems.
3. Social change.   HM291 K96b]
HM24.K86   301.1   75-2069
ISBN   0-13-073924-3

PRINTED IN THE UNITED STATES OF AMERICA

PRENTICE-HALL INTERNATIONAL, INC., *London*
PRENTICE-HALL OF AUSTRALIA, PTY. LTD., *Sydney*
PRENTICE-HALL OF CANADA, LTD., *Toronto*
PRENTICE-HALL OF INDIA PRIVATE LIMITED, *New Delhi*
PRENTICE-HALL OF JAPAN, INC., *Tokyo*
PRENTICE-HALL OF SOUTHEAST ASIA (PTE.) LTD., *Singapore*

Contents

Preface

F ew people can face the upheavals of our time with equanimity, for too much of the present and too much of the future are at stake. Indeed, it is tempting to say that wherever we turn we are confronted by the erosion of old norms and values, by institutions being shaken to their foundations, by new ways of life and thought taking on permanent and perhaps disconcerting forms. But today we cannot afford to think in terms of old analogies which all too often lead to inaction and despair. Rather, we must seek new perspectives and ask questions about the basic characteristics of man and society, their dynamic aspects, and man's role in the design, modification, and guidance of social life.

Knowledge of individuals and social systems, and especially their dynamics, is not only intrinsically interesting but also of great potential utility. Any analysis of society, any dream of designing a better world, any attempt to solve social problems, and any program to initiate, accelerate, direct, or reduce social change, no matter how idealistic or humanitarian its impetus, must begin with general ideas about the nature of man and social systems, their amenability to change, and those agencies, including man himself, that have the power to effect change. The quality of our assumptions about man and society, as well as of our conceptions of their dynamics, greatly influences the probability that the formation of designs and the implementation of programs will be successful. In this book we will describe how such images and conceptions can be evaluated and improved, and how they can be applied to the analysis of social problems and the designing of social programs.

The comprehensive study of social problems and the designing of effective programs for their solution are large-scale undertakings that require the cooperative effort of experts in several fields. No one book can attempt to do justice to the complexity of these topics, and indeed the best volumes in these areas are collaborative achievements. The aims of this book are twofold. First, we will present a behavioral perspective of social problems and plans, based on a model of man derived from principles of social learning. Second, we will outline a set of procedures that are useful in analyzing particular social problems and their causes. There will be sufficient detail and illustration to enable interested readers to engage in the study of those social problems that concern them. In addition, we will outline the steps that should be taken in the designing of effective social programs. A number of comprehensive examples of varying complexity will show how one might devise programs in areas of one's interest, or at least evaluate the adequacy and likely outcomes of programs discussed in the mass media. Hence the book will provide a sound basis for active participation in the analysis and solution of today's social problems.

The learning principles underlying the perspective of this book have been a major concern of psychology for several years. So far, most researchers have been content to discover, test, and elucidate behavioral propositions and their immediate implications; but recently a few hardy souls have leapt boldly from basic principles to philosophical points embracing such issues as freedom and dignity. The courage of these adventurers is admirable indeed, but those who watch them cannot help but ask whether their leap is valid, whether their description of the landing place is accurate, and whether that place foreshadows man's future.

This book surveys the terrain beneath the leap. Our point of departure is today's knowledge of behavioral principles, and our path is laid out by the logical ramifications of these principles for various aspects of social life, and especially for social problems and plans. We will proceed slowly and carefully, without regard for those who have jumped and are before us.

Most of this book was written while I held a fellowship at the Center for Advanced Study in the Behavioral Sciences, at Stanford, California. I wish to express my appreciation to the Center's staff and my colleagues there for providing a halcyon atmosphere unequalled anywhere. To my colleagues and friends who read and advised me on the manuscript, and especially to Albert Bandura, Reuben Hill, Orrin Klapp, Ronald Perry, and Kenneth Westhues, I extend my deepest gratitude.

J. H. K.

Behavior, Social Problems, and Change

1
Models and
Social Life

W hy do best intentions, hard work, and an indomitable spirit so rarely succeed in creating the land and life of our dreams? A significant part of the answer lies in the assumptions we make about human nature and the character of social life, the images of man and society we build into our programs, and the visions that populate our dreams. Only when our assumptions, images, and visions reflect reality or come reasonably close to it might success come to our efforts; when they markedly differ from reality we cannot help but fail. In this book we will examine some of these assumptions and images, describe their roles in social analysis, and indicate how valid images of man can be used to design and implement effective social programs.

As we look at the world, we cannot escape the question of how we should react to the social problems and changes that surround us. We may accept the problems, try to reduce them, or seek to build a society in which they no longer exist. We may accept change, attempt to stifle or accelerate it, or seek to channel it to create a better world. However we react, whether we are interested in solving social problems, in guiding social change, or even if we only want to understand what is going on in today's world, we must know the answers to some fundamental questions: To what extent are social problems and change due to the basic character of man, and to what extent are they the results of societal factors? Do individuals play a significant role in guiding change, or do social forces predominate? Since our answers will influence our analyses, shape our policies, and direct our efforts, we must be sure that they reflect the best of what is known today rather than merely what we wish to believe.[1]

If societal forces are significant, then we must know them in order to circumvent, guide, or accept them; but if human characteristics determine problems and change, then we must take them into account in our analyses and programs. Only on the basis of accurate knowledge in these areas—rather than philosophical speculation or wishful thinking—can we hope to intervene successfully in solving social problems and in designing a viable future. Effective policies and programs depend on our attempts to alter what is modifiable and on our accepting whatever cannot be changed, no matter how unpalatable this may turn out to be. The proportion of social life which can be changed and over which man has some control is as yet unknown; we *do* know, however, that simplistic hypotheses at any of the extremes—that man is either omnipotent or impotent, that social forces are either the sole determinant or without significance—are incorrect. Furthermore, not only are the nature of man and the character of society relevant here, but so also are the kind of man, the time, the place, and the circumstances; in the words of Mills, "men are free to make history, but some men are much freer than others."[2] Hence it is important to ask: How good are our observations and analyses, what do they add up to, and how do they contribute to our understanding of social life?

In the past, answering these and similar questions was regarded as an end in itself, significant in that it helped us delineate the character of society. Today, however, other questions are being added, centering on what we might do to solve or reduce the many problems which confront us in our own country and abroad. Knowledge of social life by itself is increasingly considered irrelevant, and social scientists are asked with growing urgency to use their knowledge for humanitarian purposes.[3]

Today we face questions not only about the definition of "problems," the meaning of "irrelevance," and the assessment of "humanitarian" purposes, but also about the character of our knowledge of social life. When knowledge becomes the foundation and source of policies and programs, and when sociological propositions begin to give birth to action rather than articles, it becomes necessary to evaluate the accuracy of information and the validity of interpretations. The first step in this direction is the recognition that, when it comes to complex phenomena, especially those of social

[1] For a discussion of these considerations, see Geertz (1965); Gerth and Mills (1953). The titles of references are located in the bibliography section at the end of the book, under the author's name and publication date.

[2] Mills (1959), p. 181.

[3] For the classic discussion of this topic, see Lynd (1939).

life, we usually think not only in terms of concrete events and facts but also in terms of more general and abstract images or models.

MODELS OF SOCIAL LIFE

In scientific discourse a "model" is a set of assumptions one makes about any particular phenomenon in order to describe and explain the structure and operations one observes. It is much more limited and specific than a theory, although many theories contain models.[4] In astronomy, for example, the "Ptolemaic model" of our planetary system which placed the earth in the center, dominated man's view of the universe until the sixteenth century. Today we accept the "Copernican model," which tells us not only about the paths and velocities of planets and their satellites, but enables us to predict conjunctions, eclipses, and the courses interplanetary rockets must take.

When information about a subject is scant there are likely to be several models attempting to explain it, but as knowledge accumulates some of the models turn out to be inadequate and drop out, until finally only one is generally accepted. For example, today there are several models of stellar evolution, two major models of the universe's origin, but only one of our planetary system's operation. In the social sciences, information about social phenomena is as yet incomplete and subject to different interpretations, hence we find a number of models about the character of man and society.[5]

One cannot study societal structures and processes, social problems and their causes and solutions, or be interested in guiding social change, without models of man and of society. Even when one does not use the term "model" as such, the assumptions one makes about man and society are an inextricable part of the analysis; in fact, "the models with which we work, apart from being useful tools, determine to no small extent our general perspectives, our selection of [analytical] problems, and the em-

---

[4]While models may be part of a theory, they are not equivalent to it. Models are generally rather small sets of propositions referring to a limited number of characteristics of a phenomenon, while theories are usually more comprehensive sets of interrelated propositions, mainly concerned with the *explanation* of larger wholes or the relationship between these phenomena and others. Models are often descriptive but may develop into or give rise to full-fledged theories. The Copernican model of the planetary system, for example, relates various observations and events without really explaining them. The explanations depend on propositions outside the model, in this case the Newtonian laws of physics. At the same time, of course, the model is a reflection of the operation of these laws. Thus models are usually rather small parts of theories, which influence them to some extent, as we will see in the following chapters.

[5]For an example, see Wrong (1961).

phasis of our explanations."[6] Thus, while sociologists still debate the existence or even the possibility of value-free social science, there can be no doubt that a model-free sociology is impossible.[7]

Models of man are sets of propositions about those selected characteristics of human beings which one deems to be important elements of social systems and their dynamics. The variety of such models is large, and the differences among them are quite profound.[8] For example, Freud's model of man includes the assumption that aggression is largely the result of natural internal forces, while Bandura's postulates that aggression is largely the result of learning. Both models have their followers, and both have been used in explanations of social events as well as in individual therapy.

The assumptions one makes about various aspects of man's nature both determine and limit much of one's view of social life.[9] For example, if one believes that man is basically "good"—leaving aside, for the moment, problems of definition and empirical referents—one will evaluate societies and design communities accordingly. That is, one will probably criticize many presently existing features as "repressive" or excessively limiting, and, in designing a new social system, one will probably want to eliminate many traditional rules and sanctions since the natural goodness of man makes them unnecessary. Conversely, if one postulates that man is basically "evil" or sinful, it is rather difficult to criticize restrictions as such; hence the policies one advocates and the utopia one designs are likely to have a considerable number of rules, sanctions, and means of enforcing them.

Models of society are sets of propositions—sometimes called "domain assumptions"[10] —about those aspects of society which are assumed to determine and limit both its own character and the nature and quality of human existence within it.[11] For example, if one views society as an organism developing in accord with its own internal laws, the roles which man can play are small and the future is predetermined. But if one believes that society is a dynamic system without a preordained course, man's role in determining the character of his society is very much greater, and he can participate in designing the future.[12] In the case of the organism-model there is little that can be done about social problems and policy options

        [6]Dahrendorf (1958), p. 125.

        [7]Warshay (1971). For a general discussion of models of man, see Kunkel and Garrick (1969).

        [8]For examples, see Hitt (1969); Simon (1957).

        [9]For examples, see Bendix (1970), chapter 1; Kunkel (1967; 1970).

        [10]Gouldner (1970).

        [11]For examples, see Bendix (1970), chapter 5.

        [12]Boguslaw (1965); Kunkel (1966).

are severely restricted, while in a systems-model deliberate human intervention in social processes can be quite effective.

Citizens, public officials, and social scientists, cannot help but employ models of man and of society in their descriptions and analyses of social phenomena, processes, and problems. In fact, much of the information that comes to us in the course of daily life is imbued with sense only insofar as we view it within the context of our models. For example, when we read that the crime rate is rising, we usually react in terms of our own models. "Well," we might say, "what can you expect from evil man . . . from a city machine which is unresponsive to social needs . . . from a society which perverts the inherent goodness of man?" It is from such reflections that we derive "obvious"—but not necessarily effective—solutions to the problem of crime.

The need to exercise care in selecting our models can be illustrated by the fact that it was once fashionable to regard aggressive behavior as stemming from a quantum of internally generated aggressive energy. It followed from this premise that we should encourage people to vent their aggressions in acceptable ways in order to make them less aggressive in the future. But impressive evidence supports a contrary model, which assumes that aggression is learned and maintained by positive consequences, so that aggressive acts, if successful, lead only to further aggression. It follows that, in deciding how to react to aggression or in designing a social system to cope with it, we should employ the second model, discouraging expressions of aggression and eliminating its positive consequences.[13]

As we look at the role played by canneries, oil refineries, and sewage plants in the pollution of lakes and rivers, we might conclude that organizations, being by nature benevolent, forward-looking, ecology-minded, and altruistic, will change their operations on their own volition. It is only when we have a rather different model of organizations that it even begins to make sense to establish the Federal Water Quality Administration and a series of heavy fines. In general, laws without teeth are based on rather benevolent and altruistic models of organizations and of man, while stringent laws postulate quite different models. The differential effectiveness of the two types of laws tells us in no uncertain terms which type of model is the more valid one. Indeed, the failure of many utopian communities has been ascribed to the implicit, inconsistent, and often invalid models of man on which they were based.[14]

To illustrate the variety of models available, their implications, and the kinds of contradictions among them, we will consider some aspects of two well-known models of man and of society. First, according to Ashley

[13]Bandura (1973); Berkovitz (1973).
[14]Boguslaw (1965), pp. 60 ff.; Richter (1971); Veysey (1973).

Montagu, "it is not evil babies who grow up into evil human beings, but an evil society which turns good babies into disordered adults, and it does so on a regimen of frustration. Babies are born good and desirous of continuing to be good."[15] Sigmund Freud's assumptions were quite different; he thought that "men are not gentle, friendly creatures wishing for love, who simply defend themselves if they are attacked, but that a powerful measure of desire for aggression has to be reckoned as part of their instinctual endowment. . . . [Hence] civilized society is perpetually menaced with disintegration through this primary hostility of men toward one another. . . . Culture has to call up every possible reinforcement in order to erect barriers against the aggressive instincts of men and hold their manifestations in check."[16]

According to Montagu's models, society is the major source of individual and social difficulties, while man is basically innocent. Adults would retain some and perhaps all of their natural goodness if there were less frustration, *i.e.*, if there were less repression and fewer barriers.[17] Presumably, such good adults would then create a less evil society containing less frustration for future generations to deal with. According to Freud's models, man himself is the major source of individual and social difficulties. Society protects him from his own destructive instincts. Thus, while one might want to alter some political and social features of a particular nation, many barriers and a considerable amount of repression will always be needed for man's own good, and any program of action will have to take man's aggressive nature into account.

A number of interesting questions arise when we compare these two sets of models and their implications. In order to determine why they are contradictory, we might ask on what evidence they are based. Here we would not only have to evaluate empirical studies but also consider the model builder's selective perception and his interpretation of his own and others' experiences and observations. Furthermore, it is possible that the builders had some *a priori* conceptions which they fortified with data that seemed to fit. Hence it is difficult to know whether these models consist of postulates taken for granted or of hypotheses which have been carefully tested.

The two models of society are consistent with the models of man and may indeed be viewed as their logical correlates. Again, however, we will want to know on what independent evidence these models are based; the answers involve the same difficulties and are likely to be similar.

When we take a superficial look at empirical evidence, be it experi-

---

[15]Quoted in Dobzhansky (1959), p. 80.
[16]Freud (1930), pp. 85–86.
[17]Montagu (1955), chapter 12.

mental research, observations, or historical facts (as we know them), we are likely to find some support for *both* sets. At the same time, however, it will be quite difficult if not impossible to accumulate convincing evidence to fully support *either* set. Since the social environment begins to affect human beings at birth (and indirectly even before), it is impossible to determine whether man is "by nature" loving or aggressive; and since a social system consists mainly of adults who have learned their ways in one or another part of that system, it will be difficult to demonstrate that society is "naturally" benevolent or evil.

IMPLICATIONS OF MODELS

The models of man and of society we use affect our conception of the world, our views of current and future events, and our beliefs about the role of man in solving social problems and guiding social change. All of these enter into practical questions concerning the nature of policies and the character of social programs large and small. In any attempt to determine a model's implications, we face two major uncertainties: the validity of propositions and the adequacy of logical deductions. But if our model and logic are valid, then the implications we derive must be correct, no matter how strange or unpalatable they may be.

As an illustration, let us consider three propositions commonly found in psychodynamic models of man: "Behavior is largely a function of a person's internal state," "the internal state is formed largely before the age of ten," and "once formed, internal states can change only slowly, if at all." We also have a proposition about society: "A social system consists largely of the activities of individuals." What implications follow?

When we observe people around us, it is evident that most adults do not change their behaviors, life styles, and ways of thinking very much or very quickly. An explanation would focus on the inertia of man's internal state, and the characteristics of society would be deemed largely irrelevant, for they are the *results* of this inertia. If we observe rather slow rates of fundamental social change (for example, in the area of race relations), the determinants of this rate must be sought in the slowness with which behaviors and beliefs change. Any major changes in thought and action are likely to take place between and not within generations.[18] If we now add the societal proposition, we see that low rates of behavior change lead to slow changes in the social system. Within any one family, change will occur in spurts, as manifested in the generation gap. Since the causes of low rates of social change lie in the nature of man, it makes little sense to

[18]As described by Inkeles (1959).

even attempt deliberate guidance on the societal level. No such effort can be successful since it cannot influence anyone above the age of, say, ten or twelve. The overall conclusion is likely to be some variant of the phrase that one cannot legislate change or morality.

But let us consider another model of man, based on learning theories. Here the relevant propositions are: "Behavior is learned," "learning is largely a function of external events," and "learning continues throughout life." We will retain the proposition that social systems consist of behavior patterns. What implications follow?

Now when we are asked why most adults do not change their behaviors, life styles, or ways of thinking very much, the answer lies in the overall continuity of the fundamental social context, *i.e.* in the fact that most adults do not, and need not, learn much that is new in order to get by in their daily lives.[19] For example, fancy types of appliances do not require different basic behavior patterns from those which existed when simpler appliances were the rule. And, while there is some social mobility, most people die in the same class into which they were born. Thus, the determinants of rather low rates of fundamental social change (for example, in the area of race relations) must be sought in the various factors which influence the structure and operation of the social system itself. Since new activities are learned when the social context changes, significant changes in behavior and beliefs can occur within individuals as well as between generations.[20] Consequently it is possible to initiate and guide social change and to "legislate morality" within the constraints imposed by principles of learning. Programs of successful action are theoretically possible and can be attempted within the limitations arising from ethical and practical considerations.

It is evident, then, that the model of man we use determines to a large extent what we consider to be the causes of both stagnation and change —either man or the social system itself—and what one might be able to do about it—very little or quite a bit. Furthermore, the expertise required for outlining a policy and the techniques needed for the implementation of programs are greatly dependent upon our model of man. The first model described above focuses our attention on psychological methods such as individual and group therapy, while the second requires us to understand the structure and operation of social systems and to work for their modification. The proposition about society—that it consists of people's activities —then directs attention to behavior change which, according to learning models of man, is quite possible if we know the principles of behavior and can apply them.

[19]Lipset (1963), pp. 102–103.
[20]For illustrations, see Becker (1964; 1968).

As we consider what might be done about social problems and the guidance of social change, we may be tempted to limit our choice to only two quite different paths. First, we can insist on trying to find the real cause of a particular problem and on dealing with the problem at its roots. We would begin by developing a causal theory, or using someone else's theory, until we are sure that we have firm grounds for proposing a particular course of action. Second, we can simply go ahead and do something to ameliorate a serious situation, if necessary without any explicit theoretical justification. Here we would disregard "causes" and concentrate on action instead. But neither approach is likely to bring about the development of effective policies and successful programs at the time they are needed. There are two major reasons for this. First, the development and testing of complete and, in the social sciences, necessarily elaborate causal theories requires much time and effort. Second, actions which are more or less "blind" are usually no more effective than inaction and may indeed be worse, as we will see in later chapters.

But there is a third alternative, which should be carefully considered. Here we reject the assumption that a complete and tested causal theory must underlie a program, or even that we should have a "quasi-theory."[21] Instead, we propose that a valid model of man (and, to a lesser extent, one of society) is one part of an adequate foundation for general policies and specific programs. The other part consists of accurate knowledge of past and present events relevant to the subject of interest, be it a particular social problem or the guidance of a specific aspect of society. Together they will allow us to make predictions and to design programs. A valid and complete causal theory would be good to have, of course, but in its absence a model of man and of society with solid empirical foundations will do, particularly since such models will be important parts of any theory that may be developed later on.

For example, if one assumes that organizations are basically altruistic and benevolent, then society need not regulate them, and any policy of restricting their operations would be not only redundant but possibly harmful for society itself. But if the model of organizations includes the proposition that they are basically self-serving,[22] then both regulations and strict surveillance are necessary to protect the interests of individuals. Similarly, if government is seen as a benign instrument for bringing about the coordination of diverse interests and activities, men need not distrust or fear the state. But if one views government as the servant of certain interests against others or as a set of self-centered organizations, every man must be on his guard lest others get the better of him.

[21]Hewitt and Hall (1973); Schorr (1971).
[22]For a classic statement, see Michels (1949).

MAJOR USES OF MODELS

Both models of man and of society, once their validity has been established in terms of available empirical evidence, play a major role in the three steps that lead to the solution of social problems, the designing of better societies, and the guidance of social change; that is, they are essential for the evaluation of the present situation, the definition of future goals, and the design of programs to reach them.

Models of man and of society provide the significant criteria—and perhaps the only ones—for the evaluation of existing institutions, customs, governmental and other programs, and even current philosophies of change. For example, if one's model of man holds that self-actualization and personal growth are fundamental human drives, and if one has reason to conclude that these can be achieved only in a free environment, then a relatively unstructured classroom and a flexible curriculum are required. Many existing schools, therefore, would be judged inadequate if not injurious. Models also provide an important basis for the general definition and the specific delineation of goals which policies and programs are designed to achieve.

In general, a model can be used as a basis for evaluation of actual circumstances and delineation of goals only when it is explicit and consists of empirically founded propositions. Implicit models make the assessment of existing social phenomena and historical events difficult and extremely unreliable, while the lack of empirically well-founded propositions within the model give both the assessor and the evaluation process an aura of idiosyncracy. Furthermore, models containing vague terms, such as "universal love" or "spirit," cannot readily be tested as to their validity, and therefore make it difficult to design specific programs and to set up criteria for measuring the success of these programs. Yet such models are sometimes inspiring even when the policies to which they give rise often are not. Explicit and specific models and the goals we derive from them, conversely, often provide little inspiration, and the necessary policies and programs, which are usually just as specific and hence have a prosaic air, are rarely popular, if only because they tell us what must be done and who must do it. Vague goals and implicit models provide a certain degree of comfort and security.

It is only a small step from the assessment of the present situation and the delineation of a goal to an outline of appropriate programs. The model of man usually indicates *what* should be done, while models of organizations and of society indicate what *can* be done and *how* it might be done. For example, the self-actualizing proposition tells us what schools should be like, while the school model and the community model tell us what can be done and how—whether to issue demands or to lobby, whether to rely on pressure extended by students or by psychologists, whether to argue on the basis of facts or opinions, whether or not to threaten the school board with the next election, or what combination of these and other methods are most likely to be effective.

A good illustration of the roles that models of man play in the designing of social structures and operations—and of the need to revise a model when it turns out to be incorrect—is provided by the two models which are assumed to underlie modern industrial organizations.[23] Model "X" postulates that man is weak and dependent, cannot take care of himself, shuns responsibility, and seeks external controls. Management, therefore, must not only operate in terms of material incentives and extensive controls but must also provide security and other forms of psychological reinforcement. Plants that operate on such a basis, however, continue to have labor problems, and workers in general have been quite dissatisfied. Since factory and office operations are always based on a particular model of man, the problems and failures they encounter are obviously a consequence of the model, or at least of some of the propositions within it. An alternative is model "Y," which holds that man is independent, seeks responsibility, and works not only for wages but also for the more or less intrinsic satisfactions inherent in the job, be it on an assembly line or in an office. Thus management should structure working conditions so as to include responsibility; individuals should have some control over what they do and how they do it; and there should be some means for providing satisfaction in the work itself. Peter Drucker has examined the "Y" model in the light of recent evidence and has described the ways in which work might be organized in accordance with human requirements derived from the model—for example, by the creation of "work modules."[24]

Even when we have an explicit model whose constituent propositions are based on good empirical evidence, we are a long way from a better world or even an improved organization. The *implementation* of a design based on a valid model of man is a difficult and arduous task that requires much work, patience, and willingness to experiment, reject, and start again. This can be done in industry and on the level of individual organizations, but similar programs on a societal level have yet to be seriously considered.

CONCLUSION

In this chapter we have discussed some of the difficulties which confront modern attempts to solve social problems as well as historical attempts to construct problem-free societies. The major problems are a

[23]McGregor (1960).
[24]Drucker (1974).

reluctance to recognize the significance of models of man and society and the widespread failure to examine their validity and implications. He who does not evaluate his model, be it for political, ethical, philosophical, or religious reasons, in effect bets on his omniscience and perfection. So far, most who have done this have lost.

We are led to the conclusion, therefore, that one must ask—and answer—a series of questions concerning every description and analysis of social phenomena, every policy and program of problem solution, and every design of social change:

1. What model of man is being employed?
2. What model of society is being employed?
3. How valid is each of these models?
4. Could better or more valid models be used?
5. How would these new models change the descriptions and analyses?
6. What policies, programs, and designs can be derived from the new models?

In the following chapters we will describe some procedures for answering these questions. We begin by examining models of man.

2
Models
of Man

The study and evaluation of models of man are often difficult, for when we look at human beings illusions are rife, wishful thinking and disappointments are common, and inarticulate dreams often overwhelm us.[1] Not until we make our model of man explicit and objectively assess its propositions can we shed illusions, reduce wishful thinking, and awaken; and it is only when we confront, evaluate, and, if necessary, modify a model of man that dreams for the future have a chance of being transformed into reality rather than nightmares. Consider, for example, the model proposed by Maslow: "The human being is so constructed that he presses toward fuller and fuller being and this means pressing toward what most people would call good values, toward serenity, kindness, courage, knowledge, honesty, love, unselfishness, and goodness."[2] This view of man may inspire us, but it is vague and difficult to validate and will be of little use in the analysis and design of social systems. Well-founded propositions which give us answers to important questions, conversely, will be of great value even when they consist only of prosaic phrases and contain no inspiring words.

[1] For a good discussion, see Langer (1969). Historical and literary interpretations of models of man are found in Lowenthal (1957); for a variety of modern views on the nature of man, see Doniger (1962).

[2] Maslow (1959), p. 126.

BASIC CHARACTERISTICS OF
MODELS OF MAN

In his *Essay on Man* the philosopher Ernst Cassirer proposes that "man's outstanding characteristic, his distinguishing mark, is not his metaphysical or physical nature—but his work. It is this work, it is the system of human activities, which defines and determines the circle of 'humanity.' Language, myth, religion, art, science, history are the constituents, the various sectors of this circle."[3] But while it is sometimes desirable for the sake of perspective to be aware of these marvelous complexities of man, students of social systems only rarely need such a comprehensive image in their work. They have been able to accomplish much with relatively small sets of propositions about limited aspects of man.

When we are interested in a very general understanding of political parties and their operations, for example, a rather simple model will do, while an explanation of social change will require a considerably more complex model. Students of population need one set of propositions, while he who studies religious movements will need another. Deciding which components will be included ultimately depends on the requirements of a particular analysis, and it is to be expected that different problem areas will require different models of man.[4] The choice of components will also be influenced by the builder's theoretical perspective, perhaps by his religious, political, and philosophical ideas, as well as by the tenor of the times and thus may seem to have a somewhat idiosyncratic cast.[5] Yet, while no useful model will contain all human characteristics, ideally the elements which are included will not conflict with those that are left out.

There are two dangers which must be avoided. First, many builders and users of models do not take into account the often significant variations found in any large population. A model's supporting evidence should come from a wide range of studies in order to make sure that what one calls a "model of man" does not turn out to be much more restricted—a "model of *western* man," for example, or even a "model of *nineteenth century males*."[6] A middle-class, white, college-educated American businessman or government official, for instance, may well see the world in terms of a model which does not at all represent "human beings in general" but rather a particular type of man whose specific characteristics largely reflect himself.

The second danger lies in the opposite direction; here one views some characteristics as being unique to a time or place, or the results of a

[3]Cassirer (1944), p. 68.

[4]For an examination of this question, see Dahrendorf (1958).

[5]For illustrations, see Bendix (1970).

[6]For a discussion of such limitations in Freud's model of man, see Jung (1966).

particular situation, when they really are aspects common to all human beings. Feelings of anxiety, alienation, and powerlessness, for example, have been thought to be the consequences of urban life, technology, and bureaucracies. If one believes, in addition, that members of primitive tribes, peasants, people who lived during the Middle Ages, and farmers of the nineteenth century did not have these feelings, one might conclude that it is possible to design societies without alienation and widespread feelings of being powerless to determine the course and quality of one's life.[7] Yet some philosophers—notably Camus and Kierkegaard—have argued quite persuasively that anxiety and powerlessness are part of the human condition rather than of life in urban-industrial society and are, therefore, inescapable. Indeed, anthropological accounts of life in primitive and peasant communities are replete with evidence—in people's behavior, words, and thoughts—that individuals see themselves as being governed by fate and supernatural powers,[8] and other commentators have also recently questioned the presumed correlation between alienation and urban life.[9]

A model of *man in general* can include only common elements and capacities plus those characteristics which *all* human beings acquire through learning. As soon as cultural elements are included, the model's applicability is restricted to those individuals who learn these specific elements as a matter of course—which may or may not include large numbers of people. The separation of innate from cultural characteristics is possible only in the case of explicit models, but even there it is difficult. The best model to build and use, then, will consist of some general propositions applicable to all human beings and other specific propositions which are interchangeable with one another and depend on the specific time, culture, and group with which one is concerned at the moment.[10]

Models of man are not equivalent to descriptions of human nature, for these are generally much broader and more complete than any particular model. Yet the fact that a model of man admittedly concerns only a small part of human nature should not be taken to mean that a model inevitably "distorts" or "perverts" that nature.[11] Neither does "model of man" necessarily refer to personality, personality theory, or personality development. Theories of personality and its development are usually much broader in scope and include many more elements than are found

---

[7]For a good example of a model of man of this type, see Berger *et al.* (1973).

[8]For illustrations of peasant ways and views of the world, see Foster (1965; 1967); Guiteras-Holmes (1961); and Lewis (1964).

[9]For example, see Fischer (1973).

[10]For a discussion of these problems, see Wrong (1961).

[11]This point is often disregarded by critics of "empirical" psychology, for example by Chein (1972).

in most explicit models of man, for these theories must stand by themselves whereas a model of man is only a part of theory and need not stand alone.[12] Yet there is a close relationship between personality theory and models of man, for many if not most of the propositions which make up a model of man are derived from one or another personality theory. Thus we have a classical Freudian model of man, along with neo-Freudian, Jungian, Hullian, and Rogerian models, to name a few.[13] Each model represents a part, and often only a small part, of any theorist's total work.

REQUIREMENTS FOR
A USEFUL MODEL OF MAN

Analysts and designers of social systems, molders of policies and solvers of problems, as well as mere observers, cannot work with just *any* model of man; those presented by biologists or theologians, for example, would probably be of little use. What, then, are the characteristics a model must have if it is to be of use to us? The basic requirements are that it contain *valid propositions* in those areas in which we need to have information. In general, these areas concern man's *behavior* rather than his physiological or spiritual characteristics—except insofar as these might affect his activities. Furthermore, we need detailed information about the *determinants* of behavior, for these are crucial for any understanding of social systems, their structure and operations, and social problems and dynamics. Finally, it is necessary to have considerable knowledge of the ways in which people *interact,* since isolated individuals who go their own ways are rare indeed and contribute little to the structure and operation of communities.

Behavior

An individual's activities not only vary over time but also depend on the circumstances in which he finds himself. New behaviors are learned throughout one's life, other actions are maintained over decades, and some disappear. A useful model of man therefore will be concerned with the issues described below.

1. THE ACQUISITION OF BEHAVIOR. When the frame of reference centers on the individual one usually speaks of learning, and when the person's behavior patterns are emphasized it is common to speak of estab-

---

[12]Langer (1969).

[13]The best descriptions of these and other models are in Hall and Lindzey (1970).

lishing. In any case, the major question for a model to answer here is: How are new activities acquired?

2. THE MAINTENANCE OF BEHAVIOR. Some activities are repeated often, others are seldom performed; some are remembered for a long time, while others are quickly forgotten. A second major question about behavior, then, is: How is it maintained?

3. THE EXTINCTION OF BEHAVIOR. If one learned new activities but never forgot old ones, or if one insisted on daily engaging in every action one had ever learned, organized social life as we know it would not exist. We say that a person is "mature" in part because he does not behave in ways he formerly did, and some problems of old age arise because people continue in their accustomed ways. When we speak of individuals, we may speak of "forgetting"; but when behavior is emphasized it is better to speak of extinction. A third question arises, therefore: How is behavior extinguished?

4. THE MODIFICATION OF BEHAVIOR. Only rarely do activities, especially complex patterns, appear *de novo* or fully developed. Rather, old activities are slowly modified and new complex patterns are gradually built up. In essence, the modification of behavior involves the successive establishment and extinction of a series of activities, until the final activity pattern has been achieved. The need for a specific sequence of events and the fact that the alteration of activities is one of the most common observations of social life give rise to the fourth question: How is behavior modified?

Determinants

These four questions about behavior can be approached in at least two major ways.[14] First, the "how" can be answered on the basis of determinants which are viewed mainly in terms of an individual's internal psychological characteristics, such as needs, motives, complexes, or personality; here we would speak of "psychodynamic" models of man. When one uses such an approach, the establishment of behavior might be explained in terms of infantile wishes, the maintenance of activities accounted for by fixation, and the extinction of behavior viewed as a result of unconscious suppression.

A second approach emphasizes human learning and views the determinants of behavior mainly in terms of preceding and contemporary *external* events and characteristics; here we would speak of "behavioral"

---

[14]For another typology, see Langer (1969).

models of man. When one uses such a model one might say that activities are likely to be extinguished when they are no longer rewarded, or a behavior will be maintained as long as it is reinforced. Thus, if one knows the external conditions—for example, a situation similar to one in which a person was previously rewarded for an activity—we can predict what will happen: he will probably perform that activity again. Answers to specific questions about particular behaviors are considerably more complex, of course, but their common element is a temporary disregard of, or at least a minimal concern with, the internal structure and operation of the most complicated of all black boxes—man.

Given these different approaches, it is only natural that those attempting to answer the four questions listed above will rely on social factors to varying degrees. Psychologists, especially those who favor what we have termed "psychodynamic models," usually consider the individual's social context as given. Social psychologists generally venture a little farther afield and attempt to specify the immediate external conditions under which particular activity sets, such as leadership and group cohesion, are maintained or modified. Most sociologists, finally, will be interested in the behavioral approach and emphasize the structure and dynamics of the wider social context as the major determinants of specific activities. Planners and designers, problem solvers, and those who seek to understand society need not, however, worry much about the fine distinctions among the various approaches. To them, and to us, the overriding consideration is: Which answer works best out there in the real world?

Relations

It is generally agreed that social life consists of individuals who interact, who influence one another, and who are tied together by exchange relations.[15] From a slightly different perspective, it makes sense to say that an individual is affected by his upbringing, for example, or that it is difficult to withstand social pressure. Most if not all external determinants of behavior, therefore, can be viewed in terms of social relations.

But how is one to conceptualize, measure, and analyze the relations of one person to another, and of an individual to his context? More specifically, how and why do people interact and influence one another? And what is social pressure—how is it to be conceptualized and how can it be measured? If it cannot be measured, is there any point in using the concept?

[15]The components of social systems are described by Parsons (1951); exchange relations are described in Homans (1974) and Emerson (1972).

MAJOR SOURCES
OF MODELS OF MAN

Several models of man currently in use are either implied by one or another theory or are based on research results in several related academic disciplines. In social psychology, for example, "Dissonance" and "Balance" theories imply that man is quite aware of his surroundings, evaluates his social context, makes rational decisions on this basis, and attempts to maximize the congruence of his ideas, behavior, and definitions of his context including other people.[16] A large number of experiments can be summarized by saying that as inconsistencies between beliefs and activities increase, individuals will attempt to reduce these inconsistencies in various ways, in spite of the fact that later consequences of such attempts are often unpleasant.[17] If we ask what human characteristics are implied by this conclusion, the answers will include such propositions as "man finds cognitive dissonance aversive," and "inconsistency is more unpleasant to him than many other things."

A source of some major components is biology. Man's physiological make-up, his limbs and organs, his nervous system and brain provide him with both opportunities and limitations. In the words of the geneticist Dobzhansky, "the genetic equipments of the human species do not make all men inherently good or irrevocably bad, virtuous or wicked, clever or stupid, cheerful or morose. They rather provide man with a range of potentialities, to be realized according to circumstances."[18] While man must *learn* to make use of these opportunities—for example, by learning how to speak and read—human limits constitute important parameters of social systems. Many people are reluctant to admit biological components into their models of man, based in part on the belief that much of man is the result of learning and thus somehow independent of his physiology. Yet the major *limitations* of human beings arise precisely from their membership in a biological species.

Finally, some components of models are the results of a person's own experiences and interpretations of the world. A pleasant childhood, popularity and success in high school and college, and a "good job" thereafter cannot help but influence one's conception of man, just as the opposite experiences will. Yet experiences do not exist by themselves; they are always interpreted. Thus a model of man not only derives from one's

[16]Aronson (1968); Newcomb (1968).
[17]Aronson (1968), p. 26.
[18]Dobzhansky (1959), p. 84.

experiences but also influences the interpretation and memory of those same experiences. Model and experience, then, interact, but not necessarily in the same way throughout life. Once a model has been firmly established, one is likely to view experiences through it. For example, if we have a more or less "positive" view of man, theft and injustice will be viewed as exceptions, as something one can try to eliminate, whereas a negative image of man would lead to the conclusion that these phenomena are natural and unavoidable.

If we ask where any one proposition of a model of man comes from, the answer of, say, "psychology" or "Freud" does not tell us all we want or need to know. When we then ask where psychologists, or Bandura, got this idea, the most common answer is from observations of human behavior. General propositions are derived from a large number of observations by a process of induction. This method of derivation, however, has recently been shown to be considerably less precise and more mysterious than had been assumed so far. Hempel[19] and Popper,[20] to mention only two philosophers of science, have pointed out that the derivation and formulation of a generalizing proposition from diverse observations is impossible to describe or teach, for it is essentially a creative act. "Scientific hypotheses and theories, then, are not mechanically inferred from observed 'facts': *they are invented by an exercise of creative imagination.*"[21]

The essentially nonobjective sources of propositions lead to special problems when one attempts to build models of man, for it is difficult to view man without the biases of experience and predilection. As Jung has pointed out very well, "every psychology which is the work of one man is subjectively colored . . . [and] every psychology—my own included—has the character of a subjective confession."[22] Problems of selective perception and idiosyncratic interpretation often become serious barriers to objective analysis, resulting in dissentions even among members of the same "school." Thus it has been said that Freud's major error consisted "essentially in the fact that he attempted to build a general theory of human nature on the basis of a particular type of neurotic personality."[23] Other builders of psychodynamic models have encountered similar difficulties, so that the acceptance or rejection of these models of man depends more on one's own personal predilections than on any model's data base.[24]

If the sources of propositions and the processes of their genesis are reflections of personality and individual ingenuity, how can we be sure

[19]Hempel (1966).
[20]Popper (1959).
[21]Hempel (1966), p. 115. Italics are in the original.
[22]Jung (1961), p. 336.
[23]Progoff (1956), p. 67.
[24]Progoff (1956).

that propositions about behavior—and by implication the components of any model of man—reflect reality rather than overactive imagination, wishful thinking, dreams, or despair? According to Hempel, "although no restrictions are imposed upon the *invention* of theories, scientific objectivity is safeguarded by making their *acceptance* dependent upon the outcome of careful tests."[25]

Not everyone, however, is willing to make the necessary tests. A model of man is often so close to the heart of him who builds or uses it that he cannot bear the thought of changing or dropping it. For example, there is considerable evidence that Freud was so emotionally involved in his theories that he could not accept major criticism of them.[26] If one postulates in one's model that man is basically good, for example, then contrary evidence and the consequent discarding of this model are likely to have severe repercussions for the individual as well as for his view of society and the future: perversity is natural and not an accident, the future may appear gloomy, and the solution of social problems may well be impossible. Hence it might be argued that it is easier, more pleasant, and perhaps even healthier to retain the old model and to protect it by making or keeping it implicit and vague.

The catch, of course, is that hazy and incorrect models cannot lead to effective policies and successful programs to solve social problems or to guide social systems. Comfortable models of man rarely increase the long-run comforts of men.

THE ASSESSMENT OF MODELS

The great number and variety of models both in the behavioral sciences and in public circulation raise the problem of evaluation and the question of which models one should select for a particular analysis, policy, or program design.

Many psychological theories and the models of man implied by them, and certainly those dealing with personality, often are vague yet fascinating, lacking in rigor but still full of insight.[27] As long as one is reading a theory simply for pleasure, it matters little whether the implied model of man is valid. But questions of validity become important when one undergoes long and expensive treatment based on the model. A person who expects that the symptoms of his illness will disappear on the basis of treatment founded on a vague or partially incorrect model of man is likely to be disappointed. Yet if he can spare the money and time, he may

[25]Hempel (1966), p. 116. Italics are in the original.
[26]Jung (1963), p. 150.
[27]For description of personality theories, see Hall and Lindzey (1970); Langer (1969).

have gained some insight into his nature and that of his analyst and may well be reasonably content with the arrangement and outcome. In general, the application of an incorrect model of man on an individual basis does not hurt many people, and the pain which results is in most cases minor and ephemeral.

But when a model is taken up by social scientists, government officials, policy planners, designers and managers of programs, and the public which supports and funds a project; and when the model is incorporated into legislation concerning change and solutions of social problems—then the rigor and validity of the model become extremely important. Few nations have the time or money to start many programs anew with different models, and few citizens are likely to long forgive blunders in policy. Finally and most significantly, a weak program based on questionable models of man and society will in the course of its failure hurt large numbers of people. The victims, of course, will be neither the planners and managers, nor the model builder, for in a large and complex program any failure can be assigned to "other factors"; rather, the victims will be those who were to be helped, whose aspirations were raised, and whose hopes have been dashed.

The major solution to the problem of validity is to assess one's models in terms of five criteria.[28] First, the model should consist of elements and relationships which have clearly stated empirical referents and are connected to them by generally accepted logical procedures. Second, a model should contain as few untested assumptions and inferences as possible. Third, the several propositions should be testable, verifiable, and —most important—refutable. Furthermore, they should have significant empirical support or, when this is lacking, at least be consistent with empirical evidence. Finally and most important, a model should have considerable explanatory and predictive power. A model which does not enable us to make accurate predictions is useless, and indeed it has been proposed that predictive capacity is the most significant criterion.[29] The accurate prediction of future events is at the root of any successful program of action and design for the future, and every procedure we might employ toward those ends is based on the assumption that "if we do this, then that is likely to happen." When we cannot predict with considerable confidence what the consequences of our planned actions will be, there is little point in implementing such programs. A major problem in the testing of prediction is the self-fulfilling hypothesis or prophecy. For example, if one assumes that a certain group of people is incapable of being educated, and if as a consequence one provides them with inferior schools, the existence

[28]Based on Dumont and Wilson (1967).
[29]Gibbs (1972).

of poorly educated adults among this group would not be due to their incapacity but their poor schooling. These poorly educated adults, however, might be cited as "proof" of the validity of the original proposition. In order to eliminate this problem, models of man must be evaluated in terms of criteria which are *independent* of the programmatic and other consequences to which the model leads. These criteria—self-evident platitudes to many people—unfortunately are often diregarded in the excitement of research, the heat of intellectual debates, and the quest for understanding the world.

THE NEXT STEP

In the first chapter we pointed out that any analysis of social phenomena, and indeed any understanding of social life, is greatly influenced by the underlying assumptions about man and society. The preceding pages were devoted to an examination of models of man, their sources, characteristics, and implications. We briefly described the two major models of man available today and indicated the criteria in terms of which they should be assessed. The next step consists of selecting a model of man on the basis of these criteria. We must then describe it and investigate its utility in the analysis of social problems and change.[30]

Psychodynamic models are well known and have been used by a large number of researchers in several fields. Consequently, man's internal states have been significant components in many analyses of social problems, in the designing of programs for their amelioration, and in discussions of social change. Increasingly, however, questions are being raised about such models' validity and applicability to social analyses and programmatic efforts.[31] For methodological and practical reasons, then, it is worthwhile to consider other models which have been developed in recent years.[32] In the following two chapters we will describe a model of man which meets the criteria mentioned earlier, based on principles of learning derived from a large variety of human studies.

While explicitly behavioral models have not been widely applied, learning principles and an emphasis on overt behavior have been significant in much recent sociological work. Among the best-known precursors of an explicitly behavioral approach are Neil Miller and John Dollard in their work on imitation and learning in social settings[33] and the application

[30]For a discussion of criteria and problems of model selection, see Marx (1963). For a comparison of models, see Kunkel (1970), chapter 2.

[31]For examples, see Bachrach (1962); Hall and Lindzey (1970); Marx (1963); Skinner (1972).

[32]For summaries and evaluations of these models, see Hilgard and Bowers (1966).

[33]Miller and Dollard (1941).

of learning principles to psychotherapy.[34] Even Montagu,[35] in a book about the role of and need for love in human relations and development, finds it necessary to devote an appendix to "learning theory." Whiting's and Child's studies on personality development in various cultures, finally, illustrate the cross-cultural applicability of learning principles.[36]

The behavioral model to be described below is a formal model which emphasizes relations rather than specific content. For example, the statement "past consequences affect future behavior" is formal rather than content-oriented, because it does not specify the nature of the consequences or of the future behavior. Freud's Oedipus hypothesis, conversely, is content-oriented rather than formal, because it specifies the people involved and the particular behavior patterns of each.

When one is interested in studying social systems, it is preferable to have formal models of man, for those which are primarily content-oriented often are culture-bound or otherwise limited to particular times, places, and groups. Furthermore, a specific content may obscure the essential character of the relationship between behavior and its social context. A good illustration of this difficulty is provided by Malinowski's examination of the Oedipus complex. According to Freud, the love-jealousy-hate syndrome growing out of the father-mother-son triangle is universal, and not a reflection of the nineteenth century, middle-class, central European culture to which most of Freud's patients belonged. But Malinowski did not find the Oedipus complex among inhabitants of the Trobriand Islands.[37] Rather, he observed close and friendly ties between fathers and sons as well as strained and difficult relationships between boys and their maternal uncles. He concluded that this was due to the fact that uncles discipline their nephews and in general play the same kind of authoritarian roles which fathers do in our society. Hence Malinowski proposed that the behavior patterns of sons and their fathers which Freud labeled the "Oedipus complex" were the results of authority relationships rather than of sexual jealousies. Similarly, Holmberg[38] found that among the Siriono (a poor and half-starving tribe in Bolivia) food played as significant and fantasy-laden a role as does sex in our society. When we speak of "authority relations" or "deprivations" we are close to making formal statements which can be applied to many different situations and people, while hypotheses about "father-son-mother triads" or "sexual repression" have a specific content and are applicable to only a few situations and individuals.

[34]Dollard and Miller (1950).
[35]Montagu (1955).
[36]Whiting (1963); Whiting and Child (1953).
[37]Malinowski (1927).
[38]Holmberg (1968).

In the description of a behavioral model of man we will not empha-size the differences among various approaches, concepts, hypotheses, and theories, but instead look for similarities and suggestions for possible syntheses. Our basic assumption will be that students of man do the best they can in observing, describing, and analyzing. Hence they are likely to see, describe, and explain similar phenomena, and differences will arise mainly from their various philosophical perspectives, methods of research, manners of thinking, and the words—especially the word pictures—they use. Instead of aggravating and perpetuating these differences by pointing to them and commenting upon them, we will try to determine the nature of those characteristics of man which will be important for the analysis of social problems, the designing of policies, and the guidance of change.

A Behavioral Model of Man: Components

3

This chapter presents some basic ideas concerning human behavior derived from the recent psychological literature, and their important sociological implications. While we do not pretend to describe all of man, most of what people do and much of what they are can be accounted for by the principles discussed in this and the following chapter. Future research will no doubt require reformulation of some relationships, redefinition of some variables, amplification of some statements and the addition of new ones, but the eventual picture is not likely to be significantly different from what we now see.

Most behavioral models of man are based on one or another learning theory and have considerable empirical underpinnings. The major differences among these theories, and thus among models of man, are due to the various assumptions, postulates, and inferences which are made about the nature and processes of learning and the internal events and processes which mediate between external stimuli and behavior.[1] Some theories provide much detail—for example Hull's formulas of what occurs in man —while others, such as Skinner's, have little to say on this topic. Because we are interested in the social implications and empirical soundness of a

[1] For discussions of behavioral models of man, their empirical foundations, and the differences among them, see Bandura (1969); Hilgard and Bower (1966); and Staats and Staats (1963).

model rather than in constructing a rigorous and complete theory of behavior, which of necessity would involve a large number of inferences, the model of man developed here will be based more on the work of several experimental psychologists than on the ideas of any particular learning theorist.

Like any formal model of man, this one is only a partial representation of human characteristics. Consequently much of what one might consider to be uniquely human—such as the capacity to appreciate music and poetry, or to be deeply moved and to weep—will be of only peripheral interest. This does not mean, however, that those who employ this behavioral model of man cannot love or weep or are themselves insensitive. Rather, it means that interest centers on that part of man which is significant for the structure and operation of social systems. Readers who are disturbed by the austerity of our treatment and its possibly mechanical overtones may add enriching and human factors as long as the original relationships among variables remain intact.

In the past, much of the evidence about learning and the determinants of behavior came from animal studies; only in the last decade or two has considerable human evidence been collected.[2] There are now literally hundreds of experimental and naturalistic studies concerned with human learning and behavior. Their settings range from institutions to the free environment—from small experimental rooms to schools and mental hospitals, from homes to playgrounds, offices, factories, and communities; the subjects range from normal to psychotic and include men and women in every age group, from children to the elderly; the behavior under investigation ranges from simple laboratory tasks to complex skills and includes most of the activities performed in everyday life, such as eating, driving, working, and utilizing language and gestures. In short, no area of human endeavor seems to have been overlooked.[3] It is from such human studies that the principles described in this chapter are abstracted; similarities with formulations based on animal work are merely coincidental and need not detain us here.

It cannot be said, by any means, that all behavior of all people at all times can be explained solely in terms of these learning principles, for neither the principles nor their applicability and limitations are completely known at present. What we do know today is that *most* behavior patterns of daily life can be explained by learning principles operating within a social environment.

[2]Good illustrations of this development can be seen in Hilgard and Bower (1966), and in a comparison of the several editions of this book.

[3]For examples, see such compilations as Bandura (1969); Barron and Liebert (1972); and Ullmann and Krasner (1965).

The activities of daily life do not consist of discrete units, are rarely performed in isolation, and are subject to a myriad of influences, many of which may be unknown to the observer. Hence it is often difficult to indicate which specific principles affect any particular activity that one might arbitrarily point to in the course of a day. At any one moment a number of factors operate simultaneously, and it is their combined effect that influences a person's behavior. Consequently the activities which constitute daily life will usually require rather complicated explanations consisting of several interacting principles as well as past and present circumstances, even though the basic principles themselves are relatively simple and straightforward.

COMPONENTS

In order to describe the establishment, maintenance, extinction, and modification of behavior within a social context in a reasonably clear and simple fashion, our discussion is divided into three parts: Concepts, Influences, and Sociological Implications. The symbols which are commonly used by psychologists will be employed in this section and hereafter; for example, the letter R will stand for any behavior pattern, be it simple or complex, and not for "response" to a preceding stimulus.

Basic Concepts

STATE VARIABLES: SV_1 OR SV_2.   Individuals at one time or another are subject to various kinds and degrees of deprivation and satiation. For example, in the morning one is usually "hungry," a condition of physiological deprivation; after breakfast, one is in a state of physiological satiation. Such momentary conditions are collectively labeled *state variables,* (SV). When their basis is physiological, as in the case of food, drink, clothing, shelter, etc., we speak of *primary state variables,* or SV_1. When their basis is cultural, or learned, as in the case of popularity, flashy cars, or diamond rings, one speaks of *secondary state variables,* or SV_2. The line between the two types is not always clear-cut, however, because a person might consider himself deprived of basic physical needs unless he has a medium rare filet mignon, a dry martini, stylish trousers, and lives in a splendid house with a swimming pool. Nevertheless, the distinction is useful because primary state variables are usually quite limited in variety and degree and can be changed relatively quickly. Secondary SV vary greatly in character and kind, in their stability and the number of "rewards" which are necessary to alter them significantly, from one person to another, and from one situation to the next. An income of $10,000, for example, may leave one person deprived and another quite satisfied, and ten visits a week may lead to one person's feeling "lonely" (or deprived of sufficient human contact), while two visits may be "more than enough" for another person. However, while such variations are possible and should always be expected when there is no evidence to the contrary, most individuals with similar cultural backgrounds and social characteristics are likely to have similar secondary state variables, especially when their life histories have been much the same.

A rather different kind of deprivation has been discussed by philosophers, psychologists, and other writers in terms of various needs and values. Fromm, for example, postulates needs for relatedness, for transcending one's passive state, for rootedness, for a sense of identity, for intellectual orientation, and for an "object of devotion that gives meaning to his existence and to his position in the world." [4] Maslow holds that every human being desires affection, respect and self-respect, and self-actualization. When these are denied or suppressed, people become physically or psychologically ill.[5] And Ashley Montagu proposes that "human beings are born good—'good' in the sense that there is no evil or hostility in them, but that at birth they are wholly prepared, equipped, to function as creatures who not only want and need to be loved by others but who also want and need to love others." [6]

The needs described by these and other thinkers help define the goals men seek or the reinforcers they value. The need for "relatedness," for example, would make human warmth and protection a reward, and solitude and constant change aversive.

The relationship between needs or values and behavior is close, for it is usually postulated that needs can be fulfilled and values achieved by means of a relatively limited range of activities. According to Fromm, for example, "the need to be related can be satisfied by submission, or by domination; but only in love is another human need fulfilled—that of independence and integrity of the self. The need for transcendence can be satisfied either by creativeness or by destructiveness; but only creativeness permits of joy—whereas destructiveness causes suffering for oneself and others." [7]

The analytical problems posed by these kinds of philosophical needs —and by implication, deprivations—are formidable indeed. In the first place, we cannot be certain that these needs, or values, or whatever one wants to call them, actually exist. Maslow, for instance, explicitly "as-

[4]Fromm (1959), p. 161.
[5]Maslow (1968).
[6]Montagu (1955), p. 289.
[7]Fromm (1959), p. 162.

sumes" a tendency toward (or need for) self-actualization, and other writers imply a similar source for their descriptions of human requirements. Furthermore, the terms are usually vague, so that it would be difficult to specify their empirical referents; it is one thing to cite a need, but quite another to demonstrate a "need for transcendence." At the very least, specification robs the words of their inspiration while still not completely clarifying their meaning. Finally, although it is assumed that these characteristics are natural or innate, it remains to be shown that in fact they are not learned or somehow dependent on one's culture.

Yet it cannot be denied that Maslow, Fromm, and Montagu, to mention only the men who have been quoted, make considerable sense and may be on to something. But while words such as "self-actualization," "love," and "joy" are pleasant, they are difficult to incorporate into a scientific analysis where we constantly ask, "What precisely do you mean by this?" "How do you know this is true?" and "Now what do we do?" In the following pages, therefore, we will hew closely to the empirical path, for it is here that we are most likely to find propositions with explanatory power and theories which help us to predict and guide the future.

We will assume, then, that deprivations are primary or secondary, that their magnitudes vary, and that this will be true not only of food but also of companionship, love, and transcendence. It should be noted, however, that while deprivation can be established with some certainty for SV_1, secondary state variables do not easily lend themselves to accurate measurements which remain consistent over time. In the case of human beings, most state variables have a societal or subcultural origin, but a few are idiosyncratic. Hence it is wise to adopt the rule of thumb, that "people can feel deprived of the most outlandish things at the craziest times to the strangest degree."

CONTINGENT STIMULI: S^r, S^a, AND S^o.   The consequences of behavior—usually termed *contingent stimuli* or simply *contingencies*—are considered to fall into three major groups: positive, negative, and neutral. In the study of contingencies we concentrate on their origin, their nature, and their effects on future behavior, and generally classify them on that basis. Since their effectiveness depends to a large extent on the individual's state variables, analysis of contingencies proceeds mainly in terms of those characteristics.

A *reinforcing stimulus* (reinforcer)—or S^r—is a consequence of behavior, originating in a person's social and physical environment or self-administered, which maintains or increases the probability that a behavior pattern will be repeated in the future. Once an S^r has been determined in this way—for example, a piece of candy or a smile—it may be assumed to operate for other behavior patterns as well. In short, most reinforcers are transsituational.[8] An S^r may also be defined as anything that reduces an individual's deprivations. Candy and a smile, indeed most reinforcers, fit both definitions.

An important category of S^r—and probably the most significant in human societies— consists of a variety of *generalized reinforcers.* Although not intrinsically reinforcing (*i.e.,* they do not themselves reduce any deprivation), they can be easily exchanged for a variety of effective S^r (*i.e.,* objects or actions on the part of others which *do* reduce deprivations). The possibility of such an exchange must be learned, of course; hence the specific character of a generalized reinforcer depends on the culture. In industrial societies, money is the most common and important example, while in other cultures and communities one's prestige may be more significant. Both money and status can be used to obtain other S^r—such as food, or deferential behavior from others. The major advantage of generalized reinforcers is that they are effective regardless of the individual's momentary state variables. A person may not be hungry now, but he is still willing to work for money; and the status accruing to him at one point can later induce a variety of activities from others. Furthermore, generalized reinforcers often can be divided and given in small amounts, thus making it possible to present reinforcers after relatively short series of activities, or when intrinsic reinforcers are not readily available. Hence, generalized reinforcers enable the individual to accumulate small S^r from a number of different activities and to exchange them for a larger and more significant reward.

Finally, we must recognize that reinforcers are not restricted to external phenomena or events. Many behavior patterns are intrinsically reinforcing in that their performance is in itself rewarding to the individual.[9] For example, toddlers are thrilled by early explorations of their world, and many adults take pleasure in contemplation, fantasy, and even such arduous and vexing activities as learning to play tennis or puzzling out a difficult passage in a book. While human beings frequently find their own activities rewarding, the origin, character, and extent of these gratifications is as yet obscure. In some cases, no doubt, an act is enjoyable because it triggers associations with previous pleasures; the labor of perfecting one's tennis game, for instance, might summon up recollections of one's childhood delight in motor activity; and at least part of the reward for wrestling with a hard book might stem from associations with a warm family environment in which one was encouraged to develop intellectual skills. More complex explanations are also feasible, yet the possibility remains that

---

[8]Hilgard and Bower (1966), chapter 14. For a discussion of tautology problems, see Burgess and Akers (1966b).

[9]Premack (1965). See also Bandura (1969), chapter 4.

some people simply find certain activities intrinsically pleasant, while others are indifferent to them. In any case, the effectiveness of external reinforcers and the wide range of activities which have been shown to be subject to their influence lead to the conclusion that the proportion of intrinsically reinforcing activities in daily life is probably quite small and of relatively little interest to students of social problems and change.

An *aversive stimulus*—or S^a—is a consequence of behavior, originating in a person's social and physical environment or self-administered, which reduces the probability that a behavior pattern will be repeated in the future. Like an S^r, an S^a may be assumed to be transsituational; once established, most S^a appear to operate for other behavior patterns as well. An S^a may also be defined as anything that maintains or increases a person's deprivation, or causes pain. Thus the direct costs of a given behavior as well as whatever positive experience one must forgo because of the behavior contribute to making a particular consequence aversive. Again, an S^a appears to operate as it does because of its effects on deprivation.

A *neutral stimulus*—or S^o—is a consequence which does not affect the probability of behavior repetition or the individual's state variables. In actual life, however, completely neutral consequences of an action are rare indeed. Rather, what at first glance appears to be an S^o usually turns out to be an S^r or S^a. For example, a child may steal a cookie without his mother's catching him at it, hence there is no punishment. The consequence is not neutral, however, for the eating of the cookie is pleasant. The R of cookie-stealing, then, in effect is followed by an S^r and not an S^o. As a rule of thumb, we should assume that there are no true or longlasting S^o, and that an apparent S^o will sooner or later turn out to be an S^r or S^a.

The term *total contingency* refers to the sum of the consequences which follow any behavior pattern. While it makes sense to speak of an S^r or an S^a for a particular laboratory task, the behavior patterns which constitute daily life are usually followed by several stimuli, some reinforcing and others aversive, some immediate and others which do not occur for some time. A total contingency can be positive, if it includes a preponderance of S^r, or it can be negative, if there are many S^a, and it is this sum of consequences which determines the probability that an activity will be repeated. Thus, while we will continue to speak of an activity's consequence, the total contingency will be implied by that term.

We should also remember that there are two major ways in which S^r and S^a can occur. One has been described above when we spoke of the environment's presenting of contingencies. But S^r and S^a can also be self-administered, and in fact self-reinforcement is a major component of many total contingencies. A person can treat himself to a beer or be proud of his accomplishments, and he can cut down on his consumption of sweets or call himself a fool, depending on whether or not his preceding behavior comes up to his standard or expectation.

Difficulties. While the formal definitions of these concepts are reasonably simple and precise, it is often difficult to determine whether or not a specific event, object, or action is an S^r or an S^a, or in some way affects a person's state variables. The significance of a particular stimulus depends so frequently on surrounding circumstances that it is unwise to jump to conclusions, even when the incident involves members of one's own subculture or society. For example, the expression "Why, Jack, you old s.o.b." may well be an expression of endearment at the nineteenth hole—hence an S^r—although "s.o.b." ordinarily is an S^a; here it is the place, the facial expression, and the immediately preceding events which help establish the phrase as an S^r.

A related difficulty arises because any behavioral analysis depends upon two major points of view, the subject's and the observer's. As cross-cultural studies demonstrate, perceptions of SV and of reinforcers vary greatly, and the existence of subcultures and generation gaps in modern societies illustrates the necessity of taking various perspectives into account. Even when the observer knows the person's assessment of contingencies, however, their interpretations may differ because of narrow perceptions or limited time horizons; one may not see all the contingencies that the other predicts, or may not look as far ahead as the other. Finally, both may attach different weights to the various S^r and S^a which make up the total contingency. For example, a person who believes in salvation as the ultimate reward for a pious life may behave in a way that appears unreasonable to an observer who understands the other contingencies in the case but who has not placed the same emphasis on spiritual considerations.

In short, the determination and assessment of state variables and contingent stimuli pose major problems for those who employ a behavioral model of man, problems which must be faced at the beginning of every investigation. Since our major data are observations of behavior, we must in the end rely on inferences—either our own or those of others—and recognize the tentative character of any hypothesis about contingencies. Yet we need not despair. Psychologists have wrestled with these problems for a long time without being able to resolve them, and yet they are able to predict and modify behavior patterns with relative ease and with sufficient accuracy to make behavior therapy quite successful.

CONTINGENCY SCHEDULES. A *contingency schedule* indicates the distribution and frequency with which S^r or S^a are presented once the associated behavior pattern has occurred. While pure schedules are found mainly in laboratories and a few facets of daily life, such as periodic pay checks, many events which constitute social behavior are reinforced on a mixed or complex schedule. For present purposes, however, a recognition of "pure" schedules will be sufficient. The major types of such schedules are:

1. Continuous schedule, or CS: an S^r is presented after every R (particular behavior pattern);
2. Fixed-ratio schedule, or FR: an S^r is presented after a fixed number of R have occurred (*e.g.,* some types of payment on a piece rate);
3. Variable-ratio schedule, or VR: an S^r is presented after a varying number of R have occurred (*e.g.,* hitting the jackpot);
4. Fixed-interval schedule, or FI: an S^r is presented after a fixed interval of time, but is still contingent on the occurrence of an R (*e.g.,* monthly salary checks);
5. Variable-interval schedule, or VI: an S^r is presented after variable intervals of time, but still contingent on the occurrence of an R.

Schedules are important determinants of the rate and overall number of activities as well as of the speed of extinction. When reinforcement occurs on a continuous schedule, for example, the number of rewards and activities will be the same, and upon the cessation of reinforcement, extinction is quite rapid and likely to be accompanied by considerable emotional reactions. Conversely, a variable ratio schedule will result in a very high and stable rate of behavior, require minimal reinforcement, and extinction is likely to be a slow and unemotional process. In the study of social behavior, therefore, we must look at the schedules of reinforcement provided by a person's or a group's social environment, for many of the peculiarities and problems we observe in daily life are a result of societally determined schedules and their changes.

DISCRIMINATIVE STIMULI: S^D OR S^Δ.   Human behavior always occurs within a social and/or physical environment. Over a period of time, a person with normal intelligence and awareness of that environment learns that certain activities are reinforced in particular circumstances, and others are not. Eventually, some specific aspects of his surroundings become, so to speak, "signals" for him that particular consequences are likely to occur if he behaves in a particular way. Those characteristics of the momentary environment which have acquired such a "signaling" property are known as *discriminative stimuli*. An individual *learns* to recognize and interpret discriminative stimuli; they are established on the basis of observation and/or experience, and are not inherent properties of the environment itself. Furthermore, the same event can lead to different persons' behaving in different ways; a yellow traffic light might be a signal for one person to stop and for another to speed up to beat the red. Once a discriminative stimulus has been learned, its occurrence in the environment, even if it is not consciously recognized by the individual, is likely to be followed by the activity which has previously become associated with it.

There are two major types of discriminative stimuli. The first, S^D, is a characteristic or element of an individual's social and/or physical environment in the presence of which a particular R has previously been followed by a reinforcer. Thus R is likely to be repeated whenever the S^D recurs. Any particular S^D may consist of several specific characteristics of the environment, all or most of which must be present if the associated R is to occur. S^D, then, are subtle and complex phenomena, whose existence on a given occasion might escape the recognition of the person, the observer, or both. Hence the determination and analysis of discriminative stimuli often requires a number of observations and inferences and at times considerable insight.

A good illustration of common complexities surrounding S^D is provided by motorists' responses to road signs. Ideally, a "25 mile speed limit" sign should be an S^D for a person's driving at that speed. Actually, it often becomes an S^D for a quick glance to determine whether a patrol car is parked nearby. Thus the S^D for a reduction of speed may well be a combination of the sign, the presence of a patrol car, the town's reputation as a speed trap, and an earlier sign about radar control. Here it is the individual's past experience, perhaps combined with hearsay evidence, which contributes to his perception of an effective S^D for slowing down. Still, despite the S^D, he might not slow down if he judges the probability of being caught to be low, or worth the risk. It is evident that an observer would have to have considerable information in order to predict a driver's actions accurately. He might be able to predict the behavior of 80 percent of the population by knowing the license manual alone, and that of an additional 10 percent by knowing the reputation of the town, but to increase his accuracy beyond this would require steeply increasing amounts of information about the individuals concerned. In actual practice, therefore, the student of social behavior may have to be content with knowing that a particular sign is an S^D for "most people."

The second type of discriminative stimulus, S^Δ (pronounced ess-delta), is a characteristic or element of an individual's social and/or physical context in the presence of which a particular R has not been followed by a reinforcer in the past. Hence, if the S^Δ is present now, R is not likely to be repeated. From the point of view of the individual one could say that an S^Δ is a signal in his environment which indicates that if he behaves in a particular way he is not likely to be rewarded.

An S^Δ may be either a specific characteristic of the environment or the absence of an S^D. Many children, for example, are less likely to cry when they are alone than when an adult is present, for they quickly learn that adults can be expected to extend sympathy. The adult, then, is an S^D for crying (*e.g.,* after a child falls), while the absence of the adult is an S^Δ for crying—or an S^D for simply getting up and resuming his play. The labeling of contextual properties as S^D or S^Δ is to some extent a matter of choice. Since the discussion of S^Δ requires negative and often awkward statements, it is frequently preferable to speak of the "absence" of something as an environmental characteristic, and hence an S^D for certain other activities, such as "continuing to play."

Probabilities. An important term in the above discussion is probability: an S^r increases the probability that R will be repeated, an S^a decreases it, in all but the continuous schedules there are varying probabilities that any one R will be reinforced, and an S^D indicates a high probability that a specific R will occur and that it will be reinforced. As we will see in later chapters, the existence of these probabilities and the absence of certainties in social life are significant for the structure, operation, and change of social life. Students and designers of social systems often have difficulty remembering that people must learn to live with probabilities and that it is on the basis of both experience and observation that probability expectations are established. Variations in such expectations are likely to result in differential definitions of the same environment as "benign" or "hostile," and in significantly different behavior patterns. For example, infrequent praise when one expects little is likely to be viewed positively, while the same frequency for someone who is used to a higher probability of praise will be seen as "lack of appreciation." Many of the activities subsumed under the general heading of "social problems" are affected by differences between actual and ideal probabilities of rewards for behavior, by variations of probability based on class position, and by the fact that people must learn to expect and live with the often low probabilities inherent in social life.

Influences

Whenever an individual behaves, he affects and manipulates his social and physical environment, which usually reacts in some way. Most of these reactions take the form of presenting or withdrawing aversive or reinforcing stimuli, or of failing to present expected consequences, be they positive or negative. Future behaviors and a person's view of himself and of the world are greatly influenced by such often complex reactions and the person's interpretations of them.

Let us consider, for example, a child who breaks one of his mother's vases. He can expect negative consequences to follow his behavior, as his mother might scold him (present an S^a) or take away his toys (withdraw an S^r), or do both. We can assume that the child will worry about what is going to happen to him. But what if his mother fails to notice the broken vase, or blames it on the cat, or is in a good mood and decides to overlook the matter? What if, in short, the environment fails to present a consequence for the child's behavior? Obviously, we cannot simply dismiss the lack of punishment; only the most callous and hardened child would feel or subsequently behave as if not being scolded or deprived of toys were the normal course of events. We can effectively analyze such an incident in terms of the presentation and withdrawal of reinforcing and aversive stimuli. Though the facts of the case are not the same as if the mother actually initiated punishment and then reversed herself or was overruled by the father, the net effect is similar, if somewhat more complex. A complete analysis of the dynamics of the incident would take into account at least the fact that the child's anxiety about being punished functioned as a self-induced aversive stimulus; that the diminution of anxiety as he came to realize that he would escape punishment functioned as the kind of reinforcement that occurs when an aversive stimulus is withdrawn; that the scolding and loss of toys he foresaw, though imaginary, affected him in a way analogous to real aversive stimuli and deprivation; and that the failure of these consequences to materialize influenced him much as if a real aversive stimulus or a real deprivation had been removed. The point is this: the non-appearance of consequences is significant in terms of behavior when consequences were expected; in such cases, by dealing with the anticipated consequences as if they were real, we can speak in terms of S^r, S^a, their presentation and withdrawal, to generate an analysis of such complex states of mind—and influences on future behavior—as anxiety and relief or, conversely, hope and disappointment.

Turning now to the basic ways in which the reaction of the environment to behavior influences future behavior, we can schematize our conclusions as follows:[10]

	S^r	S^a
Presented	reinforcement (positive)	punishment
Withdrawn	punishment	reinforcement (negative)

It will be noted that there are two types of punishment and two types of reinforcement. This accords with common sense, which tells us that one can punish a child by taking away his dessert or making him eat his spinach, and one can reward him by giving him dessert or taking away his

[10]Based on Holland and Skinner (1961), p. 245.

spinach. To some extent, it does not matter whether the punishment or reinforcement concerns reality or expectation—*not* giving a child an expected treat can be as effective a punishment as physically depriving him of something he already has.

In general, contingencies become linked with the immediately preceding R rather than with more distant behavior. Hence a delay in presenting the consequence may result in the punishment or reinforcement of activities that were not intended to be so treated. For example, a child who is deprived of dessert at dinnertime for misconduct early in the afternoon may associate his punishment with what he has just been doing rather than with what he is actually being punished for. Verbal statements are often used to try to link the punishment with the misbehavior, but there is no guarantee that the child will understand the connection.

As we pointed out, both punishment and reinforcement depend in part on the individual's state variables, for the state variables help define the S^r and S^a which are effective at any moment. In general, the greater the intensity of a S^a or an S^r, the higher the level of behaving to avoid or induce its recurrence in the future; and the greater the success of future R in avoiding S^a or in inducing S^r, the greater the resistance of that R to extinction. Furthermore, it follows from the close relationship between punishment, reinforcement, and state variables that the same caveats that were given regarding the assessment and measurement of state variables apply to the interpretation, and especially the utilization, of reward and punishment. What an observer views as punishing or rewarding may not be considered as such by the individual. A mother's scolding, for example, may be an S^r rather than an S^a if the child believes that he is "getting even" by making her angry, or if this is the only kind of attention he is able to get from her. Thus one must be cautious and tentative in dealing with rewards and punishments, whether as an observer or as a social planner. Effectiveness in these areas requires careful and detailed analysis of the individual's culture, learning history, and immediately surrounding social environment. Punishment in particular is often followed by emotional reactions, and the anticipation of punishment is usually accompanied by anxiety. Both emotional reactions and anxiety frequently affect the individual in ways that are detrimental to the purposes intended by the process of punishment; hence this procedure must be applied with great care.

In the study of social problems and the designing of policies, variations in societal and subcultural definitions of SV, S^r and S^a—hence what constitutes reinforcement, punishment, and deprivation for any one person—are of major significance. Conflicting definitions and the resulting inconsistent reinforcement, for example, are not only important topics by themselves but have broad repercussions for the genesis and solution of social problems, as we will see in later chapters.

Conclusions

The major determinants of activities not only exist by themselves but are also seen by the behaving individual and by observers. Hence there are at least three perspectives of determinants, as illustrated in the following table:

Objective Reality	Individual	Observer
A. the existing S^D	perceived by the individual	seen by an observer
B. the existing SV	felt by the individual	inferred by an observer
C. the contingency probability (S^r or S^a)	predicted by the individual	perceived by an observer
D. past associations of S^D, R, and S^r	learned by the individual	perceived by an observer

The existence of these three perspectives has several significant methodological and analytical implications. Although behavior is influenced by a person's actual environment through his perception of it, perception and reality do not always correspond. Sometimes the discrepancy between them is negligible and we can safely talk as if the individual were indeed responding to reality directly; but at other times the discrepancy is greater, resulting in inappropriate actions. Furthermore, it is not necessary that a person be able to describe the discriminative and contingent stimuli which affect him. A person can also make errors in predicting contingencies, or he may not see an S^D. Hence we cannot assume that the sources listed in the first two columns present the individual with the same facts on which to base his selection of behavior. Observers, finally, be they social scientists, officials, or mere bystanders, sometimes "know" more about reality than the behaving person, and sometimes much less. When observers do not know the facts of a person's social environment or are unfamiliar with his perception of them, or when they see reality in terms of their own biases, they cannot predict his behavior accurately, will judge him to behave "irrationally," and formulate programs that cannot be effective. Subcultural differences in a complex society, class-based restrictions on perspective, and the inability to "put oneself into another's shoes" have frequently led to the incorrect causal analysis of behavior and the design of programs dealing with inappropriate variables. As sociologists have long pointed out, what is *perceived* as real has real consequences in terms of people's behavior, and thus must be regarded as "real" by the observer, even if he thinks he knows better. Both

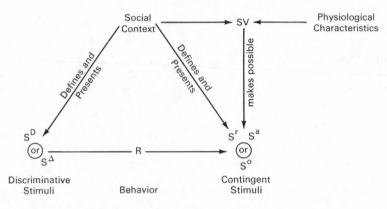

FIGURE 3–1 A Behavioral Model of Man

R=behavior; S^r=reinforcing stimulus (loosely speaking, reward); S^a=aversive stimulus (loosely speaking, punishment); S^o=neutral stimulus, or absence of any consequence; S^D=stimulus in whose presence R has previously been reinforced; S$^\Delta$=stimulus in whose presence R has not been reinforced; SV=state variables (*i.e.*, conditions of deprivation and satiation)

a causal analysis and the design of programs, therefore, may have to be performed initially on two levels, one involving individuals' perceptions and the other reality as seen by the observer. To be successful, of course, the analysis and any design based on it must eventually fuse the two levels into one. In chapter 7 we will see how this can be done.

The several influences of the environment on behavior are presented schematically in figure 3–1, which shows how the various determinants are interrelated. The psychologist's major interest is focused upon the nature of relationships represented by the horizontal arrows, while the sociologist is more concerned with the character of the social context and its influence upon man, symbolized by the diagonal arrows. Hence the questions which each asks are quite different: "Why does praise increase the probability that an activity will be repeated?" is of little interest to sociologists, and "Why does a society encourage large families?" matters little to psychologists. For our purposes, the relationships indicated by horizontal arrows are among the major "given elements" which characterize the human components of any social structure or process. They are of interest to the psychologist, but we will not be concerned with the whys and hows of human learning. Rather, our interest centers on the many kinds of SV and S^D defined and presented by a particular social system, the various consequences of individuals' activities, and the factors involved in their modification.

As we examine an individual's activities within his social context we cannot help but see that the environment does not operate independently of him in providing discriminative and contingent stimuli. In fact, the individual himself plays a significant role in creating the specifics of his own surroundings and thereby affects the determinants of his own later actions. A person who smiles often and is friendly in other ways, for example, usually receives similar reactions from other people, while a morose and silent person is likely to receive few friendly gestures from those who make up his environment. There is, then, substantial reciprocal influence between an individual's behavior and the social context; individuals, "far from being ruled by an imposing environment, play an active role in constructing their own reinforcement contingencies through their characteristic modes of response."[11] The parameters of such an active role, in the form of subcultural and societal values and norms, will be discussed in a later chapter.

SOCIOLOGICAL IMPLICATIONS

The behavioral model of man we have just outlined has a number of implications for analytical procedures, sociological concepts, and the study of social problems. We will now take a brief look at some of these.

Procedures of Analysis

A behavioral model of man—not only the one we have described but any approach which focuses on learning and observable activities—forces us to look for overt or measurable behavior on the part of individuals and groups. In addition, we are obliged to study the several important phenomena associated with the learning, maintenance, and modification of behavior, such as discriminative and contingent stimuli, state variables, and schedules of reinforcement. These are usually rather specific aspects of the structure and operation of people's social environment, and thus a researcher's initial individualistic questions sooner or later require that he turn his attention to both sociological concerns and social issues.

The study of any kind of social behavior—no matter whether it is regarded as "normal" or labeled a "social problem"—necessarily begins with a careful description of all the specific activities comprising it. The required specification is sometimes difficult to perform, for it forces us to dissect a complex set—for example, "doing poorly in school"—into its constituent elements, such as "being reprimanded," "receiving poor grades," "being inattentive," and so forth. We will call these activities "principal" or "primary" to indicate that they constitute the focus of our study. After specification, we ask of every element in the set a number of questions that arise directly from our model of man:

[11]Bandura (1969), p. 46.

1. What are the discriminative stimuli of this activity and where do they come from?
2. What are the consequences of this activity for the individual concerned and where do they come from?
3. What are the schedules of these consequences and where do they come from?
4. What state variables are involved in or implied by these consequences and what are their determinants?

Most answers will involve other people's behaviors and these we will call "secondary." As we follow the trail of "who does what to whom," we are likely to be led away from the individual or group with which we started and toward the structure and operation of the larger society. Yet the behavioral perspective does not allow us to stop with this realization, or to resort to amorphous concepts such as "community" or "class structure." The fact that any social system consists, basically, of people and their activities provides us with a hint of why and how any particular system operates as it does. Thus, for each of the several secondary behavioral components of any individual's or group's wider social context, we should ask the same four questions we did of the primary activities with which we started. Most answers will again concern other people's activities, and these we will call "tertiary." While we will be able to be specific in some cases, we are likely to encounter a number of rather vague answers as well. If we wish, we can ask similar questions of these and other behavior patterns which are still farther removed from those with which we began; in practice, however, most social analyses need not be carried out beyond tertiary activities, if only because it makes little sense to design programs from such a distance.

A good case to which these analytical procedures might be applied is *Elmtown's Youth,* the classic study of a smalltown high school.[12] A major question of this study was: Why do students from working-class families generally end up in blue-collar jobs and thus remain in the same class, while students from middle-class families tend to enter better occupations and thus either remain in the same class or rise in status? Part of the answer lies in the differential drop-out rate and in the early educational careers of students, especially in the fact that most working-class pupils choose a "general curriculum" while middle-class students usually select a "college-prep" curriculum. If these activities, together with academic performance, are defined as "primary" activities, a search for S^D, contingencies, and their sources reveals the following: most counselors advise students on the basis of their parents' class membership rather than on the students' desires or capacities; teachers often grade on the basis of the curriculum the student

---

[12]Hollingshead (1949).

is in rather than on the basis of his performance; administrators use punishment selectively, basing it on the student's class background rather than on his behavior—*e.g.*, a middle-class boy is likely to be viewed as expressing "youthful enthusiasm" and a working-class boy as showing "incipient delinquency" when they break the same window; and middle-class students in general react negatively to working-class students (except star athletes). Children from working-class families thus meet few reinforcers for remaining in school or even for studying hard, and find relatively few opportunities for "bettering" their position.

When we investigate the "secondary" activities of counselors, teachers, administrators, and fellow students, we find that the S^D, S^r, and S^a bearing on the behavior we have just described are provided by various citizens in the community, members of the school board, other students and teachers, and generally held beliefs about the nature of people in various social positions. The "perpetuation of classes," then, can be seen to operate through the behavior patterns of large numbers of people, some of whom may well have good intentions.[13]

The questions listed above focus on the behavior patterns, individuals, and/or groups which make up the center of our interest, as well as on the activities and people who presumably play important roles as determinants. In the course of analysis we are likely to find that there is considerable reciprocal influence, that the behavior patterns with which we started also affect the individuals and activities which constitute their social environment. Thus we should ask of the secondary and tertiary activities:

5. How are their discriminative stimuli related to the primary activities?
6. How are their consequences related to the primary activities?
7. How are the schedules of these consequences related to the primary activities?
8. How are the associated or implied state variables related to the primary activities?

The questions which provide the framework for our analysis cannot be answered by single observations of isolated behaviors, for these would not enable us to distinguish between functionally related activities—for example, S^D and R—and those which simply happen to occur at roughly the same time. What is required, instead, is a *number* of *careful, longitudinal* observations, ideally including repetitions in both similar and slightly different circumstances. When this is done, we will be able to distinguish between an actual S^D and something which simply happens to precede an R, between actual S^r and events which simply happen to occur subsequent

[13]For a study of public schools in general, see Coleman *et al.* (1966).

to the performance of an act. The more observations we make, the more confident we can be that we have isolated, say, an S^D or S^r, but it is not until we have made successful predictions that we can be reasonably certain of having isolated the relevant components of any behavior triad.

In the initial stages of our investigation we have to rely on hunches as to what constitutes an S^D or an S^r of observed behavior, and even later on we will not be able to free ourselves entirely from the necessity of having to make inferences or relying on hypotheses. If we can experiment, isolate the individuals and activities in which we are interested, and keep accurate records of events, we will be able to state with considerable confidence that "A is an S^D for B," or that "C is an S^r for B." But when it is impossible for us to experiment, and especially when we are restricted to limited observations in quite similar settings, we will have to be content with the formulation of hypotheses: "A is likely to be an S^D for B," or "C is probably an S^r for B." Such hypotheses in effect will be tested by later observations and by the success of predictions and programs based upon them, and must be revised when necessary. Unfortunately, the fact that much time usually elapses along the way, and that the people who do the predicting may not do the subsequent observing means that the testing may be haphazard and that the necessary reformulation may not be done.[14]

A major advantage of these behaviorally oriented procedures of analysis is that we are not forced to make a premature selection of competing causal theories which would affect our alternatives of action. Neither are we required to subscribe to one or another "global theory" which purports to explain all aspects of a phenomenon, such as discrimination or poverty.

For example, there are two major approaches to the explanation of poverty, each with its implications for solutions.[15] Situational theories emphasize various aspects of the societal context, such as the lack of access to well-paid and steady work, inadequate educational opportunities, or poor nutrition and the resulting physical and mental debilities. Cultural theories emphasize the values and life styles which individuals acquire by virtue of having grown up and living in a "culture of poverty."[16] Depending on the theory to which one subscribes, a program of income maintenance can be expected to succeed, or to fail. One or another type of guaranteed annual income, for example, would help alleviate the problem of poverty due to the first set of factors, for both the belief in and the willingness to engage in work are assumed to exist already.[17] But such a

[14]For examples of such attempts to reformulate ideas, see Samuelson (1961); Carey (1967).

[15]Spilerman and Elesh (1971).

[16]Lewis (1966).

[17]For good illustrations of this position, see Liebow (1967).

program would be ineffective in dealing with poverty due to the second set of factors, for the mere provision of money would not change the individual's value structure and might simply reinforce the existing life style. Thus it is important to know which theoretical explanation of poverty is correct, whether both are valid, and which individuals are affected by which factors.

A behavioral perspective does not require us to subscribe to either theory but allows us to make use of the insights found in each. It forces us to examine the lives of individuals, families, groups, and neighborhoods to find the determinants of those behaviors which contribute to and maintain poverty. By following the procedures outlined above, by finding answers to the several sets of questions, we can determine whether the contingencies of these behaviors come from the larger world (the situation) or from the immediate context (the subculture). Once we know the causal factors we can design an appropriate program, involving the modification of existing behavior patterns and the restructuring of the social environment.

Sociological Concepts

The fact that sociologists have always been concerned with human behavior means that most sociological concepts and propositions can be easily and profitably viewed in terms of a behavioral model of man. Such a perspective will engender two major types of questions. The first has been asked in one or another form by many students of society: "What are the empirical referents of this concept, term, or proposition?" As long as one is interested in social behavior, the answer would include descriptions of one or another measurable—or at least observable—facet of individual or collective activities.[18] The other type of question has been asked less frequently: "How do the social phenomena referred to by the concept, term, or proposition affect people's behavior?" Since we consider activities as being determined largely by discriminative and contingent stimuli, we will want to phrase any answer in terms of these elements of the behavior triad.

When we follow such procedures, most answers will be in close agreement with commonly employed concepts and generalizations. The major difference is an increased specificity of the concept and a heightened awareness of its ramifications in the form of more precise statements concerning the relationship between social phenomena and individual and group behavior.

Let us take, as a simple example, the important sociological concept of "norm" and some of the propositions associated with it. According to

[18]Homans (1964a, 1964b). For examples, see Kunkel (1970), chapter 4.

one popular text, norms are "guides to conduct, specifying what is appropriate or inappropriate, setting limits within which individuals may seek alternate ways to achieve their goals".[19] Blake and Davis define a norm as "any standard or rule that states what human beings should or should not think, say, or do under given circumstances."[20] They point out that inner and outer compulsions (or sanctions) are as much a part of norms as the rules themselves, and that orderly conduct is largely "a result of assessing the consequences for nonconformity rather than a result of the 'internalization' of the norm".[21] According to Williams, "social norms are rules for conduct. The norms are the standards by reference to which behavior is judged and approved or disapproved."[22] In all three definitions the empirical referents of norms include the verbal statement of a rule and the link between behavior and its consequences (which exemplifies the rule).

The behavioral perspective does not tell us how to analyze norms or how to solve the problems we are likely to encounter in such an effort;[23] but it does tell us to look for $S^D \longrightarrow R \longrightarrow S^r$ triads and the kinds of variations—for example in S^D and in short- or long-term contingencies—that are important. Furthermore, the behavioral perspective will protect us from the fallacies of reification and normative determinism, i.e., from viewing norms as something "real" out there which "cause" behavior. As we have seen in this chapter, behavior is determined by a number of factors, some arising in the present and others stemming from the past, some associated with the individual and others with his social context. The proposition that "norms determine behavior," a view which in one form or another is quite popular, we now see to be not only vague and misleading but, more importantly, impractical, for it does not suggest any procedures we might use in a program of action.

Social Problems

A behavioral model of man allows us to use the most common definition of "social problems" as those activities or lack of activities which the members of a society or subculture consider to be social problems. These behaviors (for example, crime)—and deficits (for example, illiteracy)—will be viewed as the "primary activities" of our analysis and provide the starting point of any study. Both the immediately surrounding and the more widely distributed determinants of these activities and behavior deficits will bring us face to face with a number of more or less "social"

[19]Broom and Selznick (1968), p. 55.
[20]Blake and Davis (1964), p. 456.
[21]Blake and Davis (1964), p. 466.
[22]Williams (1968), p. 204.
[23]Gibbs (1965; 1968).

phenomena which should also be dissected into their behavioral components.

Most people have little difficulty seeing social problems in terms of behavior and its determinants, but some practice in thinking about behavior *deficits* may be necessary. As long as social problems involve one as much as the other, action programs must be concerned with both. Many deficits in basic skills, such as functional illiteracy or lack of "social graces," have as their major determinants the inadequate operation of schools and families and the fact that young people can live "reasonably well" in their subcultures without encountering severe difficulties—until they attempt to enter the labor market.

By emphasizing the role of individuals' social environments, the behavioral perspective leads us to the study of social factors and processes and their implications for social problems; thus it favors so-called structural explanations rather than individualistic explanations (many of which have a psychodynamic basis).[24] For example, poverty has often been said to be due to largely individual characteristics such as laziness, shiftlessness, lack of thrift and foresight, loose morals, and so forth.[25] Or it may be viewed as being a result of structural factors, such as inadequate educational and job opportunities, discrimination, and poor medical services. A behavioral perspective would emphasize the latter factors and suggest, in addition, that many of the "individualistic characteristics" are the results of learning within a social context and thus have significant structural roots.

The activities which contribute to and indeed constitute social problems not only have been learned in the past but are maintained in the present. It is the task of behavioral analysis to determine the relevant factors, for it is here that we will find a major key to the solution of problems. For most behaviors in this "problem" category, maintenance results from the operation of structural factors. For example, the consequences of delinquent acts in most cities are hardly aversive, while, for many youths, the results of being law-abiding and hard-working are hardly reinforcing.[26] Severity of punishment cannot be viewed by itself, for it is inextricably bound to the probability of being caught; and if the latter is low, even severe penalties will not be aversive. According to one estimate, a youthful gang member with average skills faces a probability of only .04 of being arrested for criminal incidents involving potential violence.[27]

[24]For an application to the problem of poverty, see Feagin (1972).

[25]Rischin (1968) discusses several examples of this view and its detrimental consequences.

[26]For a general description of this situation, see Banfield (1970), chapter 8.

[27]Strodtbeck and Short (1964).

The solution to social problems will usually require the modification of several existing behavior patterns and the extinction of some old behaviors. This implies that we can specify which activities people should engage in. The task is easy in the case of "reading," but quite difficult if we want people to have greater "freedom over their destiny" or if we want to give individuals more "opportunities for self-actualization." Abstract goals will not be helpful in the designing of effective programs, because the procedures of any program must be specific and concrete if they are to be instituted. It is best to delineate a goal—for example, the rehabilitation of delinquents—in terms of activities, both those which we think should be present (*e.g.,* literacy) and those which we think should be absent (*e.g.,* fighting). Any attempt to define a program's behavior goals involves value judgments, however, and thus is subject to considerable debate. The preference for literacy over fighting, for example, may be viewed as an expression of middle-class bias; yet the definition of goals which are completely or even largely value-free may well be impossible.

One partial solution is to list those activities and skills which are likely to enable a person to do "reasonably well" in our society; yet here too we may run into difficulties. Reading skills are quite specific and surely would be on everyone's list, but many other items will probably be quite vague and subject to debate, such as "having a long-range point of view." Furthermore, the implicit assumptions in this procedure are that we live in a sane society and that individuals would benefit materially *and* psychologically by adjusting to it. Even if it were agreed that we should consider only the sane aspects of our society, there would be arguments as to what should be included.[28]

Another solution is to list those activities and skills which will enable the individual to take advantage of the many choices and opportunities provided by his society. An educated and courteous person has more alternatives, in terms of jobs, for example, than an illiterate person who has never learned to get along with people. The sociologist then has two tasks before him. First, he must determine the ways in which a society's variety and distribution of opportunities and behavioral requirements can be matched with the variety and distribution of potentialities and skills of its members. Second, he must describe and design the types of social structures and operations which will enable individuals to acquire and maintain the necessary skills.[29] In order to do this well, one must understand the dynamics of learning within a social context. This is the subject of the next chapter.

[28]Fromm (1955).
[29]Becker (1970), Part 3.

4
A Behavioral
Model of Man:
Processes

In the last chapter we looked at the several components of a behavioral model of man and considered the major types of events which affect a person's behavior. In this chapter we will be concerned with individuals, their environments, the processes of social learning, the best conditions for learning, and some sociological implications.

SOCIAL LEARNING PROCESSES

The nature of human learning, *i.e.*, what "actually happens" in man when one of his activities is reinforced, is still a subject of debate, and new information becomes available almost daily. Psychologists, neurophysiologists, and biochemists—not to mention philosophers—have proposed various theories, but no explanation as yet enjoys general acceptance. For those who are interested in the analysis of social systems, the study and solution of social problems, or the designing of policies, this unsettled state of affairs is of relatively little concern, however, because their interest does not lie in man but in social life. What matters is not *how* people learn but *what* they learn; not how the *brain* functions but how the *social context* operates.

"Learning" is usually defined in terms of new behaviors and probabilities of repetition within a certain context; we say, for example, that a person has learned a skill when he can and does perform it more often or better than he did before, in appropriate circumstances.[1] The results of literally hundreds of studies performed by psychologists over the last few decades can be summarized by the proposition that "the selection and performance [of behavior] is mainly governed by anticipated outcomes based on previous consequences that were directly encountered, vicariously experienced, or self-administered."[2]

The Establishment of Behavior

DIRECT LEARNING. When an activity is followed by an S^r on a number of trials, the probability of repetition in similar circumstances increases and eventually approaches certainty. For example, in the course of daily life an individual may perform a number of behavior patterns, say R_1, R_2, R_3 ... R_{12}. If an S^r follows R_3 but not R_2 or R_4, then the probability of R_3 occurring in the future increases, while that of R_2 and R_4 declines. The selective reinforcement of certain activities and not of others is known as *differential reinforcement* and is responsible for the fact that individuals engage in limited numbers of activities—usually those defined as "good" or "necessary" or "proper" by the particular subculture and society to which they belong. Many complex behavior patterns do not occur "naturally" and are gradually learned by means of *successive approximation.* That is, activities which are vaguely similar to those which are ultimately desired are reinforced initially; once these are established, only those which are more similar to the desired end are reinforced, until the final activity is eventually performed. In learning Spanish, for example, the student is at first rewarded for an approximate pronunciation of "ferrocarril"; later he receives praise for moderately correct sounds of, say, the double "r"; and eventually he is rewarded only for perfectly enunciated words. Behavior is said to be established when it occurs with the desired frequency in appropriate circumstances.

Experiments and naturalistic observations indicate that a number of requirements must be met if behavior is to be established by means of a person's direct experiences:

1. In order for behavior to be reinforced, it must first occur. Language makes it possible to issue instructions, but in natural settings and without communication the activity that is to be reinforced may occur rarely if at all; hence there are severe limitations to direct learning.

[1]Hilgard and Bower (1966), chapter 1.

[2]Bandura (1969), p. 132. For other propositions of a formal model, see Kunkel and Nagasawa (1973).

2. In order for reinforcers to operate, some degree of deprivation must be present in an individual.

3. In order for behavior to be reinforced an S^r must be available.

4. In order for such a presentation to occur the environment must somehow "know" whether or not the "right" activity has occurred.

5. Reinforcers must be consistent; that is, over time a particular R should be followed by either an S^r *or* an S^a but not by both. The greater the consistency with which contingencies are presented, the more rapidly and effectively the behavior will be established.

6. The $R \longrightarrow S^r$ link must be repeated several times.

7. The time interval between behavior and its consequence should be short. The smaller this interval, the more effective the contingency is likely to be during the learning process.

When we consider these factors we come to the conclusion that the establishment of new behavior is by no means an easy or automatic process; in fact, a number of specific and not necessarily widespread conditions must be met if learning is to be rapid and effective. The absence of any one—for example, a delay in the presentation of a reinforcer, or the inconsistent presentation of S^r—will reduce the effectiveness of a learning program. Nevertheless, the usual result of daily experiences is the establishment of literally thousands of sequences of discriminative stimuli, activities, and contingencies, which we can schematize in this general form:

$$S^D \longrightarrow R \longrightarrow S^r$$

MODELING. The processes and procedures described so far emphasize an individual's direct personal experiences. Fortunately for man, the learning of new behavior patterns does not occur only by means of personal trial and error. In fact, if learning depended solely on the exhibition of an activity before it could be reinforced, learning would be slow and life quite dangerous. The activity which is to be established initially might not occur frequently enough to be reinforced, and errors could be costly; for example, few people learn to drive an automobile by trial and error alone. Rather, most human learning occurs through *modeling*. By this we mean that the activities which are to be established are either described to the person (*e.g.,* "you shift into first") or demonstrated to him (*e.g.,* "this is how you shift"). Equally important, the consequences of the new behavior (driving successfully) are usually demonstrated or are at least apparent, so that an individual knows what the eventual outcome is likely to be even when his own behavior is still somewhat awkward. Another major type of modeling occurs when a person simply observes the actions of other people and the consequences of these actions, and then attempts to repeat these actions himself. Parents model behavior—often inadvertently—for their children, older siblings for the younger, and public figures for the "common man." Thus modeling not only helps establish behavior but contributes to the definition of discriminative stimuli and the learning of contingency probabilities as well. Instead of slowly and laboriously acquiring complex new behavior patterns by means of actually experienced differential reinforcement and successive approximation, it is possible and indeed common to learn through "vicarious reinforcement," *i.e.,* the observation of others' behavior and its consequences.[3]

A large number of studies show that ordinary behavior is not the only type of activity which is subject to successful modeling. Abstract concepts such as "honesty," as well as "innovative behavior, generalized behavioral orientations, and principles for generating novel combinations of behaviors can be transmitted to observers through exposure to modeling cues."[4] Extinction, too, can occur through modeling, and behavior modification is also possible by means of a combination of vicarious reinforcement and punishment.

Whether or not a particular person comes to be defined as a model depends on the observer's past experiences, hence the definition is learned. If the behavior one adopts from a model because the model is rewarded is not reinforced when one later exhibits it, chances are good that the new behavior will not be maintained and that the model will be redefined. The nature of the modeling situation and the characteristics of the model, of the observer, and any similarities between the two affect the probability of the observer's replication of the modeled behavior. At present, however, research indicates that the reinforcement of observed activities is more important, generally, than the effects of variations in observer characteristics and model attributes.[5]

The Maintenance of Behavior

Once a behavior pattern has been established, it is usually maintained by the presentation of S^r on one or another schedule, and less commonly by the avoidance of punishment. Differential reinforcement still occurs—*i.e.,* R_3 rather than R_2 or R_4 is followed by an S^r—but it is no longer necessary that rewards occur often or immediately. When a long time span is involved, however, it is useful to provide instructions for linking the S^r or S^a to the relevant behavior; for example, instead of simply saying "good" one might say "you did a good job washing the car."

[3]Bandura (1969), chapter 3.
[4]Bandura (1969), p. 148.
[5]Bandura (1969), pp. 136–138.

As we briefly indicated in the last chapter, some reinforcers can be self-administered (*e.g.,* "I did a good job"), and others can be intrinsic (*e.g.,* an activity one "likes to do"). While such reinforcers operate in the learning of new behaviors—as when one "feels good" about having mastered a new skill—they are especially significant for the maintenance of activities. Bandura summarizes a large number of studies as indicating that "people generally adopt the standards for self-reinforcement exhibited by exemplary models, they evaluate their own performance relative to that standard, and then they serve as their own reinforcing agents,"[6] using either goods or, more frequently, symbolic expressions.

When we observe that activities recur over long periods of time without apparent reinforcement, we must consider a number of possible explanations. The behavior may be intrinsically reinforcing or be followed by an activity which has that character for the individual; self-reinforcement may occur; or there may be external reinforcement which we do not recognize as such. A "habit," for example, may be maintained simply by the fact that the activity "works" or is successful, as when we drive the same route every day because it is pleasant and gets us to the store. The final alternative is that the reinforcement schedule is drawn out, with very infrequent rewards.

While the learning of new behavior usually requires a continuous schedule—*e.g.,* an S^r whenever R_3 occurs—maintenance does not. In fact, intermittent schedules are much more effective, easier to operate, and engender fewer problems for the individual and the environment than is the case with continuous schedules. The major disadvantages of the latter schedules are that (1) it is difficult to maintain sufficient deprivation (hence effective S^r), and (2) when reinforcement ceases, emotional reactions are common and the rate of behavior declines quite rapidly. Conversely, intermittent schedules, and especially variable-ratio schedules, produce high rates of behavior, make it easier to provide effective S^r, and do not require complete and accurate information concerning the individual's every action. Furthermore, upon cessation of reinforcement there is less likelihood of emotional reactions and the rate of extinction is lower. While some behavior is maintained by rather frequent reinforcement—for example, the weekly paycheck—other activities, and sometimes rather complex behavior sets, are maintained by schedules which promise rewards in the quite distant future—for example, salvation upon the completion of a pious life. In order for such schedules to be effective for the maintenance of behavior, however, it is usually necessary to have a series of intermediate reinforcers—such as periodic ceremonies which indicate one's state of grace.

[6]Bandura (1969), p. 33.

One of the inescapable "facts of life" which everyone faces is that he must learn to "live with" the several schedules found in the operation of his social environment; and one of the inescapable "facts of life" which students of society face is that in heterogeneous social systems the schedules which members of various subcultures learn are not necessarily congruent with one another or, for that matter, the ones which actually operate in the social system. Middle-class adults, for example, often tend to forget that schedules *differ* and must be *learned,* and consequently may have some difficulty understanding the "impatience"—as well as the "equanimity"—of those who come from different backgrounds.[7]

CHAINING. Few activities of daily life are discrete units followed by actual reinforcers. Rather, activities are usually combined into chains of varying length and complexity, at the end of which reinforcement occurs. A simple example is the writing of a letter; here a number of activities are chained together to form a unit which is reinforced by, for example, the individual's avoidance of reminders of negligence. Conceptually, a behavior chain consists of activities where each is the conditioned reinforcer for the preceding and the discriminative stimulus for the following activity— hence S^{rD}:

$$S^D \longrightarrow R_1(S^D) \longrightarrow R_2(S^{rD}) \longrightarrow R_3(S^{rD}) \longrightarrow R_4(S^{rD}) \longrightarrow R_5(S^r) \longrightarrow S^r$$

In this example, R_2 is an S^r for R_1 and also serves as an S^D for R_3; only R_5 is actually reinforced. The behavior chains which constitute daily life vary greatly in length and complexity, from a drive downtown (and ultimate safe arrival) to job performance (and ultimate pay check) to a pious life (and salvation after death). The procedure (or process) of chaining usually begins at the end and works backward, so to speak, except when specific verbal descriptions of the whole chain are available. In terms of the illustration, R_5 is established first by being followed by an S^r. This makes R_5 itself a conditioned reinforcer which, by being presented after R_4 has occurred, helps establish R_4. R_4, in turn, becomes an S^D for R_5 and a

---

[7]Principles in the area of behavior maintenance are mainly concerned with schedules of reinforcement and their effects on overall performance and variations in behavior rates. For example, S^r presented on a continuous schedule lead to rapid learning and rates which vary with the degree of deprivation. When S^r are presented on a fixed-interval schedule, the result is a pause after reinforcement and a gradual increase in the activity rate as time for the next S^r approaches. When S^r occur on a variable-interval schedule, a low and nearly stable behavior rate is the usual result. In general, the longer the intervals of a VI schedule are, the lower the activity rate is likely to be. When S^r occur on a fixed-ratio schedule, the result is a pause after the S^r (brief for low ratios and long for high ratios) and an abrupt change to a constant, high behavior rate. Finally, when S^r are presented on a variable-ratio schedule, a very high and nearly constant activity rate is the probable result.

conditioned reinforcer for preceding activities, such as R_3. The building of chains is slow and requires much care and patience; and while the later links—such as R_4 or R_5—are usually well established, the earlier links— *e.g.*, R_1—are often difficult to learn and maintain. For example, many children have trouble understanding why they should take piano lessons, and adults are often less than keen on living a virtuous life; in both cases the chain is rather long, requires much work and sacifice, and the pay-off is uncertain. The problem of long and complex chains is especially note-worthy when we do not actually experience a chain but must rely on general descriptions of it. For example, it has been said that the taking of mathematics courses in high school will increase one's chances of eventu-ally entering a good graduate program in physics, which in turn will affect the quality of job offers after one acquires a Ph.D. The acceptance of such long chains and schedules usually requires some experience with relatively long chains, relevant observations of other people's lives, or trust in some-one's descriptions—all of which are slowly acquired, require some training, and are not accessible to everyone.

In order to facilitate chaining, to prevent discouragement, and to forestall the rupturing of lengthy chains, it is advisable to include activities which are intrinsically reinforcing or to break the chain into several shorter but connected segments, each with its own intermediate reinforcer, such as good grades at the end of a course or graduation ceremonies spaced throughout one's educational career. In general, the greater the distance, in both time and number of links, between any activity and the terminal of a behavior chain, the less effective it is likely to be, both as an S^D and as a conditioned reinforcer.

The Extinction of Behavior

When the rate of activities and the probability of repetition decline and approach zero, extinction is said to occur. Three major factors are usually responsible for extinction: the cessation of reinforcement, the application (or threat) of punishment, and the elimination of the discriminative stimu-lus.

The cessation of reinforcement can be direct, as when previously available S^r are eliminated, or indirect, as in the alteration of an individual's state variables, which effectively changes the power of previously opera-tive and still available S^r. As we mentioned above, the rate at which extinction proceeds depends on the previous schedule of reinforcement and the rigor with which the new schedule of zero frequency is main-tained. When the S^r provided by a person's environment cannot be manip-ulated, extinction sometimes can be produced by reducing the deprivation with which the S^r is associated; such satiation procedures result in the effective "elimination" of the reinforcer. Emotional reactions, *e.g.,* anxiety or frustration, often attend the cessation of reinforcement and reduce the effectiveness of an extinction program.

The application of punishment, and eventually the mere threat or high probability of an S^a, contribute to at least a temporary decline in the rate of behavior. The side effects are often so severe, however, that punishment is, generally speaking, a relatively ineffective method for producing extinction. Fear, anxiety, and other emotional reactions often attend—and eventually precede—punishment, thereby interfering with the individual's learning of alternative behavior patterns, or at least with his learning *not* to exhibit the old activities. Spontaneous recovery (the reappearance of the activity) is a rather common feature of extinction produced by punishment alone.

Since most activities are associated with particular preceding discriminative stimuli, it follows that when there are no S^D the R will not appear either. If, however, the behavior should be attempted in a new context (*i.e.,* in the absence of the old S^D) and be reinforced, R will simply become associated with a new S^D. The disappearance of an S^D, in short, must be associated with the cessation of reinforcement in that and other contexts.[8]

The Modification of Behavior

The alteration of behavior involves the application of one or more of the processes and procedures just described. The old activity is extinguished and the new behavior is established while most other activities remain the same. For example, if R_2 is to be modified, say into R_{14}, the following steps would be taken:

1. The maintenance of R_1, R_3, etc.;
2. The extinction of R_2, by one of several methods;
3. The establishment of R_{14}, by means of modeling or differential reinforcement. Whether or not successive approximation is required depends on the complexity of R_{14} and the similarity betwen R_2 and R_{14}.

[8]Presently available evidence, derived from both experiments and naturalistic observations, can be summarized in a number of generalizations. For example, when reinforcement ceases consequent to a continuous schedule, the behavior rate declines rapidly, accompanied by emotional reactions. The greater the similarity between the maintenance schedule and extinction, the slower the extinction; a variable-ratio schedule of low frequency, therefore, will lead to behaviors that are most difficult to extinguish. Furthermore, the greater the magnitude of the reinforcers or the number of reinforced activities, the greater the amount of time and number of nonreinforced activities required to reach a low, terminal rate of behavior. Conversely, the greater the number of previous extinctions, the more rapidly will subsequent extinctions proceed.

Other Processes

The establishment, maintenance, and alteration of activities involve three additional processes which serve to facilitate or hinder the learning and expression of behavior.

MAXIMIZATION.   As we indicated in the last chapter, many activities have several consequences of various weights and valuations; hence it must be assumed that people usually act in terms of total contingencies rather than simple S^a or unitary reinforcers. Another important proposition of our model of man, derived from both psychologists' experiments and economists' observations, which has significance for the operation of social systems is that, in general, people behave so as to maximize the total contingency of their actions. That is, most individuals tend to sum up the various consequences of the several alternatives confronting them and to select that behavior pattern which promises to result in the most beneficial total consequences. The usual consideration of costs and profits, however, while applicable, is probably too restricted for the analysis of behavior in complex social systems. A more adequate view of the total contingency would include, from the point of view of the behaving individual:

1. his time horizon, which determines the consequences that are included and excluded in his summation;
2. his view of the schedules and probabilities with which the contingencies occur;
3. his impression of the environment as a predictable and stable source of various contingencies;
4. his knowledge of the relationship between his behavior and various reactions and future events emanating from his environment;
5. his present and presumed future state variables, which determine not only whether a particular future event will be an S^r or an S^a, but also its weight;
6. his scale of values in terms of which he assesses the sum total of the contingencies, including the probabilities of various risks;
7. his ability to combine and evaluate all of the relevant contingencies of any one activity;
8. his selection of one behavior on the basis of one or another decision rule;[9]
9. his ability to effectively perform the activity which has the "best" predicted consequences.

When we look at this list it is immediately apparent that maximization is a matter of judgment. A person could, for example, behave so as to maximize the S^r regardless of the S^a; or minimize the S^a regardless of the

[9]Ofshe and Ofshe (1970); Simon (1957).

S^r; or minimize the S^a and maximize the S^r within certain limits. In addition, perfect maximization is quite rare. Limitations of an individual's knowledge of his environment, restrictions of experience, narrow parameters presented by a short-range point of view, and the perception of a turbulent world in which long-range predictions are hazardous, would indicate that maximization is usually a matter of degree and depends on estimates. Furthermore, an observer may well have information which differs from that of the individual concerned. The observer may know more, or less, or may interpret contingencies differently; salvation in the distant future, for example, may be a very real and powerful S^r to one person, while a nonbelieving observer might assign little weight to this reward or might not even consider it. Observers may also be unaware of a person's self-administered censure or gratification. Thus maximization is a matter of perspective. Finally, the behavioral consequences of maximization depend on whether the individual acts alone or is a member of a group. The perception of what is optimal for a person varies with the objectives, size, and structure of the group to which he belongs, hence maximization is a matter of contextual characteristics.[10]

Good illustrations of the role of rewards, costs, and maximization are provided by some recent discussions of deviance. DeLamater, for example, points out that "to the extent that the deviant can prevent detection and/or punishment by agencies [of social control], or to the extent that they 'overlook' the deviance, the rewards . . . will regularly exceed the deprivations resulting from deviance."[11] After initial deviant acts, which more often than not are individual rather than social occurrences, their repetition "depends on the responses of others, both deviants and primary relations, and the reward-cost balance which the individual experiences. . . . A strong force in preventing deviance is the response or anticipated response of those with whom one has primary relationships."[12] In his discussion of crime in large cities, Banfield notes that for many individuals, both young and old, the probable benefits of occasional criminal activities far exceed the probable costs and that, as a general rule, despite what one often hears and observes, crime does pay.[13] The contingency changes necessary for behavior modification, therefore, include not so much an increase in the cost of criminal activities (which would also increase the community's outlay for police, courts, and jails) as an increase in the benefits of non-criminal activities.

[10]Olson (1971).

[11]DeLamater (1968), p. 448. For a comprehensive discussion of deviance from a behavioral perspective, see Akers (1973).

[12]DeLamater (1968), pp. 449, 451.

[13]Banfield (1970), chapter 8.

It is a small step from the discussion of maximization to the treatment of rationality. A person is usually labeled "rational" when his actions tend to maximize external contingencies as evaluated by an observer, while "irrational" indicates a departure from this standard. The common occurrence of self-administered consequences (such as self-approval, or feeling depressed when one has not done as well as one had hoped), together with the fact that an observer and the behaving individual are likely to have different points of view, greatly reduce the usefulness of such terms as "irrational." Rationality assumes that people take into account all external and self-administered contingencies known to them and evaluate them to the best of their abilities. When an observer labels a person's behavior "irrational," this is likely to be simply a reflection of different assessments of contingencies and decision rules, or of the person's inability to perform a different or "better" activity, perhaps because he never learned one or has no opportunity.

DISCRIMINATION. This is the process by which an individual learns to define and distinguish the "signals" in the environment which indicate whether or not a particular activity is likely to be reinforced. Some discriminations can be very crude, as when we distinguish between "strangers" and "friends" and act accordingly. Other discriminations have to be very fine, as when one attempts to "sort out" the people one meets at a cocktail party where gate crashers abound; here "stranger" and "friend" are only part of relevant discriminative stimuli, for "cocktail party" is itself an S^D for being moderately friendly even to strangers. The discriminations required for ordinary life are varied and complex, and are usually established by means of reinforcement which follows specific activities in particular contexts and circumstances. A "smooth operator" has learned to discriminate well—he does the right thing in the right place at the right time— while a "boor" has not and thus behaves inappropriately.

GENERALIZATION. This process is roughly the opposite of discrimination, for here a particular behavior pattern that was associated with one S^D comes to occur also in other similar contexts. Deference which originally was shown toward one's grandmother, for example, may come to be directed toward other old people as well. Studies indicate that there are generalization gradients, usually based on similarity, which vary with the particular S^D and R and depend on the individual's learning history as well. While some generalization is quite common, the maintenance of behavior based on generalization depends greatly on the later reinforcement history. Thus, if deference toward other old people is not reinforced, generalization from the grandmother to "others" is likely to cease. In practice, generalization is one of the major processes of learning, for it obviates the necessity to define anew every context in terms of relevant S^D and to shape anew the appropriate R.

Ideal Conditions

This discussion of basic processes and the available experimental evidence may be summarized in statements describing the best circumstances and procedures for the establishment, maintenance, and extinction of behavior. When daily life is characterized by conditions which differ markedly from the ideal, one should expect that both the establishment and extinction of behavior will be slow, laborious, and not necessarily successful ventures. In general, we should expect that, particularly in heterogeneous, complex, and dynamic societies, even the maintenance of the "right" behavior patterns is likely to be quite difficult. Conversely, when a society's characteristics approach ideal conditions we should expect learning to be easy and behavior maintenance to be a simple thing. When these circumstances prevail and when these procedures are employed, a behavioral program should be successful.

As far as is known today, the ideal conditions are as follows:[14]

FOR THE ESTABLISHMENT OF BEHAVIOR:

1. If R is complex, there must be a logical sequence of successive approximation.
2. There should be opportunities for modeling, especially for complex R.
3. There must be opportunities to exhibit R.
4. There must be a stable context and opportunity to define S^D.
5. Some deprivation must be maintained.
6. Contingencies must be applied immediately.
7. Contingencies must be applied consistently.
8. Contingencies must be applied frequently, initially on a continuous schedule.

FOR THE MAINTENANCE OF BEHAVIOR:

1. Reinforcers should occur intermittently (with the particular schedule depending on the rate of R that is to be maintained).
2. Contingencies must be applied consistently.
3. There must be some deprivation, or generalized reinforcers must be available.
4. Schedule changes must be gradual.
5. The S^D must occur whenever R is supposed to occur.

[14]Based on Bandura (1969), chapters 3–6.

6. There must be opportunities to exhibit R (*i.e.,* there must be no restraints).

FOR THE EXTINCTION OF BEHAVIOR:　Because of uncertainties and unresolved debates surrounding the subject of punishment, it is difficult to
list one set of best conditions. Presently available data suggest the following elements:

1. Cessation of reinforcement.
2. Elimination of deprivation.
3. Presentation of S^a.
4. Opportunities to engage in other activities which are reinforced.

These eighteen conditions and procedures have definite implications
for the operation of an individual's immediate social context and, indeed,
for the structure of a viable social system. Consistent contingencies, for
example, require that both S^r and S^a must be available and can be presented
quickly. Furthermore, these conditions assume that there are criteria for
the evaluation of R, that there are some means of comparing R with these
criteria, and that this information is passed on to whoever provides the
contingency. The maintenance of deprivation, indispensable for the existence of reinforcers, requires a social philosophy which does not advocate
immediate and complete gratification of most human wants as a matter of
right. Effective differential reinforcement, finally, requires that people are
willing and able to punish as well as reward, and that they reward and
punish quickly and consistently on the basis of behavior rather than the
individual's status, physical characteristics, or other considerations.

One cannot expect the easy and rapid learning of complex activities
in a social environment which lacks several of the above characteristics. At
the same time, a society which makes ideal conditions possible is not
necessarily one whose members are interested in or conversant with the
employment of the basic procedures. As we will see in later chapters, a
detailed analysis of the differences between ideal learning conditions and
existing circumstances enables us to locate the major determinants of social
change and many significant social problems. Excellent illustrations of
such discrepancies and their consequences for individuals, as well as of
programs designed to eliminate such problems, are found in Hamblin's
study of schools.[15] Interestingly enough, the title of this book—*The Humanization Processes*—indicates not only that learning transforms the human organism into a person, but that empirically grounded principles and
their application are the essentials of any humane approach to the solution

[15]Hamblin *et al.* (1971).

of individual and social problems. It is mainly by providing more logical and humane environments, in terms of the above criteria, that action programs will have a chance to be effective, and that we will be able to design better and viable social systems.

The Internal State

Our concern with the structure and operation of an individual's—or group's and even subculture's—social context, rather than with feelings, hopes, frustrations, and other aspects of the internal state, should not be viewed on an all-or-nothing basis. As we have pointed out several times, our behavioral model of man does not deny the existence of an internal state. Many of the processes assumed to occur in behaving, such as maximization, expectation, or perception, obviously imply an internal state, and our discussion of state variables makes explicit reference to it. We have tried, however, to minimize our reliance on internal processes by postulating relatively simple ones and by relating them to external events whenever possible. Thus we viewed expectation in terms of probabilities of S^r and S^a as perceived on the basis of past experiences.

In short, we have thought of man as a system: events, other people, and various other stimuli provide "inputs," and the resulting "outputs" are behavior patterns. What goes on within the system is still largely a matter of debate. While there is a possibility that it includes psychodynamic forces and processes, it is also possible that the system actually contains other elements. In this and the following chapters we subscribe to the view that we simply do not know enough about man's internal state to make many detailed statements about it. We cannot say precisely what it consists of, but we also know that it is not empty. We shall have to rely on future research by psychologists and others to tell us about man's internal structure and operations, or at least to provide us with valid schematics. Today we have some ideas about these things, we make educated guesses and subscribe to various theories, but there is as yet no general agreement as to the content of the internal state besides the several elements of maximization described above, decision rules, plans, and the memory implied by these.[16]

The area in which our lack of specific, validated knowledge about the internal state is especially detrimental is that of state variables, particularly the area of nonphysiological deprivations. The range of hypotheses, in-

---

[16]For discussions of rationality and decision rules, see Meeker (1971) and Rapoport (1966). Miller, Galanter, and Pribam (1960) describe some of the processes which presumably occur when an individual confronts a situation and "decides" to engage in a particular action. Bandura (1969) emphasizes such internal processes as symbolic mediation and covert rehearsal in behavior modification. Scott (1971) presents a behavioral perspective of the internalization of norms.

cluding the ideas of Fromm, Montagu, and Maslow, to mention only a few students of the subject, is wide indeed. Some hypotheses can be stated in specific, empirically relevant form with relative ease, as Montagu has so admirably done with "love."[17] Other concepts, such as "self-actualization," are difficult to phrase in terms of observable or measurable activities or events without appearing idiosyncratic.

Yet, as long as we recognize the difficulty and remain on the lookout for hints and suggestions from different fields and specialists, and as long as we evaluate them in terms of empirical evidence, we cannot go too far wrong. By using a behavioral model of man we certainly will be no worse off than we would be by blindly accepting everything that people have had to say about man's internal state during just the last hundred years alone. The point to remember is that even if such a presently vague state variable as the need for "self-actualization" were to be definitely established, and thus would have to be incorporated into our model, the propositions outlined in this chapter would not be materially affected. A smile would still be a reward, and one person's greeting would still be a discriminative stimulus for a friendly response by another. All that we would have to do is add a new "reward" and perhaps a new set of intrinsically reinforcing activities, *i.e.,* those which result in or signify a person's "self-actualization."

While many social scientists prefer to stay away from the question of what the specific nonphysiological state variables of man might be, such a concern is inescapable because, while physiological deprivations are being reduced for an ever larger number of people, neither happiness nor tranquility can be proven to have increased;[18] as Berthoff points out, the problems of America lie not so much in a deprivation of material goods as in the loss of roots, of community, and of a meaningful life both in work and at home.[19]

Summary

The learning processes described above operate within parameters determined by the individual's physiological, neurological, and chemical structures.[20] While some of these structures are the same for all members of a population or even species, there are individual variations which expand or constrict the "normal" parameters, as in the case of persons with prodigious memories or low intelligence. For present purposes it is sufficient to postulate that human beings are characterized by limited perception, cog-

[17]Montagu (1955), chapters 9 and 12.
[18]Berger *et al.* (1973).
[19]Berthoff (1971).
[20]Seligman and Hager (1972).

nition, time horizon, and memory (which can be expanded slightly through learning). Additional parameters arise from the individual's experiences, and thus are determined by social class, subculture, and society. While these two major sets of parameters are often irrelevant—as in the case of the ordinary behavior which make up daily life—they are quite significant in many complex behavior patterns and contingencies which involve a long time perspective or the complex interplay of physical, social, and ecological systems.[21] Behavioral variations even within a group, therefore, are facts of social life which should surprise no one, least of all the designers of social programs.

The significance of heterogeneity of behavior and of physiological and psychological characteristics within a population have not yet been fully explored or even described. One major implication, however, is that in any group there are likely to be individuals with what are often labeled "grossly deviant" behavior patterns, "distorted" perceptions, and "abnormal" cognitions. These will play important roles in the operation of a group, organization, or subculture—and through them affect the total system and its transformation.

A superficial reading of this chapter may remind one of hedonistic theory, utilitarianism, and Jeremy Bentham. Indeed, one may be tempted to reject a behavioral model because of the criticism which has been applied to these views over the decades and centuries.[22] Here one should remember three points.

First, every generalization discussed in this chapter is based on considerable direct, significant empirical evidence in the form of studies dealing with human beings both in the laboratory and the free environment. Any similarity with hedonistic or utilitarian theory and philosophy is coincidental and essentially irrelevant.

Second, most of the criticisms which have been leveled against such theories and philosophies are inapplicable to the behavioral model of man because the model is not derived from them. The best basis for criticism would be an attack on the empirical evidence from which the several generalizations are abstracted. The fact that behavioral principles have been found to be extremely effective in the shaping and maintenance of "normal" activities and in the modification of "abnormal" behavior, however, would make criticism a rather difficult enterprise.[23]

Third, a behavioral model of man is theoretically and philosophically neutral and does not logically lead to the conclusion that man is materialis-

---

[21]For a description of this problem, see Simon (1957).

[22]For an example of such criticism, see Abrahamsson (1970).

[23]Bandura (1969) describes and evaluates more than one hundred studies in these two areas.

tic or selfish. To be sure, people can be and have been moved by food, drink, and money—who can deny it? But a person can also be moved by honor, love of country, and the smile of a child. In fact, self-administered reinforcement can outweigh external consequences and enable a person to submit to prolonged maltreatment rather than submit to what he regards as unjust or immoral. In short, reinforcers can be many-splendored, and whether or not human beings are seen as base or selfish depends on the eye of the beholder.

SOCIOLOGICAL IMPLICATIONS

The dynamic aspects of the behavioral model of man we have outlined in this chapter have a number of significant implications for both sociological analysis and for the design of policies and social systems. We will now take a brief look at some of these, especially insofar as they tell us something about the possibility and nature of effective programs.

1. Human Behavior Is Malleable

In spite of the large number of studies which indicate that human behavior can be maintained or modified with relative ease, the popular belief persists—based on a psychodynamic perspective—that personality and its resulting behavior patterns, once they have been established in childhood, remain roughly the same throughout life. Such a static conception of behavior cannot help but produce a rather pessimistic view of society and man's role in its transformation. If today's experiences cannot affect tomorrow's behavior because of yesterday's personality, why worry much about today's events? If the only beneficiaries of societal alterations are coming generations, why not simply talk about and hope for a better future? Or we can agree with Rousseau or Freud that civilization—without specifying particulars—perverts the noble savage or naturally engenders discontent. The postulate of a static internal state allows one not only to give up on the present generation, but makes it easy to blame the past or invariant personalities, to absolve the present, and to abstain from large-scale collective efforts to modify existing social systems on the grounds that such efforts could not change people anyway. The fact that behavior can be modified leads to a rather optimistic view of the future, at least on theoretical grounds. Individuals beyond their teens are *not* "lost," the alterations of today's social systems *does* affect our behavior tomorrow, and yesterday's sins of omission and and commission need *not* burden us in the future. While much of man's inner being may still be beyond his understanding and power of remaking, as psychoanalysts, philosophers, and theologians are wont to tell us, man's ability to reshape his social environment and thus to affect his own behavior now appears to be quite real and significant. Furthermore, the postulate of malleability removes a major justification for present inaction and makes it increasingly difficult continually to blame the past for present woes. More disturbingly, perhaps, we are now faced by questions which were irrelevant in the past but which we must now answer prior to any program design: What should be done, how should it be done, and who should do it? Many of the simplistic and mystical answers of the past, including those centering on revolution or the reconstitution of society, turn out to be inadequate when viewed from the perspective of our model, for now we must be concerned with the specifics of construction. The empirical generalizations described in these two chapters provide us with a general outline of the requirements for constructive action, involving careful analysis, specific projects, rigorous adherence to learning principles, and willingness to experiment in the design and execution of programs.

2. The Recent Past Is Significant

While behavior is maintained by present contingencies, it has been learned in the past; hence an explanation of activities and an important guide to modification lie in a person's previous experiences and environmental conditions. The more we know about the past and the more carefully we have studied past events, the better will be our understanding of the present and the more specific will be our prescriptions of what needs to be done in the future.

The behavioral model does not require us to delve into a person's earliest life, however, and it is not necessary to know the precise origin of an idea, belief, activity, or institution. A study of the past is necessary only to the extent to which it provides information about a person's state variables, definitions of S^D, and effective contingencies. If we were to meet a speechless stranger today and begin our observations immediately, we would have sufficient data after a few weeks to provide us with at least preliminary hypotheses concerning the major determinants and possible modification of his behavior patterns.

Psychodynamic models generally require us to seek the origin of an activity in the distant past, and behavior modification, if it is to be genuine and lasting, will require either the removal of the causal factor through a better understanding of it, or a clinical reformulation of it. Since the search for origins is crucial for undertaking ameliorative action, the fact that it can be exhausting and is not guaranteed of success prevents the prompt initiation of policies and programs. But the behavioral perspective does not require us to be concerned with the original causes of an activity; its interest in the past centers on the elucidation of the conditions which are more proximate and accessible, and less obscured by selective memory.

In our study of the immediate past we will be interested not only in the specific determinants of a behavior but also in the general circumstances of learning. Thus, in order to gain an understanding of sex discrimination and what might be done about it, we would look at the role-models provided for little girls by their parents, neighbors, and teachers, and by books, verbal definitions of "what girls do," and by the activities encouraged in the community.[24] We must also look at the divergence of actual learning conditions from the ideal ones described earlier, for such conditions provide the general setting for a large number of behavior problems. Many city schools, for example, especially those located in slums, often provide environments which practically guarantee that the traditional functions of education, such as the transmission of basic skills and a society's cultural heritage, cannot be performed;[25] as a consequence, behavior deficits occur which enter into several social problems.

3. The Present Is Significant

Whether or not behavior patterns will recur in the future depends not so much on past learning histories as on present experiences. As was pointed out in this and the last chapter, today's events are the major determinants of future probabilities; if we should begin punishing even well-established activities today, or at least cease rewarding them, or provide models of conflicting activities, the current behavior will be affected in the future.

In practical terms this means that we must be careful in our dealings with others, and that we must evaluate our policies and programs not in terms of what they are supposed to accomplish but in terms of the actual behaviors they help shape, maintain, and extinguish. As Hamblin and others have pointed out,[26] for example, when teachers concern themselves with loud and aggressive students in a class room they in effect reinforce such behaviors by their attention. Teachers may think that their punishment and their display of anger are aversive, but in fact threats and verbal abuse soon loose their force and the teacher's expression of anger often becomes a rewarding experience for the student. Hence the real effects of teachers' actions and the environment they provide are often the opposite of that expected: loudness and aggression continue, while being quiet and studious—hardly noticed or rewarded—are reduced in frequency.

The presently wide acceptance of at least implicitly psychodynamic models of man affects the way we behave, our reactions to others and thus the way they behave later, the laws we promulgate, and the operation of

[24]For examples, see the anthology edited by Maccoby (1966).
[25]For illustrations, see Hamblin et al. (1971), and Kozol (1967).
[26]Hamblin et al. (1971); Thomas et al. (1968).

many institutions. For example, the belief that an individual has personality disorders such as a weak ego or an unresolved Oedipus complex often
excuses and may even justify activities which would otherwise arouse
censure; it becomes increasingly difficult to blame individuals, to hold
them responsible, and—most important—to react in appropriate ways
which would lead to corrective behavior modification. We become increasingly reluctant to punish or even to censure, and prefer to pass over the
event quietly, thereby effectively encouraging the individual to repeat his
actions. For example, the notion that aggression is instinctive or has one
or another deep psychological source practically condemns us to inaction
in the immediate situation, whereas a behavioral view of aggression opens
the way to various kinds of ameliorative projects, including more appropriate reactions on the part of the people exposed to an individual's aggression.[27]

A behavioral model of man alerts us to the fact that everything we
do, everything that occurs, is likely to be a discriminative and/or contingent stimulus for some behavior, though it is sometimes difficult to know
precisely what the implications for later activities will be. Especially when
we choose to do nothing—be it on the basis of ignorance, ambiguity, pity,
charity, or deliberate decision—what we see as an S^o is likely to be seen
by others as an S^r or S^a for their behaviors. Because individuals are always
engaged in some activity, any person's present context provides continuous and inescapable contingencies which exert important influences on
future behavior.

The analysis of present social environments and the learning conditions they set up provides us with information about the alterations, if any,
that should and can be made in the structure and operation of any person's
or group's social context. If the ideal conditions for learning and behavior
maintenance are not met, we will at least know toward what end the
context should be restructured to make it more effective. The "how" is
another matter, of course, but even the methods we might employ are
likely to become clearer when we know the kind of structure we are trying
to produce.

Finally, when one looks at present events from the perspective of a
behavioral model of man, some light is cast on several rather amorphous
and abstruse problems and phenomena one may experience or read about.
At the moment we are forced to generalize, for there are few immediately
relevant empirical studies, but learning principles and their implications
provide some intriguing and insightful suggestions. In an affluent society,
for example, and especially in a nation whose citizens subscribe to a belief
in immediate gratification and the rights of individuals to a host of material

[27]Bandura (1971; 1973).

possessions, few strong deprivations will be acceptable, *few significant reinforcers will be available,* and the links between behavior and its consequences will often be quite weak. As far as contingencies of behavior are concerned, therefore, very poor and affluent societies are quite similar: poor countries offer the general population few rewards; in affluent societies few rewards will be perceived; and in both there will be many people who believe that their activities have few or no positive consequences. While the psychological effects of a life characterized by S^r scarcity and tenuous $R \longrightarrow S^r$ links are not yet clear, feelings of "discontent," "unhappiness," and of being "adrift" and "powerless" are logical correlates.[28] We know, for example, that the lack of reinforcers is usually associated with a pessimistic view of the world and a poor self-image.[29]

Since neither the threat nor the application of punishment is conducive to long-term learning or behavior maintenance, a social system which relies heavily on this type of contingency should be expected to have considerable difficulty in maintaining the "proper" activities of its members. To put it differently, a society will be most humane and effective if it emphasizes reinforcers and employs a minimum of aversive contingencies. As Skinner[30] has recently argued, even in modern democratic societies there is considerable emphasis on punishment or its threat, and it will only be upon the general recognition of behavioral principles—and the inefficiency of punishment—that an effective restructuring of social systems can occur.

4. Behavior-Consequence Linkages Are Vital

So far we have been concerned with the effects which past and present environmental events have on a person's behavior. Another and often more important aspect of this individual-context relation is the person's conception of this relationship and his participation in it. People learn not only behavior patterns but also the fact that the world consists of behavior-consequence linkages—that in daily life one encounters not only R but also many $R \longrightarrow S^r$ and $R \longrightarrow S^a$ units.[31] In fact, "normal life" is the result of a person's effective interaction with his environment. When the links between one's behavior and environmental consequences are strong and positive, one can predict the effects of one's behavior and thus control the context's reactions. Eventually one will come to view the world and even the universe as positive, predictable, systematic, and subject to considerable control, and one will gain a sense of power as well as a positive

---

[28]Seligman (1975).
[29]Bandura (1969), pp. 85–91.
[30]Skinner (1971).
[31]Rotter (1966).

self-image. Conversely, when the links are weak, the effects of one's behavior are unpredictable and one cannot control the context by performing the "right" actions. Eventually one will tend to view the world and universe as being capricious, unpredictable, and uncontrollable, and to consider oneself as being powerless and helpless.[32] These world views, in turn, affect one's predictions of the likely consequences of one's activities; the latter view, for example, commonly results in a low level of actions, apathy, and the quick abandonment of efforts. This, in turn, will reduce the likelihood of "success," thus reinforcing the idea that one is powerless and ineffective. Hence it makes sense to speak of "benign" or "vicious circles" in the development of world view, self-image, and behavior.[33]

The behavior-consequences linkages that an individual perceives are more or less accurate reflections of the $R \longrightarrow S^r$ and $R \longrightarrow S^a$ units which constitute social life. That is, the social structures which surround us give rise to a large number of these units, but we must activate their operation through appropriate behaviors on our part, as defined by our culture.[34] Most people learn what these "appropriate" behaviors are; they consequently lead lives filled with many positive consequences and are able to avoid many negative events. Some individuals, however, do not learn "appropriate" actions and then find that life is unpredictable and full of disappointments. The ability to activate the many different behavior-consequence units arising from the complex social structures of modern urban-industrial society are subsumed under the term "competence."[35]

For example, language has been viewed as the most important means by which social structures become part of one's life.[36] Without symbolic communication the operations of social structures would appear partial and distorted, one would have to depend only on one's own limited experiences, and one could not gain a wider perspective from other people's lives. More important, it is through language that many behavior-consequence units of social structures are activated, as when we ask for advice, apply for a job, give and follow orders, take advantage of the benefits and services provided by official agencies, or protect ourselves from various attempted influences by other people. The greater one's linguistic and other social skills, the better one will be able to cope with the requirements and problems of daily life. Melvin Kohn, in fact, has recently proposed that one important determinant of schizophrenia is the lack of competence in coping with the problems and stresses of modern life.[37]

[32]Rainwater (1968); Winslow and Winslow (1974).
[33]Smith (1968).
[34]A more detailed and complete description of these processes will be given in the following chapter.
[35]Gladwin (1967); Smith (1968). Hunt (1968) suggests several ways of preventing incompetence.
[36]Bernstein (1964).
[37]Kohn (1972).

There are three major difficulties which individuals face as they confront the behavior-consequence units of social structures. First, a person may lack sufficient competence in enough areas to activate existing units, as we have just described. Second, one may not be sufficiently close to these units to activate them. Social isolation, for example, is an effective barrier to garnering the benefits that organizations and clubs might offer, and class membership greatly influences a person's access to opportunity structures such as schools. Finally, the behavior-consequence links within a social system may be weak, small in number, limited to particular groups, or largely negative and aversive. Good examples of such structural inadequacies and their implications for personality and behavior are found in John Dollard's description of the racial caste system.[38]

All of these difficulties, and especially the last two, are significant aspects of several social problems. Indeed, the solution of many problems, such as crime and poverty, will have to include the restructuring of social systems so that they will have a larger number of accessible, positive, strong behavior-consequence units, ready to be activated by competent citizens.

5. There Are No Free-Floating Contingencies

The postulate that environmental events which follow an activity affect the probability of its later repetition has received major attention in this and the last chapter. So far, however, we have looked at the proposition from only one side, that of behavior; what do we see when we view it from the side of environmental events?

The postulate leads us to the conclusion that if an environmental event should occur which is defined by a person as an S^r, the immediately preceding behavior is likely to be strengthened. Conversely, if an event is viewed by someone as an S^a, the probability that the immediately preceding activity will be repeated declines. Even when there appears to be no event, the S^o is likely to be interpreted as, or to pave the way for, an S^r or S^a, with the results described in earlier sections. Thus a family's disregard of a good report card might effectively discourage a child's future efforts, and a mother's simple ignoring of her son's stealing a cookie is likely to lead to further attempts. In one case the S^o is aversive in the sense that the child expected some praise (unless there has been a history of parental indifference), and in the other the mother's S^o is more than offset by the S^r of the cookie.

These two examples illustrate an extremely important corollary of the basic behavioral postulate, namely: there are no free-floating contingencies. Many environmental events, and especially those which occur

[38]Dollard (1937).

with some frequency, regardless of how an observer may define them, affect the immediately preceding activities by influencing the probabilities of their recurrence.

On the simplest level, when we give a young child an ice cream cone we should expect that the immediately preceding behavior, no matter what it might be, is likely to be strengthened, while a slap will have the opposite effect. Verbal instructions which attempt to tie the cone or slap to other past behaviors—*e.g.*, "This is for having been good yesterday"—cannot always be counted on to be effective. More important, if we present reinforcers capriciously or on the basis of momentary emotions—perhaps we feel sorry for someone or are sad or exasperated ourselves—we cannot help but strengthen what originally may have been "random" activities. Furthermore, since anger on our part may well constitute an S^r for a person, the impersonal presentation of punishment is often essential. We see now that it is rather easy inadvertently to establish strange, irrelevant, and even dysfunctional behavior patterns in spite of our best intentions and sometimes even because of them.

The "Pygmalion Effect" provides a good illustration.[39] It refers to the fact, described in several recent studies, that many teachers treat their pupils in terms of presumed characteristics which have little if anything to do with performance. For example, a teacher is likely to pay more attention and give better grades to those students whom he simply *believes* to be more intelligent, to possess greater ability, or to come from a higher class background. Even a child's first name sometimes influences a teacher's grades, his concern with the student's problems, and the time and trouble he is willing to spend with him. In terms of our behavioral model, such teachers attach favorable consequences not to the student's activities but to other characteristics, including the teacher's expectations; hence there is no functional tie between the child's behavior and environmental contingencies. If Hubert or Bertha is thought to have relatively low intelligence and to come from the working class, then attentiveness, study, and good work are not as likely to be rewarded and thus maintained, while actions which *do* attract the teacher's notice, such as lethargy, poor performance, or improper behavior, are more likely to be maintained, simply because of the attention they produce.

A good example on the community level is provided by Banfield's study of child-rearing practices in a small Italian village.[40] Here parents punish their children quite capriciously, whenever they "feel like it." When the father is angry, or sad, or drunk, he is likely to take his emotions out on his children by beating them, no matter what they have just done.

[39]Rosenthal and Jacobson (1968).
[40]Banfield (1958).

One major result is that the child develops no sense of trust or power, and no conception of a systematic and predictable universe. The child concludes that he lives in a capricious world where he can trust no one, where "cooperation" is dangerous, where he has no control over events or even his life, and where unpredictable natural and human dangers confront him at every turn. In his description of a Southern town, Dollard[41] points out that discriminatory actions of Whites, who are often not even aware of what they are doing and how their actions affect Blacks, produce not only negative self-conceptions among Blacks but also behavior patterns which are detrimental for effective participation in the larger society.

On the level of institutions, mental hospitals provide excellent illustrations of what happens when the postulate "there are no free-floating contingencies" is consistently disregarded. By providing patients with environments that are free of conflict and stress, and in which most of the amenities of life are available as a matter of course, behaviors have few if any of the variable contingencies found in normal daily living. By providing rewards regardless of a patient's behavior, hospital operations cannot be effective in shaping or maintaining "normal" activities, for they encourage helplessness. In fact, many institutions maintain the very illnesses they are supposed to cure by providing amenities as long as patients are "sick." It is only when amenities and other rewards are attached to specific behaviors, and when contingencies are provided in a systematic way, that behavior modification becomes a possibility.[42]

On the level of society, finally, the actions of governments, schools, the economic system, and the class structure affect the behaviors of people in many hidden as well as obvious ways. A behavioral model of man sensitizes us to the fact that these influences, though they may be difficult to discern, operate throughout a person's life wherever he might be. As Myrdal[43] pointed out some years ago, the American caste system systematically reinforces Blacks' behaviors expressing dependence and extinguishes or does not even shape the actions necessary for an autonomous way of life. It lays the foundation both for Blacks' withdrawal of allegiance from the social system and for their hostility toward Whites. What is significant in this study as well as in Dollard's and others' is that while many Whites may feel guilty, they are also often unaware of the precise influence of their actions, *i.e.,* how the White-dominated social system shapes and maintains the behaviors of Blacks. More recently, the rise of the "permissive society," which is reluctant to reward and punish, accepts wide deviations and idiosyncratic activities, and attaches rewards to mere

[41]Dollard (1937).
[42]Ayllon and Azrin (1968).
[43]Myrdal (1962).

existence rather than to behavior, can be seen as the societal equivalent of
mental hospitals run on a psychodynamic game plan. The implications of
this, and whether something should be done—and what—will be examined in a later chapter.

6. Models Are Everywhere

The learning of new behavior patterns by observing models and what they
do is the most significant means for acquiring and modifying behavior;
such vicarious processes operate in many situations, and daily life provides
people with a host of models and opportunities to learn from them.[44] One
learns not only from parents, teachers, friends, and public figures when
they are deliberately on their best behavior, but also at other times; from
people of high and low status; from heroic and notorious personages; and
from the many little-known individuals one meets in the course of daily
life. Furthermore, we cannot assume that a child, youth, or adult will
consider as models only those people whom we think of as "model citizens," or who we think *should* be imitated. While the later repetition of
new behaviors depends on their consequences, the ubiquity of models
means that a myriad of new behaviors are at least available for being tried
out.

   The fact that models are everywhere and inescapable means that
special care must be taken to reinforce only those activities which the
members of a social system judge to be "proper." That is, we cannot rely
on "official" models alone but must in addition create the proper circumstances for behavior maintenance, regardless of whether the system is a
family, community, or society.

7. Man Constitutes the Major Internal
Restraints of Social Systems

Man, his "psychological nature," and the physiological requirements for
his continued existence make up the major internal restraints imposed
upon any social system. We can see this most clearly in primitive tribes
which lead a marginal existence, where mere survival is at the center of
communal interest, and where the satisfaction of basic needs constitutes
the major focus of daily life and social structure. Among the Siriono of
eastern Bolivia, for example, food is scarce, getting it requires the expend-
ing of considerable efforts, and much of society revolves around hunger
and its prevention.[45] When we view "continued existence" in terms not
of individuals but of populations, another set of restraints becomes ap-

---

[44]Bandura (1969), chapter 3.
[45]Holmberg (1969).

parent: those involved in the production and raising of offspring, or the incorporation of new individuals into the system. Sociologists refer to some of these as "functional requisites" and point out that, before anything else, a social system must satisfy these requirements within the framework of the character of its human components.[46] Only when the population is fed, when there are children, and when these are brought up reasonably well can a society afford to build temples and support astronomers or sociologists.

One's views of the "psychological nature" of man and the restraints it imposes are essentially a reflection of the model of man one chooses to employ. The Freudian model, for example, would include propositions about static personality, natural aggression, and the Oedipus Complex. What a social system must do, in light of these assumptions, is provide the means for dealing with the dark powers of the id and for channeling the forces of sexuality.[47] Other models provide other sets of constraints, hence the student of social systems can to some extent choose the limitations he builds into his analysis and the programs he advocates by his selection of a model of man.

The constraints exerted by the components of psychodynamic models of man are by now so well known that they need not be discussed in detail. Most people are aware of them and take them into account when they consider the nature of society and man's role in guiding social change. But there is another set of human elements, less well known but pitilessly firm in constraining the present operations and future possibilities of society: the learning principles discussed in this and the previous chapter. While we are admittedly dealing with an as yet incomplete model of man, the empirical evidence in support of the several propositions is impressive. For example, as we have just pointed out, there are no free-floating contingencies. This puts considerable constraints on a society, for it does not allow any long-term *free* distribution of the necessities and luxuries of life —i.e., regardless of preceding activities. In the past, the Protestant ethic and such proverbs as "a fair day's wages for a fair day's labor" defined and limited the obligations of both individuals and society. But what about today's efforts to improve society, or our visions of states we might create some day? In general, utopian communities which have disregarded this particular constraint failed because they could not cope with individuals who contributed little or nothing, and modern communes have had to institute one or another system of requiring and rewarding manual labor.[48] Another proposition—that behavior, to be maintained, must be reinforced

[46]Levy (1952).

[47]Freud (1930).

[48]For a concrete example, see Kinkade (1972); for a general discussion of this problem, see Kanter (1972); Richter (1971); Roberts (1971); and Veysey (1973).

—has sounded materialistic, hedonistic, and evil to many. Yet, while people can be taught to live with other reinforcers—for example, "the good of the group"—we often assume, idealistically but nevertheless incorrectly, that the definition and learning of symbolic rewards and processes of self-reinforcement are minor, easy, and almost automatic matters. But utopian communities which have disregarded this constraint and have assumed a simple and almost natural conversion to new rewards have had to pay the price of failure.

The learning principles contained in our model of man allow for considerable optimism regarding the modification and guidance of social systems. First and foremost, they indicate that many of the human constraints existing today are learned and, therefore, can be changed. In some societies people learn to work only for money, while in others they are willing to work primarily for the benefit of the nation. On a technical level, some people have learned to live with low frequency schedules and others are used to a high rate of rewards. Many of the constraints exerted by members of a particular society and epoch, therefore, can be altered, and this modification in turn will allow for some latitude and experimentation in the social system's structure and operation. In short, a social phenomenon which presently appears to be necessary—for example, grossly unequal incomes—may well be a reflection of a particular type and magnitude of behavioral characteristic which can be modified, leading to a redefinition of what is necessary to insure that essential jobs are performed. When the true nature of human constraints is finally known, social systems will turn out to be considerably more malleable and variable than they appear to be today.

8. Effective Programs Are Possible

The behavioral perspective described in these two chapters has been incorporated into a large number of successful programs designed to modify behavior and social environment, ranging in size from individual-oriented treatments to community development projects. Behavior therapies, as distinguished from psychotherapies, have been described in considerable detail.[49] On the level of small groups, Hamblin has studied and modified the operation of school rooms.[50] New institutional settings have been provided and found to be effective,[51] and whole communities have been fundamentally improved by the construction of new and more humane systems of contingencies.[52] While there are few studies of behavior modi-

---

[49]For examples, see Bandura (1969); Ullmann and Krasner (1965); Wolpe et al. (1964); Wolpe and Lazarus (1967).
[50]Hamblin et al. (1971).
[51]Ayllon and Azrin (1968).
[52]Dobyns et al. (1971).

fication on a societal scale,[53] there is no reason to believe that similar programs could not be instituted in many other places and on a larger scale. Later chapters will present some of the practical difficulties and ethical questions involved in any such effort.

9. Ideal Conditions Do Not Exist in Today's World

When we compare the structure and operation of society today with the ideal conditions for the learning, maintenance, and extinction of behavior outlined earlier in this chapter, we cannot help but note great discrepancies. In today's dynamic world of relative affluence, where we are reluctant to punish but implicit threats are everywhere, it will be difficult to establish and maintain behaviors. Furthermore, since much of a person's world view and self-image are derived from his experiences, especially from the successful manipulation of his social context, we should expect difficulties with the establishment of positive self- and world-conceptions as well.

Many observers of modern life have argued with great persuasion that ours is a nonsane society in which children cannot help but grow up into disturbed and unhappy adults.[54] But we now see that part of the "insanity" lies in the operation of the individual's social environment, which presents contingencies inconsistently, defines many reinforcers as rights but insists that they be attached to behaviors, keeps the necessary behaviors unavailable to many people, and destroys the $R\longrightarrow S^r$ link for others. Idealistic verbal descriptions of $S^D\longrightarrow R\longrightarrow S^r$ triads abound, yet many individuals are not presented the S^D, have not learned the R, or eventually find out that it does not really matter because the consequence is not an S^r anyway. Here we have the roots of several social problems.

CONCLUSION

As we look at these eight consequences of learning principles, we cannot help but be impressed by their positive implications for the future and man's role in shaping it: not only is it possible to change individuals' activities, but it also makes sense to think about building viable and humane social structures. The above considerations tell us much about the procedures and limitations of any such efforts. Before we discuss the designing and implementation of social programs, however, we must answer the question of how one moves from individualistic learning principles to social phenomena and processes. We will do this in the following chapter.

[53]For an example, see Papanek's description of Pakistan's early years (1967).
[54]For example, Fromm (1955); Goodman (1960).

5
Social
Relations

$\mathbb{T}$ he model of man we have outlined in the last two chapters postulates that any behavior (R) is preceded by one or more discriminative stimuli (S^D) and followed by one or more contingent stimuli (S^r, S^a, S^o). Both sets of stimuli essentially consist of events, behavior patterns, and other phenomena in the individual's physical and social environment. Since most observed activities, and especially those which have been repeated many times, are reinforced at least once in a while, the vast majority of behavior patterns may be viewed as central elements of triads ($S^D \longrightarrow R \longrightarrow S^r$).

While psychologists are mainly interested in the development and structure of these triads including the nature of the arrows, sociologists and others interested in group phenomena usually consider the triads as given and concentrate on the social determinants of the S^D, the nature and determinants of the contingencies impinging on the individual from his context, the social factors responsible for behavior modification, and the influences of one triad on others.

In most situations of daily life any activity is part of one or another behavior chain of varying length and complexity, as shown in figure 5–1. There usually are several S^D, a number of R, and several positive and negative consequences (or costs), some occurring immediately and others happening much later, some emanating from the environment and some

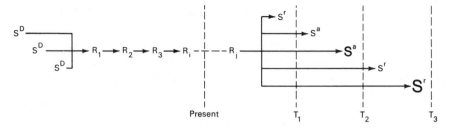

FIGURE 5-1 Contingencies and Time Horizons

self-administered. Both the behaving individual and the observer may view the various consequences separately or combined; if the latter, we usually speak of a "total contingency." State variables are implied by the nature and magnitude of the various S^r and S^a, and may be viewed in terms of the subjective utility of an S^r or an S^a in the eyes of the behaving person, but *not* in the evaluation of an observer. In most cases it will be sufficient to indicate magnitude by the size of relevant symbols. Finally, it is useful to indicate how far ahead a person sees when he evaluates the various consequences of his actions. Those who live only in terms of weeks, for example, do not take into account as many factors as do those who live in terms of years or decades.

Let us consider, for example, the hypothetical total contingency shown in figure 5-1. When the individual's time horizon extends only to line T_1 he is likely to perform R_j, for its consequence is an S^r. If he looks ahead to T_2, however, then R_j is not likely to occur, for the total contingency now includes the original S^r and two S^a, one of them of considerable magnitude. But the time horizon T_3 includes an additional powerful reinforcer; hence one would predict that R_j *is* likely to occur. Here we see that the same objective context and the actual consequences it provides lead to varying probabilities of R_j's occurrence, depending on the individual's time perspective, his probability perceptions, the values he attaches to the several consequences, and the decision rules he employs.[1] In this case, the probability that R_j will occur is high at first, then declines, and finally increases as the person's time horizon expands.

An individual's time horizon, then, is an important general determinant of behavior because it limits the specific contingencies he can take into account when he selects his activities. If one lives in terms of the present alone, one can weigh only the reinforcing and aversive characteristics intrinsic to the behavior itself; a short time perspective will add a few contingencies; only a long time perspective will provide a realistic picture of an action's probable total outcome. Since time horizons vary with edu-

[1]Thibaut and Kelley (1959).

cation and the direct and vicarious experiences which contribute to one's view of the world, we should expect that, even within an objectively identical social setting, people with different backgrounds will behave differently. Significantly, however, everyone's behavior will be "rational" insofar as decisions on various behaviors are made in terms of all contingencies known by the person.

Predictions and plans made by observers or designers of social programs will also depend on time horizons. For example, if an observer cannot see beyond T_2, or if for other reasons he does not recognize the existence of the final and most significant S^r, he would conclude that R_j will not occur and that the individual, therefore, will require "special stimulation." If R_j did occur without the special effort, he would probably call the individual "irrational."

Behavior that we call "inexplicable" or "irrational" and events which at first blush appear to contradict the principles discussed in the last two chapters are likely to be the results of inadequate data, the observer's lack of knowledge concerning other people's time horizons and views of the world, or his inability to recognize other people's perceptions and self-administered consequences. Yet we cannot assume that everyone has a complete and accurate grasp of all relevant factors which should enter into his decision-making. Rather, it is useful to remember what might be called the principle of limited capacity: "The capacity of the human mind for formulating and solving complex problems is very small compared with the size of the problems whose solution is required for objectively rational behavior in the real world—or even for a reasonable approximation to such objective rationality."[2]

Discrepancies between actual and perceived consequences, people's different time horizons and evaluations of reinforcers, and the often haphazard assignment of probabilities to contingent stimuli—not to mention the behavioral consequences of these phenomena—influence the character of social processes, enter into many aspects of daily life, and are significant components of several social problems.

SOCIAL RELATIONS

The relationship between two or more people and their behavior patterns may be conceptualized in two nonexclusive ways: interaction and exchange. The first is mainly descriptive, while the second has been found to be useful in the analysis, explanation, and prediction of numerous small-group phenomena and processes. While exchange always implies interaction, the reverse need not hold true.

[2]Simon (1957), p. 198.

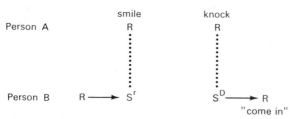

Interaction

Most discriminative and contingent stimuli of most human activities are provided by the behavior patterns of individuals who make up a person's social environment. A person's smile, for example, is an action which often has the character of a reward for someone else, and a knock on the door is usually an S^D for saying "Come in." We may visualize these relations in the diagram above. Any interaction between two people has the structure of a lattice, where the horizontal lines indicate a sequence of events and the vertical (dotted) lines indicate that one person's activity is equivalent to an S^D or S^r for the other person's behavior. For example, figure 5-2 shows that A's behavior R_3 is both an S^r for R_2 and an S^D for R_4, and thus can be shown as an S^{rD} for person B.

In any diagrammatic representation of interaction only a few of the actually occurring activities are usually shown, for it would be awkward and unnecessary to include all actions. In the illustration, R_3 actually consists of a series of movements, including the turning of the door handle, moving the door, and walking into the room. Furthermore, between R_3 and R_4 there may occur a silence, one or both persons may smile, and B may stand up. The activities which are included in any particular diagram are those which are viewed as being necessary and significant in terms of the particular study's requirements. If the above diagram were part of a study of deference, for example, it would have to include such behaviors as "standing up" and "standing in the doorway" or "briskly walking in," along with an indication of who greets whom first and in what manner.

Interactions of several persons can be conceptualized in the same

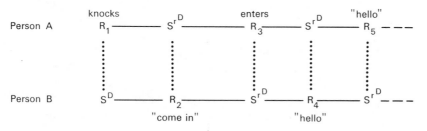

FIGURE 5-2 Diagram of an Interaction

way, except that in the case of large groups it may be convenient or necessary to combine two or more individuals into one "line," as when "children" may become one unit of a larger family group in a diagram of a reunion with grandparents.

Figure 5–2 may be viewed as a succession of "squares," each with two observable activities, $e.g.,$ R_1 and R_2, and two elements inferred from them, S^r and/or S^D. Any two adjacent squares will then be a representation of a particular norm; thus the two squares R_3—R_4 and R_4—R_5 may be summarized as the norm of "courtesy in visiting," $i.e.,$ the rule that one should greet a visitor and the implied expectation that one will be greeted in turn.

Dyadic as well as more complex interactions can be viewed not only in terms of behavior but also in terms of symbols. In our example we treated the interaction elements "Come in" and "Hello" as behaviors, but we might equally well have considered them as symbols. In fact, much of social life is made possible and proceeds by means of symbols which carry information, and it often makes sense to speak of "symbolic interaction." Whether one treats "Hello" as one person's behavior which is equivalent to an S^D for another person, conveying information about possible consequences of later actions, will depend on the focus of the analysis of which the word "Hello" is a part. As described by Rose, most of the basic principles of symbolic interaction theory are similar to and congruent with the social implications of our behavioral model of man, and differ mainly in terminology. The first three principles, for example, are: (1) "Man lives in a symbolic environment as well as a physical environment and can be 'stimulated' to act by symbols as well as by physical stimuli"; (2) "Through symbols, man has the capacity to stimulate others in ways other than those in which he is himself stimulated"; and (3) "Through communication of symbols, man can learn huge numbers of meanings and values—and hence ways of acting—from other men."[3] Other principles—for example, about thinking and the stages of human development—do not conflict with learning principles in their attempts to describe the processes which intervene between symbols and action or, as we would say, between one's awareness of an S^D and the subsequent R, including one's predictions of reinforcement probabilities.

So far we have been concerned with relatively simple situations. Figure 5–2, for example, could refer to what we have observed or to a situation which ideally should occur. Often, however, social life is or appears to be considerably more complicated; contradictory rules and ideal confront an individual or observers gather inconsistent results. We often notice that people say one thing and act quite differently, as when they say that they are not prejudiced but actually discriminate; and people may behave inconsistently over time, or when they are in situations which

[3]Rose (1962), pp. 5, 7, 9.

appear different to them although they may appear quite similar to a casual observer. Studies of attitude and behavior, and especially of prejudice and discrimination, have repeatedly demonstrated such inconsistencies.[4] Far from being inexplicable or suggestive of man's caprice, however, such behavioral inconsistencies usually turn out to be the logical results of the person's different perception of the circumstances at the moment and the associated contingent stimuli.[5]

Figure 5–3 presents an illustration of interactions among four people. Individual A makes a prejudicial remark, and this is equivalent to an S^D for varied reactions by others: B smiles, C is silent and D reproaches A. To keep it simple, let us assume that all are Whites. The reactions, therefore, are equivalent to an S^r, an S^o and an S^a for A. Let us assume that A has received such reactions in the past and therefore can predict rather well how these individuals will behave in the future. When A and B are together, R_1 is likely to occur; when A and C are alone, A's behavior will depend on extraneous factors, unless silence is aversive to him; and when A and D are together, R_1 is not likely to occur. What will happen when the four people are together? The answer depends, in large part, on whose reactions are most important to A, and which behavior he takes most seriously at the moment. (These are not necessarily the same criteria.) In short, it depends on A's frame of reference and reference group. If A

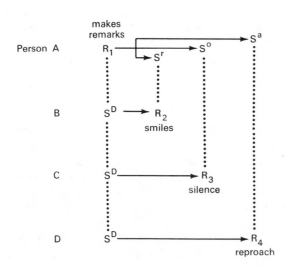

FIGURE 5–3 A Complex Lattice

[4]For example, Bem (1970); Fishbein (1966); Wicker (1969).
[5]For examples, see DeFleur and Westie (1963); Tarter (1970).

identifies with B, the S^r presented by R_2 will be important and outweigh the S^a of R_4. But if A and D are members of the same group, or like one another, then the potential S^a of R_4 will be so great as to eliminate the likelihood of R_1 occurring. If an observer is unaware of these factors, A's behavior of sometimes engaging in R_1 and sometimes not will seem inconsistent or capricious. But when one knows the situation the changes will be logical and one can predict the variations in R_1. In short, use of the label "inconsistent" is inversely correlated with the amount of information which an observer has about a particular person and his circumstances. If one wishes to predict a person's behavior, one must know something about his reference groups and the resulting weights attached to various contingencies, his learning history, his time horizon, and his evaluation of the situation (*e.g.,* A may think that D is out of earshot and, therefore, may speak to B). The behavior of a person we have just met is largely unpredictable, but after a marriage of thirty years one can predict one's partner's activities to the smallest detail, including what appear to be inconsistencies to the superficial observer.

In summary, if one dissects a person's social context and examines its operation, one usually ends up with very complex lattices including both sequential and overlapping squares. The "top of the pyramid" in figure 3–1 disappears, and the bottom line becomes part of a lattice. Conversely, if we observe the behavior of members of a group, we should be able to abstract the regularities of many triads ($S^D \longrightarrow R \longrightarrow S^r$) and thus infer the "rules" which link and order the various activities of the several members. These we would call the group's "norms." Its ideals and values, on the other hand, can be determined only by asking the members how one *should* behave, how people *should* react to others' activities, and what people *should* work for.

Exchange

An increasingly popular way of conceptualizing and explaining interaction, be it within small groups or in larger collectivities, is that of *exchange.* Thus George Homans considers "social behavior as an exchange of activity, tangible or intangible, and more or less rewarding or costly, between at least two persons";[6] Richard Emerson speaks of "reciprocal reinforcement" as the major attribute of most social behavior; and Peter Blau has described even large social structures in terms of exchange.[7]

The model of man underlying exchange theory is essentially the one which was presented in the last chapter, and the relations among activities

---

[6]Homans (1961), p. 13.
[7]Blau (1964); Emerson (1969); see also Turk and Simpson (1971).

and among individuals are viewed as just outlined. Homans, for example, builds his theory on these propositions::

1. "For all actions taken by persons, the more often a particular action of a person is rewarded, the more likely the person is to perform that action."
2. "If in the past the occurrence of a particular stimulus, or set of stimuli, has been the occasion on which a person's action has been rewarded, then the more similar the present stimuli are to the past ones, the more likely the person is to perform the action, or similar action, now."
3. "The more valuable to a person is the result of his action, the more likely he is to perform the action."
4. "The more often in the recent past a person has received a particular reward, the less valuable any further unit of that reward becomes for him."[8]

Most discussions of exchange add some elements to basic learning principles in order to sharpen the analysis and enhance explanatory power.[9] The most common additions are one or more of the following:

1. There exist limited behavioral alternatives, from which a person must select one.
2. The total contingency includes not only S^r and S^a but certain costs as well, which may be direct or simply the alternatives that are foregone.
3. The individual's perception and evaluation of behavioral alternatives and their various contingencies has an effect upon his behavior.
4. Some kind of balance between one's investments (broadly defined as what one brings into an exchange) and profits (reward minus cost) is necessary for the continuation of an exchange relationship.

In short, the explanation of social behavior based on exchange leads to a concern with an activity's antecedents and presumed effects, and this, in turn, has led some theorists to the study of internal processes, and at times to the statement of rather complicated assumptions about the human "black box."[10] Let us consider, for example, the interactions described in figure 5–3. The exchange theorist who is interested in why R_1 occurs in the presence of B but not of D would scrutinize the exchanges occurring between A and B and between A and D in terms of the investment, costs, and rewards of each of several alternative modes of action besides the ones shown in the figure. For example, person B might not want to disapprove

[8]Homans (1974), pp. 16, 23, 25, 29.
[9]For expositions and examples of the exchange perspective, see Blau (1964, 1968); Emerson (1972); Homans (1974); Thibaut and Kelley (1959).
[10]For example, Blau (1964); Meeker (1971).

because he knows that he will later on have to depend on A's good will or help.

So far, the most careful and painstaking work has been done in very small groups. Neither Thibaut and Kelley[11] nor Emerson[12] venture much beyond the dyad, and Homans[13] has relatively little to say about the "increasing roundaboutness" of exchange in larger groups, communities, and nations. While not restricted, by any means, to dyadic interaction, exchange relations are best exemplified in that kind of situation.[14]

The path from the reciprocal reinforcement of two people in a face-to-face situation to the structure and operation of large groups has been sketched by Blau[15] and Emerson.[16] Emerson distinguishes between two major types of exchange relations, simple and productive. The first is evident in relations where one person's behavior directly reinforces another's within a wide range of activities, as in the case of two friends who exchange greetings, favors, help, and so forth. The second type, probably more significant in the study of social systems, involves two or more individuals where neither one's behavior by itself is rewarding for the other. Rather, two much narrower ranges of activities unite to produce something that is rewarding to both, as in a game of tennis. More commonly, the product may mean very little to the persons involved but can be exchanged for something that is of some value to them, as in the case of factory workers who produce goods and then are paid. Here it would be useful to speak of a group-system, within which an often complex series of productive exchanges occur and whose output, while not necessarily useful or reinforcing to its members, is exchanged with the environment or other similar group-systems for goods which, upon being distributed among the members, reinforce their varied but coordinated activities.

INDIVIDUAL AND CONTEXT

The above discussion of relationships among individuals and their activities provides us with several insights into the operation and dynamics of social phenomena.

[11]Thibaut and Kelley (1959).
[12]Emerson (1972).
[13]Homans (1974).
[14]Blau (1968), p. 457.
[15]Blau (1964); McGinnis and Ferster (1971).
[16]Emerson (1969).

Nature and Operation of the Context

Generally speaking, a person's social context defines and presents him with a large variety of state variables and discriminative and contingent stimuli, as shown in figure 3–1. The "social context," however, is only rarely an undifferentiated unit; rather, as we have just seen, it usually consists at the very least of ideal values and operating norms, not to mention the people through whose activities these regularities are exemplified. Ideal values refer to a society's or group's theoretical and ideal standards of behavior —what one should do and when, the goals one should attain, and the consequences that should follow any action. Operating norms are the actual standards of behavior, the existing goals—what people actually do in various circumstances and the usual consequences of actions. The major sources of information concerning ideal values are verbal and written statements, while information about norms is abstracted, and perhaps inferred, from observations of how people actually behave and react to one another's activities. These two sets of definitions, behaviors, and consequences may coincide, but we increasingly find conflicts, inconsistencies, and incongruities between them. Hence it is not unusual or surprising to face conflicting views of what to do in a certain situation, and inconsistent provisions of S^r and S^a. The major implication of this, a lower probability of behavior repetition, was discussed in the last chapter.

The replication of behavior over time and behavioral homogeneity in a society are further reduced by the fact that most individuals are members of several groups, have had a variety of learning experiences, and have different aspirations for future group memberships. Every group in the individual's past, present, and future provides him with a slightly different set of ideal values and operating norms, of deprivations, activities, and expectations about consequences. While he probably has discarded some of them, he is likely to adhere to others, and not all of these are necessarily congruent. His immediate social context, therefore, consisting of family, friendship cliques, work groups, neighborhood, and community, provides him with several sets of ideal values and operating norms which affect his behavior no matter what his momentary role may be. The social context today, therefore, is often ambiguous, unclear, and inconsistent, and the earlier schematic representation (figure 3–1) should be revised accordingly (figure 5–4).

A good illustration is provided by Burgess and Akers' recasting of Sutherland's well-known "differential association" hypothesis.[17] Criminal

---

[17]Burgess and Akers (1966a).

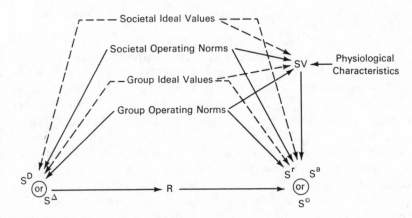

FIGURE 5-4 The Complex Social Environment

behaviors, like the activities of law-abiding citizens, are learned and maintained in ways described in the preceding chapters. The people who are a
person's major sources of positive and negative contingencies provide
differential reinforcement for criminal and other activities, hence the
groups with which one associates are significant determinants of one's
actions. Whether or not a person becomes a criminal—that is, learns and
performs activities defined as "crimes" by his society—thus depends on
the groups to which he belongs, the neighborhood in which he grows up,
the behaviors they reinforce, and, we would add, the models they provide.

One should expect that over the years most people's activities will
change when their lives' contingency structures change as a result of increasing maturity, horizontal and vertical mobility, altered reference
groups, and a widening of perspectives from the immediate neighborhood
to substantial parts of the larger society. As Becker points out, personal
changes occur throughout life, and juvenile delinquents rarely become
adult criminals.[18] Since a large portion of the youthful population at one
time or another engages in delinquent acts[19] but the number of adult
criminals is quite small, the momentary reinforcement characteristics of
particular social environments appear to be the most significant determinants of antisocial behavior.

Yet one cannot disregard the wider world which exists outside the
neighborhood and community. While the majority of contingencies of
one's actions originate in the immediate social context, the principles and
parameters governing their distribution and magnitude are greatly affected
by the more distant environment—for example, by the nation's social
structure, economy, and political system. No matter how far away or

[18]Becker (1970), chapter 19.
[19]Haney and Gold (1973).

abstract these elements may be, however, they usually operate through the immediate context. An adequate understanding of the context, therefore, and a solid basis for bringing about change, will require accurate knowledge of both types of environment.

In his famous discussion of social structure and anomie, for example, Merton[20] postulates that any society includes a set of goals (which define and determine people's major deprivations S^r and S^a) and numerous legitimate means for attaining them (R). For most people, the employment of legitimate means enables them to reach their goals; *i.e.,* there are definite $R \longrightarrow S^r$ links. On the other hand, the class structure and other societal characteristics, such as castes and unequal educational policies, provide people with differential opportunities to use or even learn legitimate means, thus leading to different degrees of goal attainment. Some individuals—for example, those with a middle-class background—know most of the right activities, can perform them, and reach their goals, such as security, through them. Others, however, do not know the right actions or cannot engage in them—*e.g.,* because they have no job—and thus do not reach the goals. To put it differently, the $R \longrightarrow S^r$ linkage, opportunity to perform R, and the frequency and kind of S^r, are greatly dependent on the individual's position in the class and caste system. The frequent result of failure is a search for new activities and/or reinforcers.

Depending on personal characteristics, environmental opportunity, and the available models, some individuals reject the nationally defined goals and seek new S^r, while others keep the old definition but try out other ways of attaining them (new R). Again we must be aware of the subjective character of perceived models, perceived reinforcement probabilities, and the perceived discrepancy between the reinforcers one expects and actually receives. Hence objectively identical social environments may lead to behavior replication for one person and a search for alternatives—*e.g.,* crime—in another, and similar opportunities for alternate actions may be accepted or rejected by individuals who perceive or evaluate the consequences differently. Thus, while it is acceptable to make general statements such as "the lower the class, the greater the probability that a person will search for new activities," we must make sure that there is the necessary empirical evidence before we incorporate the proposition into an action program. Even when there is evidence, we must make a careful study of the exceptions in order to design a proper program, *i.e.,* one which recognizes the heterogeneity of learning histories and views of the world.

In conclusion it may be said that while the establishment and maintenance of behavior is relatively fast, simple, and effective in small communities with highly consistent values and norms, the modern context does

---

[20]Merton (1957).

not come close to the ideal conditions outlined in the previous chapter. Hence the establishment of behavior in urban-industrial societies is slow, difficult, and likely to be incomplete, while its maintenance over time is far from guaranteed.

The Objective and Subjective Context

The behavioral conception of social relations as shown in figures 5–1 and 5–4 may be summarized by saying that an individual lives on a "behavior plane" consisting of several activities, S^D, and contingencies. Other people's activities, considered separately as in figure 5–2 or summarized as values and norms as in figure 5–4, exist on different "planes." An observer of social life, a philosopher, a social scientist, indeed anyone who makes special efforts, can see and study different people's planes and their inter-relations, with success depending on the degree to which he is able to liberate himself from the confines and perspectives of his own plane (figure 5–5).

He who sees life only from his own plane exists in only two dimensions, so to speak, and his view of the world and indeed of himself is quite restricted and distorted. Discriminative stimuli are merely "there," S^r and S^a simply occur, but he does not really know the whys and wherefores of what happens. In concrete terms, he does not understand the workings of the social world, things simply "happen" to him, there is little that makes sense outside his own immediate family, and much of life is a matter of chance and good or bad luck. But one can also rise above one's plane and view oneself as an object (yet still a person) who behaves in terms of probable contingencies, who is affected by other people's actions, which are influenced in turn by similar considerations in a slightly different environment. Such a three-dimensional view of the world in terms of figure 5–5 also provides a more rounded conception of oneself and leads to a better understanding of why other people act as they do, how and why their actions influence one, and what is likely to happen in the future. Mead's use of the terms "I" and "me" is an early attempt to differentiate between the person as a subject ("I live on this plane and there is little else") and an object ("That's me down there, living on one plane, affected by people on other planes"). An understanding of social life and thus of oneself, control of the social environment and thus of one's own fate, and prediction of future events and thus one's planning for them all require that one rise above one's plane, view oneself as an object, and "take the roles" of other people.[21]

As we saw in the last chapter, a person's behavior depends on his memory of previous experiences, his perception of present circumstances,

[21]For a discussion of the "I and Me" topic, see Mead (1934); Turner (1962) describes various aspects of "role taking."

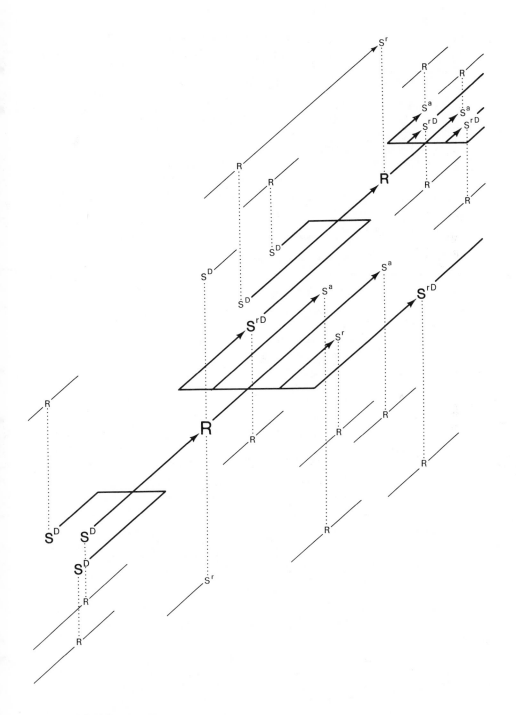

FIGURE 5–5 A Behavior Plane

his conception of future contingencies and their probabilities, and his feelings of deprivation. Yet, while all of these factors involve his own subjective views and appraisals, the similarity of learning histories among members of the same family, neighborhood, community, subculture, and, to a lesser extent, nation produce quite similar assessments of large portions of the members' planes. Once these are known to an observer, he is able to make rough predictions as to how members of various groups are likely to behave in various situations. In ordinary life, the roughly similar assessments of individuals and the rough predictions of observers are quite sufficient for the intermeshing of activities which constitute a society. But if we are interested in explaining any particulars of social life, and if we are concerned with a specific social problem and the designing of better social systems, such rough approximations are not sufficiently detailed or precise.

We must investigate the topography of the planes on which individuals live, not only as they actually exist but also as they are seen by the inhabitants. Thus we must not only look at the total pyramid of figure 5–4 from the outside, so to speak, but also from the inside; more specifically, we must look at it in terms of the configuration of $S^D \longrightarrow R \longrightarrow S^r$ triads which constitute a person's life. If we do not, errors in description and analysis are bound to be made.

For example, a person may have a short time horizon and yet believe in heaven and that he will enter it. Such a person is not likely to show much foresight in his selection of activities; yet he will have a view of life that we might call serene and optimistic, and a self-definition that is positive. A superficial observer, however, might judge his behavior to be short-sighted and irrational, his life problem-ridden and miserable, and his general attitude either inexplicable or a result of sublimation. If, in addition, the observer did not believe in heaven, then the great though distant S^r which is so much a part of the individual's life and behavior might not even be considered.

A person's conception of his behavior plane and the surrounding planes is often called his "world view"—referring to his summation of the numerous activities available to him, their likely consequences both now and later, the magnitude and frequency of reinforcers and the probability and ways of avoiding S^a, the predictability of the context which provides the various contingencies, and the kind of life and future which is a result of all these factors. If he then abstracts from this view some general operating principles both for himself and the events on his plane we usually say that he has a "philosophy of life."

At first glance it may appear strange that such abstractions as "world view," "philosophy of life," and even "weltanschauung" can be conceived in terms of our model of man and behavioral planes. Yet when we take a careful look at the meanings and empirical referents of these concepts, we usually find that experiences and expectations, the past and future events on behavior planes, are of major significance. For example, Foster speaks of a world view as including the presumed "rules of the game" of life and the principles thought to underlie the universe's operations.[22] Both result from, and are summaries of, one's own and other people's experiences in the social and physical environment. A *weltanschauung* usually includes more than this, but even Jung recognized the importance of environmental reactions in shaping one's conception of the world.[23] In their discussion of the problems faced by modern man, the Bergers make extensive use of "world view" as a definition of reality derived from experiences with the social and physical context.[24]

It is not easy for an observer to put himself onto another man's plane, to understand the discriminative stimuli and deprivations which exist there, to view time and to assess contingencies as the other person does. When anthropologists speak of "culture shock" they are referring precisely to the difficulties inherent in meeting and understanding the novel $S^D \longrightarrow R \longrightarrow S^r$ triads which prevail in other societies.

When we put ourselves onto another individual's plane we encounter not only his definitions of S^D, R, SV, S^r and their relationships, but also his view of other planes (figure 5–5), of the top of the pyramid (figure 5–4), and how these affect him. When we take the place (or plane) of a sibling, life from there will not seem very different. But when we attempt to live on the plane of a person from another class, caste, or sex, we may well suspect that we have followed Alice through the looking glass. A policeman, to use the most obvious illustration, may quickly change from a provider of minor S^r (in the form of directions, help, or feelings of security) to a source of major S^a (perhaps fear of unjustified arrest or feelings of being exposed to unpredictable power). To many middle-class individuals, a nation's social structure—*i.e.*, the very complex lattice arrangement of activities which constitutes a society—may well appear to be on the whole quite benevolent. After all, it consists of large numbers of definite $R \longrightarrow S^r$ links, provides a host of reinforcers, relatively few S^a, and few long-term deprivations. To the poor, however, the same structure, or what appears to be the same, contains fewer $R \longrightarrow S^r$ links, provides only a few S^r, rather more S^a, and many deprivations which last for a long time.

[22]Foster (1965).
[23]Jung (1969).
[24]Berger, Berger, and Kellner (1973).

Social and Behavioral Change

In any analysis of social phenomena and in the designing of social programs we must remember the planes on which people live and from which
they see and judge the rest of society. By changing all or most of a social
structure we modify these planes, but this is not the only means available,
nor necessarily the most effective. It is easy to say that we must change
the major determinants of the target behaviors; it is much harder to know
which aspects of a social structure must be changed and how this is to be
done within a given historical context. Hence we should consider at least
three alternative procedures leading to behavior modification of both the
target individuals and those who make up their context. Indeed, it is by
means of these procedures that many a powerful group has seen the "errors
of its ways" and changed both its own behaviors and the operation of
social structures.

1. EXPANDING TIME HORIZONS.   Studies reported by Bandura (1969)
show that a negative self-image and a dismal view of the world are greatly
influenced by the number and proportion of S^r one experiences. Generally
speaking, the more rewards one encounters, the higher one's opinion of
oneself and the better one thinks the world is. A short time horizon
restricts one's sense of the consequences of one's actions to those which
are immediate. Since social systems consist of many rather long and tenuous links between behavior and the eventual S^r—*e.g.,* one must attend
school for 12 years before a diploma is granted—we may expect that the
longer a person's time horizon is, the more realistic will be his view of the
number and proportion of S^r and S^a, for particular activities and for his life
as a whole.

How can we expand a person's time horizon? The major determinant
of any time horizon is the schedule of reinforcement one has experienced.
When rewards come quickly, though not necessarily often, time in effect
contracts. We could lengthen a person's time horizon, therefore, by gradually lengthening the time between behavior and its reinforcement, or by
verbally describing the long linkage between R and S^r and by following
through with the S^r. Lectures and exhortation by themselves have little
effect, however, and we should therefore provide concrete experiences
with long but definite R $\longrightarrow$ S^r links.

While it is generally true that middle-class time horizons are longer
than lower-class horizons, there are enough exceptions to require an investigation as to the kind of horizon associated with various activities, especially when we design policies and programs. Consumption patterns and
credit buying of middle-class individuals, for example, would call the
ubiquity of a long-range perspective into question. In short, time horizons

differ among individuals, vary from one behavior and situation to another, and thus may not be as difficult to change as one might expect.

2. REDEFINITION AND REASSESSMENT OF CONTINGENCIES. The proportion and magnitude of S^r and S^a in one's life can be changed by altering one's expectations and evaluation of things and events. For example, if one believes that one deserves the best in life, one expects much. Ironically, the likely result is a perceived scarcity of S^r and a tenuous relation to preceding activities, with negative consequences for one's view of life, oneself, and the world. Conversely, if one believes that "into every life some rain must fall," one expects less and, therefore, may well experience more than the expected number of rewards, leading to a rather positive view of life, oneself, and the world. To an objective observer the number, kind, magnitude, and distribution of reinforcers might be exactly the same in both cases, but the two people's perspectives, especially the ratio of S^r they expect to those they actually experience, lead to their quite different evaluations of identical events.

Affluence—a wide distribution and high frequency of the "good things in life"—makes it difficult to recognize a reinforcer as such, and a society's unwillingness to reward and punish removes the link between behavior and its consequences. Thus the more or less automatic provision of goods and the absence of "real" rewards leads to feelings of futility, a humdrum life, and a sense of powerlessness.[25] Sociologists usually refer to these conditions as "alienation," and have pointed out their pervasiveness in modern society.[26] Yet it appears that their causes are to be found precisely in what most people would call the "good" or "beneficial" aspects of contemporary existence rather than in problematic situations, such as urban life.[27]

A redefinition of the things and events which constitute an S^r and the reestablishment of definite relations with preceding behaviors will require some changes in ideas and beliefs about the "significant" aspects of life. Religious revivals often accomplish this, but only for a small number of reinforcers and behaviors. Individuals who "drop out," those who join communes, and people who speak of revitalization often appear to have taken the first steps in this direction. The problem, however, is that the temporary establishment of some new $S^D \longrightarrow R \longrightarrow S^r$ triads does not necessarily lead to a new society, for the activities of a few people do not constitute a new social system.

---

[25]For example, Seligman (1974).
[26]For example, Seeman (1959).
[27]Fischer (1973).

3. CONTEXTUAL ALTERATIONS.   When we carefully examine the social environment of an individual who shows some behavior problems or
deficits—e.g., someone who does things which harm himself or does not
do what would benefit himself—we usually find that his learning history
and present context are largely responsible for his behavior. Stuttering,
aggression, shyness, and illiteracy have been shown to be the results of
inadvertent shaping and maintenance by often well-meaning parents,
teachers, and friends. The solution, therefore, lies in the modification of
those aspects of the social environment which directly affect the behavior,
as described in earlier sections.

Reciprocal Influences of Individual and Context

As we mentioned in the last chapter, people learn to predict probable
consequences of their various actions on the basis of hearsay, observations,
or past experiences, and to choose their activities accordingly. Besides
actual behavior, then, there are potential actions in which a person and the
members of his social context could engage. These potential actions are
often referred to as elements of an individual's "behavioral repertoire."
The word "potential," in short, refers to what a person has already learned
and not what he could learn. Since most people could learn almost any
behavior, we need no special term for such theoretically possible activities.
The sociological terms "status" and "role" are useful short-hand expressions for the sets of potential activities which we can assume people to
have.[28] When we know that a person is a father, for example, we can make
rather good guesses of how he is likely to behave in certain situations. The
more we know about a person's status, the better our prediction of how
he will play his roles; if we know that he is a high school graduate and a
machinist, our prediction of how he will behave as a father will be somewhat better, but still not perfect.

When we look at an individual's past, we see that his social context
consisted of many different activities performed by various people. His
future context, and what he takes into account in selecting present behavior, consists of the potential activities of many people or, in short, his
potential environment. Since his behavior (rarely, his mere presence)
serves as S^D for other people, it follows that their potential actions cannot
become actual behavior until the appropriate stimulus—i.e., his own behavior—has occurred. For example, if I do not speak to a stranger on a bus,
he is not likely to speak to me, and his potential behavior—light conversation—will not become actual behavior. Of course, the stranger may start
a conversation, but if I do not respond he will stop after a while. Only
when I answer does the potential "more talking" become actual fact.

[28]The concept of "role" usually includes not only behavior but societal expectations
and sanctions as well. See Sarbin and Allen (1968.)

Much of the behavior of people in our environment is only potentially there until we make the effort—the right effort, at the right time, to the right people—to elicit the context's actual reactions. This behavioral variation on the old theme of reaping what one sows is of great significance in the assignment of causal properties. So far in this chapter we have treated the context as more or less "given," and the individual's behavior as a result. Now we see that social interaction cannot be viewed quite so simply, for what the context "does" is the result of both its potential activities and the individual's actual behavior. To a large extent, then, a person in effect helps produce his own consequences by determining which of the several potential activities in his context will actually occur. Hence man is far from being a weak pawn subject to immutable environmental forces.

Furthermore, the size of one's own behavioral repertoire affects the variety of the environment's reactions: in order to take full advantage of one's potential environment, one must have a wide behavioral repertoire. What has been called "cultural deprivation" refers to a small behavioral repertoire which does not enable an individual to take full advantage of his environment's potential responses and especially to experience the normal number of rewards.

The potential activities of people in one's environment may be viewed both by an observer and from the plane on which one lives. Thus most middle-class, well-educated people, like members of any other category, have a particular view of their potential environment and are wont to generalize to the social structure as a whole. For example, they may believe that behavior such as "hard work" and "being straightforward" will result in environmental reactions summarized as "success," "a good job," and a "pleasant life." Yet such a view of the potential environment may be incorrect and surely is partial. At the very least, most views of social structure implicitly disregard the fact that the S^D for an environment's favorable reaction—*e.g.*, a person getting a "good" job—consists not only of his past and present behavior—*e.g.*, his performance in school and general deportment—but also includes personal characteristics such as race, sex, or age and social characteristics like class position and power.

Yet, while these characteristics play a significant role in determining the nature and frequency of environmental reactions to a person's behavior, they are not recognized by egalitarian ideologies and have no place in the American Dream. Hence many individuals have to face the rather difficult problem of coming to understand their own failure—*i.e.*, the insufficient positive reactions they have received from the wider social context—in spite of the fact that they meet all of the official or overt requirements for success. As an alternative, a person may seek success—for example, status—by engaging in behaviors which receive approval and honor from a limited group of his peers, such as a gang, but are defined by the larger society as being illegal. Cloward and Ohlin describe some of the ways in which delinquents confront, explain, and come to terms with the discrepancy between formal and informal requirements for success in our society, and Cohen builds his theory of lower-class male delinquency on the frustrations that boys encounter in their efforts to achieve status in a middle-class world.[29]

A good illustration of the reciprocal relationship between individual and context is provided by recent discussions of "learned helplessness."[30] According to Seligman and others, people learn to have confidence in themselves and their own powers by being able to manipulate, and thus control, significant portions of their social and physical environment. Such control, however, is possible only when there is a functional tie between several behaviors and their consequences. For example, if R_1 leads to an S^r and R_6 to an S^a, one can control the environment in terms of producing rewards and avoiding punishment by engaging in R_1 and not in R_6. Conversely, if the context's reactions are capricious, not related to preceding activities, or the result of what a person is rather than what he does, one is likely to feel discouraged, powerless, and depressed—in short, helpless. Furthermore, one's view of the world is likely to be quite negative and to include such elements as being cold, cruel, unresponsive, uncontrollable, and unpredictable. One's own actions, in turn, will be congruent with these views of oneself and the world; *i.e.*, one will do very little to the context, shrink from interactions with it, and ascribe whatever happens to chance or luck. Apathy, minimal activities designed to "barely get along," low aspirations, little foresight and planning, and a short time horizon are the logical outcomes, and the result of these will be precisely an unresponsive context which produces few rewards; one's behavior will be insufficient to provide the necessary S^D for the people who make up the context. "Learned helplessness," in short, involves a self-fulfilling hypothesis about environmental reactions to one's behavior, and thus is likely to be reinforced and maintained.

There are two major factors responsible for severing the functional relationship between individual and social context. When a person does not know how to behave appropriately we speak of "behavior deficits," and when there are extraneous characteristics, such as his race or class membership, we speak of "discrimination." Many people in our society and in other countries find that their efforts and good intentions produce little of the "good life" described by the mass media, and that little if any part of the world responds to what they do. Hence they see themselves mainly as the "effects" and not as the "causes" of events. Such a life, with

[29]Cohen (1955); Cloward and Ohlin (1960).
[30]Seligman (1975); Seligman *et al.* (1971); Thornton and Jacobs (1971).

few or no behavior-consequence linkages, is dreary and hopeless indeed, imbued with both a poverty of goods and a poverty of spirit.

One example of what can happen when these linkages are cut for whatever reason is described in David Matza's theory of delinquency. He speaks of "the mood of fatalism [which] is the negation of the sense of active mastery over one's environment. It is likely to culminate in a sense of desperation among [those] who place profound stress on [their] capacity to control the surroundings." In order to regain one's sense of control, to believe again that one can make things happen, and indeed to feel one's manhood again and to rejoin the human race, one may engage in new infractions, for these at least produce reactions from one's context. Thus "the delinquent is rejoined to moral order by the commission of crime!"[31]

The lack of $R \longrightarrow S^r$ linkages as a major source of a sense of control over one's environment has often been viewed as an important part of alienation, expecially the type of alienation which is related to feelings of powerlessness. Some significant behavioral consequences of such feelings were demonstrated by Seeman's study of reformatory inmates. He found that the more powerless a person felt, the fewer efforts he made to learn materials concerning parole and life "outside," and the less he learned. Furthermore, he was likely to have lower aspirations and to engage in fewer achievement-oriented activities.[32] Coleman suggests that the behavior-consequence linkage may be an important variable in the problems faced by rural, southern migrants in northern cities.[33] In a share-cropping situation and, to a lesser extent, in any semifeudal, paternalistic setting, people are "taken care of" by others regardless of what they have accomplished; consequently, they learn to do little.

From these and other studies we may draw the conclusion that a person "is sensitive to the cues of his environment only when he believes he can have some effect upon it. He will learn only when such learning can benefit him—either in formal learning situations or in the casual cues of his [daily life]." [34] A conception of the world need not be established by personal or observed experiences, however, and many parents have little difficulty transmitting them to their children. Coleman, for example, found that minority children with low educational achievement already expressed their sense of lack of control by agreeing with statements such as "good luck is more important than hard work for success." [35] The major solution to such attitudinal problems is to increase the number of both reinforcers and behavior-reward links.

---

[31]Matza (1964); both quotations are from p. 189.
[32]Seeman (1963).
[33]Coleman (1964).
[34]Coleman (1964), p. 77.
[35]Coleman *et al.* (1966).

Learned helplessness is also found in many other groups besides the disadvantaged. For example, life in an affluent society weakens the R $\longrightarrow$ S^r links generally, but especially among those youngsters whose parents shower them with material goods. And as Friedan observed long ago, the American social structure systematically produces and maintains behavior patterns among women which correspond to learned helplessness; these actions in turn reinforce men's opinions of women and the very operation of the discriminatory system.[36] Civil rights legislation during the last few years has attempted to produce an effective solution by providing a variety of S^r and more R $\longrightarrow$ S^r links, or at least to make these possible. Finally, the behavioral and attitudinal characteristics of learned helplessness correspond to the major components of the "culture of poverty."[37]

One cannot say that all youngsters from affluent families, women, and poor people are characterized by learned helplessness, however, for it is the individual's learning history, and especially his experience with behavior-contingency links, that is of crucial importance, and such experiences vary even within a subculture or neighborhood. Yet it is interesting to find that both rich and poor can have similar experiences and come to similar conclusions about themselves, their efficacy, and the world. As a general rule, therefore, we should say that one must be careful in generalizing about people with objectively very different characteristics in income, age, caste, etc. Such individuals may have subjectively identical experiences, *e.g.,* tenuous R $\longrightarrow$ S^r linkages or few reinforcers; the particular acts and S^r will be different, of course, but the essential element of the experience—the type of link between behavior and consequences, or disappointment—may be the same.

While potential environments within a nation ideally are similar for all citizens, and while it may be said that a nation has only a small number of legitimately different potential environments (depending, for example, on a person's age), there may well be as many different subjective views of the environment as there are groups and subcultures. Rather than rely on our own ideas, then, we should ask what a person's conception of his potential environment is and what behaviors it leads to. Since the solution to many social problems requires behavior modification on the part of both the individual who is part of the problem and the people who make up his context, we must know their conceptions of the potential environment. Once we have this knowledge it may be enough to show people how the context actually operates. On the other hand, we may suggest that a longer time perspective is required, or we may conclude that the context itself will have to be restructured, in whole or in part.

[36]Friedan (1963).
[37]Lewis (1965).

The actual behavior which people exhibit depends not only on their potential activities and their environment's responses, but also on a third factor: how they are defined. The label attached to a person often restricts the number and variety of a context's reactions. If we are defined as "friendly," for example, usually on the basis of past actions, failure to greet people will probably be ascribed to our being momentarily cross, and people will continue to make overtures in the future. But if we are defined as "unfriendly," failure to greet people will be viewed as being in character, and few further efforts of friendlinesss are likely to be made.

The concerted operation of these three factors, as well as their consequences, are illustrated by the development of some types of delinquency. A youth's behavior, when it is defined as acceptable within his subculture, results in reinforcement from its members and thus is maintained. When he meets people from other subcultures, however, for example in school, these same activities—let us say aggression and boisterous behavior—result in his being labeled a "problem child." Once this label has been attached to him, teachers are likely to treat him more harshly, and to overlook less—in short, to reward him less and to punish him more. As a result he may then come to define and label himself as a "problem boy" and to seek out others in similar categories, for only they are likely to reward him for his behavior. As social psychologists say, he shifts his reference group; and when he does, the S^a presented by "good kids" and teachers become less aversive, for he no longer cares so much about them. As he continues in the activities rewarded by his new reference group, his label among teachers is likely to change from "problem boy" to "incipient delinquent," with a corresponding shift in the proportion and evaluation of S^r and S^a emanating from school authorities and others. As we saw in an earlier discussion of *Elmtown's Youth,* when a boy labeled a "good guy" breaks a window, adults will probably define this action as "youthful exuberance" and let it pass or punish it mildly.[38] But when a boy labeled "troublemaker" breaks a window, the same behavior is likely to be defined as "rebellion" and to be punished accordingly. Here we have the reverse of the "Pygmalion Effect" described in a previous chapter. We might conclude, therefore, that people often, perhaps even most of the time, react not only to a person's behavior but also to their own image of him. When this image is positive more S^r will come his way than he deserves, and when the image is negative he will receive fewer S^r and more S^a. Hollingshead shows that the origin of labeling depends not only on a person's previous behavior but also on his caste and class position. In the high school he studied, for example, lower-class children generally received less reinforcement and more punishment, and had fewer opportunities to en-

[38]Hollingshead (1949).

gage in those actions which merited rewards than did middle-class children. By small steps, then, a person acquires new labels, learns new activities (which may be considered to be delinquent), forms a new self-image or self-label and view of the plane on which he lives, and seeks new reference groups.[39] Eventually, the major determinants of the boy's behavior will be quite different from and independent of those which govern the activities of "law-abiding citizens." This is when we can no longer reach him, when scolding and exhortation are no longer effective. Punishment also, especially by itself, will not lead to behavior modification. What is required is a process of relabeling in the opposite direction, involving a restructuring of contingencies and an increasing proportion of S^r for lawful behavior. Such procedures have been found to be quite effective when tried on a systematic basis and over a period of time.[40]

The reciprocal relationship between individuals and context leads to the conclusion that there is little sense in placing the blame for social problems at the feet of either individuals and their nature or society. The search for and placement of blame reflects a desire to discover ultimate origins and causes, but this is an irrelevant endeavor which promises little success; it is reminiscent of the medical and psychodynamic perspectives, according to which problems can be traced back to a specific condition or event, the removal of which goes far toward eliminating the problem. Social life has an entirely different character, however; reciprocal relations and interactions among people have been going on for so many years— ultimately, centuries—that it is impossible to determine when, where, and how something "really started." Neither would it help us much to know this, for today's problem is also the result of numerous intervening events and relations, each of which has contributed a share to what we confront today; it can be solved best by looking at today's events and the possibilities of modifications tomorrow. This is not to say that one should not be concerned with causes, but rather that it is more useful to restrict one's analysis of determinants to the gathering and interpretation of information necessary for instituting ameliorative and preventive programs with regard to actual behaviors and deficits which concern us today.

FROM "INDIVIDUALISTIC" TO "STRUCTURAL" APPROACHES

There are two major approaches to the study of social phenomena in general and social problems in particular. One centers on individuals, what

---

[39]For examples, see DeLamater (1968); Rushing (1968); Schur (1971).
[40]Phillips (1968); Phillips *et al.* (1971).

they do and why; it views social structures as comprising a series of given, external determinants, and is illustrated by our discussion of helplessness and delinquency in the preceding section. The other approach centers on social structures, their operations and dynamics; it views individuals as incidentals caught up in social processes, and is illustrated by sociological discussions of stratification, institutionalization, and urbanization.

Adequate descriptions and complete explanations of social life require that one consider individuals, social structures, *and* their interactions. Our behavioral model of man provides a foundation for synthesis (though not the only one) because learning principles affect individuals, operate within social structures, and constitute the major link between man and context.

In previous sections we have looked at the behavior-consequence link from the point of view of individuals. The linkages which people experience, however, are actually the properties of social structures and reflect their operations. As we pointed out earlier (figure 5–2), one person's behavior is equivalent to an S^D, S^r, or S^a for another. Thus an R $\longrightarrow$ S^r unit for the individual is equivalent to an $S^D \longrightarrow$ R unit within a social structure, such as a school system or government office. For example, a person who applies for a passport sees mainly consequences (a successful request for a passport), while the social structure consists mainly of $S^D \longrightarrow$ R units (receiving and processing the request). The clerk's rewards (his salary, and perhaps a feeling of having done a good job) need not come directly from the individual who is served. Indeed, one of the problems for people within large social structures, such as bureaucracies, is precisely that the reinforcers for their activities are difficult to specify and often must be sought in other facet of life. We may visualize the important components of an individual's life and the basic units of social structures as shown in figure 5–6.

The great significance of behavior-consequence linkages for the normal life and mental health of individuals, as previously described, raises the question of how the $S^D \longrightarrow$ R units of social structures become avail-

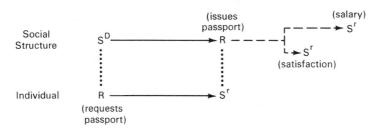

FIGURE 5–6 Behavior-Consequence Links and Basic Structural Units

able. In fact, this availability may be viewed as the hallmark of humane social structures. Accordingly, the major characteristics of humane social structures would include (a) an adequate number of $S^D \longrightarrow R$ units (in terms of numbers of people and their normal activities); (b) adequate availability of $S^D \longrightarrow R$ units (in terms of normal access for all members of a society); and (c) adequate strength of $S^D \longrightarrow R$ units (in terms of the functional tie between the S^D and R). A humane social structure, then, includes a configuration of strong $S^D \longrightarrow R$ units which covers all members of a society and all those activities which are considered appropriate by a culture. For example, a humane educational system would be accessible to everyone of any age and provide effective instruction in all areas a culture defines as appropriate.[41]

Most societies contain few truly humane social structures, in the sense that there are too few and often inaccessible $S^D \longrightarrow R$ units or that they are frequently quite weak. For example, Merton has described the operation and consequences of inconsistent goals-means structures, Cloward and Ohlin have described class-linked access to opportunity structures, and Postman and Weingartner have expressed much concern over the operations of school systems.[42]

An important aspect of inadequate access to $S^D \longrightarrow R$ units is that the S^D frequently consists not only of an individual's behavior but of other characteristics as well. Earlier in this chapter we described racial discrimination in these terms—*i.e.,* that the social context reacts not so much to a person's behavior but rather to the color of his skin. Another series of significant additional factors, which often are necessary to trigger the operation of $S^D \longrightarrow R$ units, are the various aspects of power. "Powerful people" are those who get things done, their way—*i.e.,* individuals who can influence the character and strength of $S^D \longrightarrow R$ units in social structures. The specific characteristics which constitute and determine power vary among individuals and from one time and situation to another. Yet the effects are the same: it is not the person's behavior but "something extra" that determines environmental reactions, as the diagram below shows. Here the linkage between an individual's behavior and its conse-

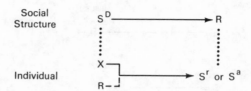

----

[41]Examples in this and other areas will be treated in chapters 6 and 7.
[42]Cloward and Ohlin (1960); Postman and Weingartner (1973).

quences is weakened because it is the "X" that leads to an S^r or S^a. In the case of discrimination, where the usual linkage becomes $X \longrightarrow S^a$, apathy is a frequent result, whereas "power" usually produces $X \longrightarrow S^r$ links, which frequently result in arrogance.

Humane social structures may develop gradually through more or less natural processes, or they may be deliberately designed. While the former is possible, the latter is much more common as legislators, officials, and citizens attempt to modify the structure and operation of various organizations. Many of these attempts are not successful, however, in large part because it is often unclear what aspects of a social structure need to be changed and how this is to be done. Here our behavioral model of man can provide some guidance, as we will see in the following chapter.

Models and the Design of Programs

In this and the following chapter we will take a brief look at the possibilities and types of concerted efforts in two major areas: the amelioration and solution of social problems, and the guidance of social change. Our emphasis will be on models of man and their implications for the designing and implementation of programs rather than on technical aspects of planning or strategies for putting plans into effect. The literature on these aspects of social planning is vast indeed, and includes comprehensive discussions of general principles and problems[1] as well as analyses of simple and complex cases, successes and failures.[2] By concentrating on the ways in which models of man influence a policy's goals, the associated programs of action, and the presumed and likely consequences (which may not be identical), we hope to contribute to a general improvement of the design process and an increase in the probability of successful implementation.[3]

Social programs generally fall into two major categories, depending on the relationship between the plan (including the planners and the

[1]For examples, see Bennis *et al.* (1969); Gans (1968); Horowitz (1971); Lerner and Lasswell (1951); Warren (1971).

[2]For example, Meyerson and Banfield (1955); Shostak (1966).

[3]For a discussion of sociological aspects of the design process, see Bauer and Gergen (1968); Boguslaw (1971); and Tarter (1973). Gans (1971) describes the major characteristics of policies, plans, and the major problems encountered by social scientists.

planning process) and the complex of social, political, and historical realities within which the plan is to operate.[4] The "abstract-rational model" of social planning focuses attention on the problem to be solved, its careful and dispassionate analysis, and the rational designing of logical solutions. The plan, in short, arises more from the analysis than from a concern with its eventual fate in the real world. The completed design is presented to the appropriate agency or sponsor with the hope that implementation will follow. Unfortunately, however, the process of acceptance and implementation occurs within communities of real people, where real political, economic, and other factors are extremely significant. Consequently, the design usually is greatly transformed, and the eventual program is likely to be very different from, and much less effective than, the original plan.

The "concrete-processual model" of social planning also begins with the analysis of a problem but incorporates the community's political and other characteristics into its design phase. Consequently, the eventual plan will be based on bargaining and accommodation as much as on objective criteria, and will involve the social interaction of various contending factions as much as the careful analysis of the problem. While the acceptance and implementation of the plan usually present few problems, its effectiveness is often low.

As Warren points out, both models have advantages and encounter difficulties, and both have been criticized for leading to ineffective programs. At present there appears to be no approach which incorporates the strong points of both models, and most planners are content to steer a course between the major problems of the two extremes. Whatever planning course one follows, however, the models of man one employs in the analysis of the problem and in the design for its solution will greatly affect the nature of the program and its constituent procedures.

Any program of social action, be it educational improvements, the reduction of discrimination, tax reform, urban renewal, or the war on poverty, includes as its fundamental attribute more or less obvious and deliberate attempts to modify the behavior patterns of individuals, be they "the poor," "the Young," "Whites," "legislators," "the establishment," or members of any other group or category. We will use the principles discussed in chapters 3 and 4 to indicate what is required in good designs, successful procedures, and effective programs. We will not be concerned with an exhaustive and detailed discussion of particular problems or types of plans, for such an attempt would require, if justice were to be done, a number of books. Rather, we will consider the general components of programs regardless of their specific content, and treat particular social problems only as illustrations. Interested readers should be able to apply

[4]Warren (1971), pp. 56ff.

these general principles to the various specific phenomena and problems that concern them.

THE DEFINITION OF PROBLEMS

Society—or, if we take a dynamic perspective, social life—consists of a great number and variety of structures and processes. Some of these are viewed as social problems and others are not, depending on one's values and perspective as well as on the people, places, and times one uses as a frame of reference. The first question we face, therefore, is: "What constitutes a social problem—*i.e.,* how do we know what needs to be changed, eliminated, or improved?"

This question has vexed both citizens and social scientists for quite some time. It has been pointed out, for example, that lists of problems vary from one population segment and time to another, and that the items on these several lists have few characteristics in common. Thus most social problems seem not to exist "out there" in nature but rather in the eyes of the beholder; that is, people subjectively evaluate the various aspects of social life, label one or another as a social problem, and then consider this aspect as something that one should do something about.[5]

The definition and analysis of social problems can be approached from several perspectives. Those who speak of "social pathology," for example, postulate that there can be, somewhere and at some time, a healthy or sane society—and that they know what its characteristics are. Our task, therefore, is to design a program which will eradicate the symptoms and causes of the social pathologies around us, much as medical experts do for organic pathologies. Others speak of "social disorganization" and believe in the possibility and desirability of a well-organized society; again, they assume that they know the characteristics and determinants of such systems. Those who think in terms of "deviance" define some aspects of social life as normal or have some other way of distinguishing deviant from nondeviant behavior. Whatever approach one uses, then, the definition of what is or is not a social problem involves a number of often implicit assumptions and evaluations, which play a crucial role in any decision to place a particular phenomenon in the category of "social problem."

Still another perspective represents an attempt to replace the rather specific assumptions about pathology or disorganization with the more diffuse values of a population or subculture. According to Tallman and McGee, for example, a social problem is "a situation which is perceived by

[5]For example, Blum (1971), pp. 177–184; Bandura (1973), pp. 5–11.

some group as a source of dissatisfaction for its members and in which preferable alternatives are recognized so that the group, or individuals in the group, are motivated to affect some change. It is a social problem principally because it occurs in a social milieu and the attributable causes are seen as existing in the [social] environment."[6]

While the question of definition has not yet been answered in a generally acceptable manner, our argument in this chapter does not depend on how or why one concludes that something is or is not a social problem. Thus we will be content to take as our working definition the last one offered and proceed from there. In other words, we will begin with any process or phenomenon which previously has been defined by others as being a problem, and go on to consider various solutions derived from our models of man and assumptions about society.

MODELS OF MAN
IN PROGRAM DESIGNS

As a general rule, *every program design of social action contains a model of man.* Even when nothing specific is said about individuals there are implied propositions about the nature of man and the determinants of behavior. For example, Banfield's thoughtful and disturbing treatment of feasible and infeasible, acceptable and unacceptable solutions to urban problems, includes several discussions of the role of models in program designs.[7] When we are restricted to implicit and amorphous models of man, many proposed solutions turn out to be clearly infeasible, but even some specific models of man lead to designs which are politically unacceptable. Among the former would be exhortations to change men's "hearts and minds," while among the latter would be payments to "problem families" to send their children to day nurseries and preschools.[8]

Models of man are important in the designing of social programs because, even though we may speak glibly of "social forces" or "men's minds," we ultimately have to work with individuals and the modification of their behaviors. The very concept of "program" implies that something be done, be it to maintain the status quo or to change it. Hence we want to be sure that the model of man we employ reflects the best available evidence; and when the model is hidden or ambiguous, we will have to bring it into the open and clarify it.

[6]Tallman and McGee (1971), p. 41. For a discussion of this definition, see Manis (1974) and Merton (1971).

[7]Banfield (1970), pp. 238ff.

[8]Banfield (1970), p. 246.

Let us take, for example, the common but vague notion that many problems would be reduced if there were a "change in the hearts and minds of men." What can we do with this idea? According to Banfield, a "class of 'solutions' must be considered infeasible because in the absence of an adequate specification of the means by which they are to be brought about it must be presumed that no one knows how and that they represent mere wishful thinking."[9] Thus we would first ask what is meant by a "change in the heart and mind," and how one is to know whether such change has occurred. The answer is that the empirical referents of such changes are behaviors, as when we say that someone has "changed his mind" when he does or says something different from what he said or did in the past. The phrase "change in the hearts and minds of men" now turns out to refer to behavior modification, and the only remaining question is how this might be accomplished. It is apparent, then, that some kind of specification in terms of empirical referents is possible for any notion and concept, no matter how vague or outlandish it may first appear to be. In the process of clarification we may even have an opportunity to select a model of man. When we speak of "hearts and minds," for example, we imply a very simple model which we can replace by that of Freud, or Bandura, or whomever we choose. We also find that silence about means is not necessarily a result of ignorance or the absence of procedures; a specific model of man will not only imply but require specific courses of action.

Psychodynamic Models

Psychodynamic models of man affect the designs of social programs in at least four different and not necessarily consistent ways. First, as we have already mentioned, they may lead to an emphasis on social processes and economic structures and a relative neglect of individuals and their behaviors. For example, it has often been postulated, though sometimes not explicitly, that man is naturally good, decent, hard-working, or whatever else we may want him to be, and that these qualities will naturally emerge without additional efforts once the opportunity is there. Hence the mere provision of opportunity becomes a major element of solutions to social problems; equal opportunity alone is seen as a major goal of social change, and income redistribution or a guaranteed annual wage as a panacea.

Second, psychodynamic models may lead to a disregard of environmental effects and an emphasis on individual characteristics, especially in efforts to explain and legitimize failure in the game of life. In an achievement-oriented society such as the United States, for example, most people have typically viewed their own and others' failure as an indication of

[9]Banfield (1970), p. 240.

personal shortcomings.[10] Rationalizations may be relatively benevolent, such as real or imagined illnesses,[11] or they may rest on more serious assumptions of personal inadequacy.[12] In any case, ameliorative programs would center on individualistic rehabilitation and alterations in the internal state, to the extent to which this is possible within the limitations of the particular model of man one uses.

These two types of emphasis—on either the social context or individual characteristics, to the exclusion of the other—are not necessarily contradictory, for they are usually found in different explanatory schemes. Different people and program designers subscribe to one or another emphasis; some social problems are viewed as being due to personal characteristics and others as the result of social structures.But what interests us here is what these two types of emphasis have in common: neither makes adequate provision for the learning and modification of activities. The first does not recognize that people *must learn* new behaviors, and thus must be taught, while the second disregards the fact that people *do* learn from the operation of their contexts.

Third, psychodynamic models introduce the idea that personality as an internal state is a significant aspect of some problems, such as deviance, and that changes in the internal state are a prerequisite for social change.[13] More generally, it is assumed that behavior modification can occur only after various aspects of the internal state have been altered. Program designs therefore must emphasize man's internal state and might be devoted to such topics as the changing of self-images, the improvement of self-confidence, or the reduction of feelings of alienation. In all such endeavors, however, the role of the present social context is seen as minimal and not as the major means of bringing about internal changes. A common problem in this approach is that the link between the social structure and the individual, and the means by which changes in the former might lead to alterations in the latter, are usually not indicated in empirically verifiable or programmatically useful ways.

Finally, psychodynamic models may influence the design of social programs by defining various human *types,* whose members are assumed to be incapable of altering their ways. Once a person has been classified as a certain personality type, there is very little that can be done for or about him. For example, in his discussion of individuals whose orientation is to the present rather than to the future, Banfield describes the "cognitive" type of person as being *"psychologically incapable* either of taking

[10]For example, Cole and Lejeune (1972).
[11]Parsons (1958).
[12]For example, Horney (1950).
[13]For example, Hagen (1962).

account of the future or of controlling impulses. . . . Adults who were brought up in a group or society whose culture does not provide concepts by which to think about the future are cognitively present-oriented by virtue of their culture."[14] Banfield points out that few individuals are of this type (there are two others); still, the implication is that little can be done with or about people in this category.

Behavioral Models

Regardless of which behavioral model of man one employs in a design, there will be an emphasis on overt activities, a recognition that behavior can be modified, and much concern with altering individuals' and groups' immediate social context. As Liebow points out in his description of *Tally's Corner,* many activities which appear to be results of cultural transmission are actually based on personal experiences;[15] hence program designs must include genuine and obvious alterations in a person's future experiences, not once but many times. When behavior patterns persist it is because the context has not been significantly altered, or at least not in the view of the individual concerned; an adult might then become a cynic, a youth may simply return to his corner, and the peasant will go back to the ways of his forebears.

Learning models direct attention to matters far beyond the target behavior. For example, it is not enough to provide merely for the opening up of jobs and opportunities; we must look beyond the skills immediately associated with a given job to those other activities and often subtle perspectives which make up the work syndrome. Similarly, any concern for education must go beyond the provision of books, meals, laboratories, and even good teachers and small classes. When we look at the activities associated with academic success we see that their maintenance depends crucially on what happens in the family and neighborhood, among peers, and on the street. As Coleman puts it, "schools bring little influence to bear on a child's achievement that is independent of his background and general social context; and . . . this lack of an independent effect means that inequalities imposed on children by their home, neighborhood, and peer environment are carried along . . . [as] they confront adult life."[16]

Along with considerable optimism engendered by the very real possibility of designing effective programs, however, there are some disturbing aspects to many behavioral models. While we now know the procedures which will lead to behavior modification, there is the question of whether and to what extent they should be employed. It is ironic indeed that

[14]Banfield (1970), p. 217. Italics are in the original.
[15]Liebow (1967).
[16]Coleman (1966), p. 325.

behavioral models, which give us effective procedures, should arouse fundamental questions concerning their use; perhaps the very ineffectiveness of psychodynamic models protects us from having to ask, and answer, such questions.

PROBLEM SOLUTIONS
AND SOCIAL CHANGE

If we think of a social problem as something which is not inevitable or a natural part of any society, but rather as something which can be modified, reduced, eliminated, or solved, we are naturally led to the subject of change, for it is only by some kind of alteration in the existing phenomena or in the labels we attach to them that we can effectively deal with social problems. While relabeling has been advocated in some areas, notably in the abolition of some "crimes" which have no victims, we will be concerned mainly with attempts and programs of guided change.

The statement that solutions of social problems involve social change is a platitude which enjoys widespread acceptance; yet its implications are not generally appreciated and often are seen from only one side. The questions "Who and what should be changed?" and "Who should do the changing?" are still being debated. Thus the reduction of poverty has been said to involve changes in the ideas and behaviors of the poor but not of the middle class; the government might help but should not threaten or stifle us with bigness; more money might be spent but my taxes should not be increased; incomes might be redistributed, but I want to keep all I have; people should not discriminate but I want to send my children to a White school. As we survey discussions among politicians, neighbors, and in the newspapers, we may well conclude that the answers are "You should be changed," "I should do it to you," and "Any change is good as long as I agree." But what happens when there are millions of "you's" and 'I's"?

Our behavioral model of man presents a different set of answers, which lead us from the individual into the social system, from target behaviors to those of people across the land. We begin by viewing change in terms of two levels—individual and social—and two major types— natural and deliberate (figure 6–1). The level and type one advocates reflects not only concern with one's own future and position, but also one's models of man and society. In its extreme form, concern with "deliberate, individual" change neglects social structures and processes, or assumes the existing social system as a given element. On the other extreme, an interest in "deliberate, social" change assumes that little need or can be done for or about individuals, but that social systems can be rapidly altered in fundamental ways. Existing programs range on a continuum between these

		Types	
		Natural	Deliberate
Levels	individual	growth	behavior modification
	social	laissez faire	planning

FIGURE 6-1 Types and Levels of Change with Examples

two poles. Many welfare programs, for example, place considerable emphasis on the modification of individuals' behavior patterns, be it in job training or early education. Urban renewal and housing projects, conversely, tend to neglect individuals and to be concerned mainly with changing people's physical environments on the assumption that better housing will lead to "better" people and behaviors.[17]

The "natural" approach to change usually assumes that neither individuals nor social phenomena are open to significant human intervention, either because of their nature or because of man's presently limited knowledge and skills. Social Darwinism as a political doctrine, the laissez-faire philosophy, and many theological systems are embodiments of these assumptions. Social programs and deliberate intervention here make no sense.

A behavioral model of man, and especially the description of the social context in the last chapter, lead us to the conclusion that the distinction between "individual" and "social" is largely a matter of analytical perspective. To change individuals we have to alter their contexts, but any alteration of contexts involves the modification of other people's behaviors. Consequently any social program must be two-pronged, concerned with the alteration of both the target behavior and its context. When we analyze social phenomena in terms of particular sets of activities, institutions, and systems operations, the amelioration or solution of problems is seen to consist of changes in these activities, institutions, and operations, regardless of where we think the ultimate causes of the problem might be located. Especially when the causes of a problem are unknown or lie buried in the past, the behavioral model of man is useful in that it leads us to a study of the present conditions and circumstances which maintain those phenomena which people call "problems." A search for ultimate causes and the placing of blame will do us no good, for the pressing question today is not whose fault it is, but rather what can be done. Just as behavior

[17]Gans (1968).

therapy is less time consuming and more effective than psychoanalysis,[18] so a concern with present conditions instead of past causes is likely to be more useful in the social area.

While this conclusion is not new, the procedures which should be employed are either yet to be specified or still a matter of debate. Should we reeducate the poor, exert force on the affluent, or exhort people across the board? Should we foment a revolution, modify existing institutions, or design completely new systems? And how, after we decide on an approach, will we proceed on a day-to-day basis? It is from our models of man and assumptions about society that answers to these questions emerge; it is from them, in conjunction with the particulars of the present situation, that we derive specific procedures. But before we turn to this subject we must briefly consider the question of whether it is right to modify behavior, to manipulate contexts, and to alter institutions.

MORAL ASPECTS OF
DELIBERATE CHANGE

Discussions of guided change and, more recently, the operation of large-scale programs have given rise to a number of moral questions concerning the goals of any such change and the propriety of deliberate alterations. But while the questions have become more pressing and the debate has ceased to be a mere academic exercise, no resolution is yet in sight. Here we can do no more than indicate some aspects of the debate.

The assessment of any program's goals is inextricably bound to one's values and one's visions of what the world could and should be like. In the case of individual problems and many of the programs which have been proposed and initiated for their solution, moral questions either do not arise or can be answered with relative ease. This is so mainly because there usually is widespread agreement concerning the definition and severity of the problem, the need for solutions, and the means which might be employed. Psychoses, phobias, illiteracy, lack of various social skills, and some neuroses, for example, are generally considered to be problems requiring treatment. There is little argument as to whether the goal of a literacy program is good or justified, and few scruples are involved in the suggestion that someone seek psychiatric help.

But as soon as we move away from such individualistic and relatively obvious difficulties and begin to look at social problems and their solutions, the goals of programs often become subjects of moral controversy.

[18]See Bachrach (1961); Bandura (1969); Wolpe *et al.* (1964); Wolpe and Lazarus (1967).

One reason is that the very definition of such problems involves the differing values of many people. Furthermore, the presumed causes are usually quite complex, involving individuals and factors which appear to have their roots in a large number of otherwise quite acceptable social phenomena. Hence we can usually think of a number of different solutions but cannot be sure which one is the best. Each solution will conflict with the values of some people and is likely to have far-reaching repercussions, many of which we cannot foresee. In addition, the specific benefits of a program are often difficult to predict and assess, and often appear to be as remote as the problem itself. It is easy to see that literacy would benefit the individual and his community, for example, but to reduce poverty by remaking the poor in the image of middle-class WASPs is a quite debatable goal. Finally, the distance between a problem and oneself increases one's perspective and thereby provides room for moral considerations. When life is brutal or merely hard, conventional morality quickly becomes irrelevant, as shown by the experiences of concentration camp inmates[19] and in deprivation experiments with conscientious objectors. Ivar Lovaas' treatment of autistic children[20] raised a storm of protest when a picture story appeared in *Life* magazine; the most eloquent defense, interestingly enough, was provided by parents of the children concerned.

The debate concerning goals cannot be separated from questions about the propriety of intervention in general and of specific procedures in particular. While many discussions are cool and rational, we also find such phrases as "unscrupulous manipulators," "self-righteous social engineers," and "self-appointed dictators." Two questions which repeatedly arise are: "Do we have the right to change people?" and "What gives us the right to tell people what to do?" It is of interest that such questions are especially likely to arise when we are not sure about the goals we are trying to achieve. Hardly anyone asks, "Do we have the right to make people literate?" But the question "Do we have the right to teach people all or most middle-class behavior patterns?" is not at all easy to answer.

Yet, at the same time that many people wrestle with the general moral question of the propriety of social intervention, it frequently seems that the resulting debates are irrelevant. Whenever there is widespread agreement that a particular phenomenon constitutes a social problem, it makes little sense, moral or otherwise, to leave it as it is. In fact, the very label "social *problem*" implies that something exists which should not, and that ameliorative action should be undertaken. On the other hand, when such labeling does not reflect a consensus, when there are some groups or individuals who do not believe that the phenomenon—for example, rapid

[19]Bettelheim (1943).
[20]Lovaas *et al.* (1965).

population increase—is indeed a problem, then moral questions become significant. In many cases, actions undertaken to solve problems which exist mainly in the eyes of the intervening agency, or the existence of which is subject to debate, are quickly viewed as attempts at manipulation. Deliberate programs of change, in short, tend to become involved in moral issues to the degree to which there are disagreements about the need for them and the ways of instituting them.

The most fascinating aspect of the continuing debate about the adequacy of goals and propriety of deliberate change is the fact that many existing programs of behavior modification are either overlooked or not even recognized as such. The raising of children, the operation of schools, and adjustments throughout life all involve procedures which are not in essence different from those which form the heart of any action program. In fact, wherever we turn we are likely to find evidence of behavior modification and more or less obvious attempts of manipulation. Well-mannered children, for example, are always the result of a long-term program of behavior modification; children do not naturally eat with utensils, speak the language of their parents, become toilet-trained, or accept the mores of their community. Any successful academic program changes at least verbal behavior; any book on child-raising is basically a guide to behavior modification; and one of the hallmarks of good parents is that they are such excellent manipulators of children and contingencies that neither they nor their children, nor visitors are aware of the underlying "personal engineering." Schools, especially in the primary grades, modify behavior and manipulate children; indeed, when we complain that after twelve years of education students still cannot read or write well, we are in effect saying that the behavior modification efforts of the school have been inadequate.

In later years our behavior not only continues to be modified through more or less stringent programs determined by the exigencies of occupation and community life, but we come to be manipulators ourselves. We not only learn new roles but see to it that others do as well, and when we say that the person we marry will change after the ceremony we express our faith in our manipulatory skills. Even when we admire someone's self-discipline and will-power, we are really commenting on the good job he has done in modifying his own behavior, in manipulating his own contingencies.

We see, then, that a behavioral model of man and the programs we might design to solve social problems do not require that people do anything which is substantially different from what they have done in the past. The rationale may be more explicit and the program may be more rigorous, but the basic ideas are the same. What is different is that when we actually want to do something, and when learning principles and the present social context have shown us what to do, then we have to go out into the world and start doing it. We no longer can hide behind ignorance about effective procedures. In fact, it sometimes appears as if the raising of insoluble moral issues allows us to put off any action in which we might otherwise engage, as if posing moral questions allows us to lower our sights concerning the building of a better future.

In this chapter we cannot answer either the moral questions raised above or others which revolve around the definition of social problems and the propriety of their solutions. Rather, we will assume that the question, "Are social programs necessary?" has been answered by a firm "Yes." Such an answer, even if we do not agree with it in a particular case, leads us logically at least to examine the procedures and assumptions which should and inevitably must provide the foundation for any action program. We now turn to this topic.

CHARACTERISTICS OF
SOCIAL PROGRAM DESIGNS

The designing of specific constructive programs of social change, and especially the designing of better social systems, has received much less attention than the description of what is wrong with the world. Such differential emphasis is ironic, for it is only in effective designs that we can find the key to a better future. Among the major reasons for this neglect of large-scale social designs are widespread uncertainties about the models of man and society built into goals and programs: the requirements of the human components of a system are not well known and quite difficult to specify, and the requirements of social systems are not well understood.[21] While many psychologists have presented general outlines of the kind of life and society required for psychologically healthy and complete individuals, it is extremely difficult to derive from their works all of the specific interrelated characteristics which social systems ought to have, and practically impossible to design programs for actually constructing a viable society. Utopian thinkers and political philosophers speak of the creation of Christian communities, humane institutions, nations of multi-dimensional men, and responsive societies; yet again we find that there are few specifics about the new social order and fewer still of the particulars one might incorporate into the design of programs for its construction.

As we listen to these men we may nod in agreement; our spirits may well be uplifted by their dreams; perhaps we share many of their visions. But as soon as we venture beyond ideals and focus on pragmatic concerns,

[21]For example, Freud (1930); Fromm (1955); Maslow (1968).

as soon as we begin to look beyond the revolution and ask precisely what must be done, and why, great difficulties arise. It is almost as if concern with criticism of the world today and with revolution tomorrow prevents us from looking to the days thereafter, or perhaps we concentrate on generalizations and resounding, if vague, ideals in order to have a reason for neglecting the specific tasks of the more distant future. When we wish to design programs of amelioration or of change, and especially when we wish to design a better community or even society, we find that there are few proven guidelines in the literature.[22] Few writers provide us with the detail that is required for actually building the better future they describe in such glowing and general terms.[23] To put it differently, most writers on problems and utopias and most social critics provide us with a two-dimensional perspective of the world, especially of the future. They give us a front elevation of their visions of the new house of mankind but tell us little about the internal arrangement of rooms, the materials to be used, and the building methods. Architectural specifications and engineering problems, such as the strength of beams and the size of wires and foundations, are barely touched upon, and those who would begin construction have to be self-reliant indeed. Builders are likely to find, furthermore, that upon completion the edifice will look different from the original plan, precisely because they had to take the characteristics of various materials into account.

As we consider the long line of well-intentioned visions and attempts at their realization—as we look at utopias, historical experiences with revolutions, observational evidence, and the results of experiments—what conclusions can we reach about the requirements of effective social program designs? We will formulate an answer in terms of a series of logical steps.

1. Specification of the Problem

The first step in the design of any social program is the definition and specification of the problem to be dealt with, the system that is to be changed, or the process which is to be guided. We will consider some examples of specification to illustrate the necessary procedures. One is a rather small part of the socialization process which has, however, important repercussions for problems such as poverty; the others are significant large-scale problems in their own right. We do not mean to imply that our analysis is complete, for such an effort would require several chapters; but it serves to demonstrate that the dissection of social phenomena forces us to consider things we may not have seen before.

[22]For examples of such guide lines, see Bennis *et al.* (1969).
[23]Etzioni (1968).

Hyperactivity in children, and especially their aggression, have been ascribed to a number of causes, including genetic, biochemical, and psychological factors, each with its implications for treatment. The usual procedure is to consider the child as an isolated individual, to look at his behavior and characteristics. Yet many commonly applied therapies, such as punishment and drugs, are not very effective; roughly half of hyperaggressive children do not respond to chemotherapy, for instance.[24] Hence it appears that one term, "hyperactivity," is used to refer to a variety of different phenomena. At the very least we must distinguish between two hyperactivity syndromes: behaviors of physically underdeveloped children, who are usually helped by drugs; and behaviors of physically normal children, who usually do not respond to drugs. Our interest will center on the latter.

Once we have distinguished between types of hyperactivity we direct our attention to the immediate circumstances; that is, we observe the child in his social context and scrutinize the operations of the environment. We will see that most children are not hyperactive or aggressive in all circumstances or at all times. When we make careful observations of children and their contexts we become aware of considerable reciprocal influence. For example, we will notice that much hyperactivity, especially in the school room, is a means of getting attention or something else the child views as a reward (*e.g.,* a display of anger from the teacher), and that teachers encourage hyperactivity by reinforcing it in many different ways.[25] Since hyperactivity affects school performance and the drop-out probability, even a small part of social life such as this deserves attention and a careful description of the "total" situation (which may, however, include only a small part of the child' life).

In the field of race relations, the distinction between prejudice (an internal state) and discrimination (a behavior) has been recognized for some time. If one subscribes to a psychodynamic model of man one is likely to emphasize prejudice and the possibilities of attitude change, while a behavioral perspective would lead one to take a close look at the various activities subsumed under the heading of "discrimination." Since the problem of race relations revolves much more around what people do than around what they think, and since attitude change has been shown to be crucially dependent on experiences—*i.e.,* one's own and others' activities[26] —one should take a careful look at the behavioral aspects of discrimination.

Discrimination by definition involves several people and is, therefore, a characteristic of social interaction. In normal social life, one person

[24]Stewart *et al.* (1966).

[25]Hamblin *et al.* (1971), pp. 99–121.

[26]For example, Bandura (1969), pp. 595ff.; McGuire (1969).

reacts to another's behavior; as we described social (or exchange) relations in chapter 5, one person's action is an S^r, S^a, or S^D for another's behavior, while personal characteristics (*e.g.,* color) are relatively insignificant. Normal interactions may therefore be diagrammed in terms of behavior alone:

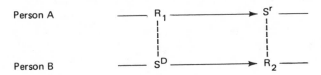

It is possible however, for a person to react not only to another's behavior but also to some of his biological and/or cultural characteristics, and in extreme cases the other's behavior may even be disregarded. When a person reacts negatively and responds not to another's behavior but to some other characteristics, we speak of discrimination. Since there are variations in the extent to which one reacts to another's behavior and other elements, discrimination is a matter of degree. In terms of our diagram, discrimination means at least two things: B's activities are predominantly negative or neutral, and the relevant discriminative stimuli are not so much A's behavior as A's physical and/or cultural characteristics (here labeled X). in the illustration below, R_2 is a reaction to X rather than to R_1:

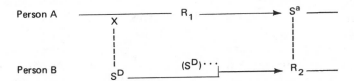

As we pointed out in the last two chapters, such a severance of the behavior-contingency links for the victim of discrimination cannot help but have severe behavioral implications, such as learned helplessness. Because of the existence of reciprocal influence, however, we should expect some effects on the discriminator as well. And to the extent to which discrimination is rewarded[27] —as it used to be by both Blacks and women who accepted their inferior status—we should expect it to continue. Indeed, until recently, and to some extent even today, discrimination has generally been followed either by S^o or S^r and only rarely by S^a, regardless of a community's expressed values. A description of discrimination, then, must include the consequences for all parties, as well as the activities themselves and their contexts.

[27]Dollard (1937) describes the several positive consequences which accrue to Whites from their discrimination, while Myrdal (1962) outlines some of the major negative outcomes for both discriminators and the larger society.

The importance of careful specification is illustrated well in the area of deliquency and crime. The image of the delinquent as a tough, lower-class, male gang member with psychological problems, who comes from a broken home or has parents who cannot control him, and who lives in a slum has been widely accepted. It is a significant determinant of both the reactions of law enforcement agencies and the efforts of ameliorative programs.[28] This image, however, is derived mainly from youths who have been caught and sent to the courts, and does not reflect the characteristics of all youths who may be classed as delinquents—*i.e.,* youths who commit major unlawful acts. But if an analysis of delinquency is to be useful as a component of program designs, it must be concerned with all instances of illegal activities on the part of teen-agers, and not just with the activities of those who are apprehended. When we look at the deliquent with this in mind, what do we see?

The study of delinquent behavior in one city (Flint, Michigan) has been quite revealing. Here a random sample of youths were interviewed to determine whether or not they had engaged in illegal acts during the preceding three years. Great care was taken to assure anonymity and reliability. The results showed that of the 522 youths in the sample, 433 had engaged in 2490 self-reported delinquent acts; yet only 3 percent of these offenses had been noted by the police. More important, there was little relationship between class and crime, residence and crime, and only a few of the crimes had been committed by gang members. In fact, middle-class white boys reported more serious delinquencies than did lower-class white boys, and for most individuals their "companions in crime" shifted from one escapade to the next.[29] Studies of youths in other cities have shown similar results,[30] and a recent survey based on a national sample of youths led to the same conclusion.[31] Furthermore, contrary to the widely held belief that middle-class citizens and Whites are the major victims of crime, a national survey for the President's Commission on Law Enforcement concluded that most crimes are of an intra-racial nature and that Blacks are the victims of crimes against the person more frequently than Whites.[32] The respondents in the study also reported at least twice as many crimes as were known to the police. In short, the problem of delinquency and crime as it appears from police and court records is quite different from that which appears when we look at the actual delinquent behaviors which occur in a community. It is little wonder that ameliorative

[28]Williams and Gold (1972).
[29]Gold (1970).
[30]Short and Nye (1957); Vaz (1966).
[31]Haney and Gold (1973).
[32]President's Commission (1967), pp. 31, 36.

programs designed on the basis of the former are rarely successful and do not touch the nature of the problem.

Even when we view problems in terms of activities—such as aggression—we must be careful to include all of the variables associated with it. Whether or not a person's behavior will be viewed as aggressive, for example, depends on the act's intensity, expressions of pain and injury by the recipients, the intentions we attribute to the person, preceding events and present circumstances (or our interpretation of them), and the characteristics of the person and the observer.[33] Thus identical activities can be labeled "aggression" or simply "horseplay," an "accident," "expressions of masculinity," "justified defense," and even "understandable expressions of frustration." If one wishes to reduce aggression, therefore, one will have to specify the peripheral elements which define specific acts. If one concentrates on generic concepts it will be difficult if not impossible to perform adequate causal analyses and to implement effective remedial procedures.

Social problems have been viewed not only in terms of people's activities but also, and more frequently, in terms of social structures and their properties. For example, we may define alienation as a problem and consider it as a characteristic of modern institutions; or we might concentrate on a society's caste system, school system, or its income distribution. In most cases, however, we will find that the empirical referents of the problematic structures and operations again involve people and their activites. Alienation, for example, is a problem in the sense that people feel powerless,[34] and, as we saw in the previous chapter, this is a function of a tenuous link between behavior and its consequences. The structural property, then, is one of the determinants of an individual's feeling of powerlessness, and is not necessarily a "problem" itself. The same can be said of the caste system and educational institutions: they are problems mainly in the sense that people's behaviors are adversely affected by them. Only a few societal characteristics might be viewed as problems in their own right—for example, a grossly unequal income distribution; but even here we eventually will have to look at people, for what makes the income distribution a problem is that some people suffer by it (*e.g.,* through malnutrition, little education, or feelings of despair).

The major advantage of looking at social problems in terms of people and their behaviors, and of reducing structural characteristics to their human components and effects, is that such a perspective quickly leads us to concrete specifications of what the social structure or institution should be like and how the transformation might be accomplished. It is difficult, for example, to outline a program of educational reform on the abstract

[33]Bandura (1973), pp. 5–11.
[34]Seeman (1959).

institutional level. But when we concentrate on people—students, teachers, administrators, and parents—and what they should do differently, we immediately are confronted by specific goals and steps for their attainment. And, in fact, when we look at proposals to solve major institutional problems, we find that they are concerned largely—at times exclusively—with the modification of the behaviors of the institution's human components. When Illich[35] speaks of deschooling society or Postman and Weingartner[36] present ways for assessing schools and improving them, for example, emphasis is placed on individuals, what they do and what they should do.

The result of Step One, them, is a careful and detailed description of problematic social phenomena, phrased largely in terms of particular individuals' behaviors, together with their context and consequences. While commitment to any particular etiology is not necessary and in fact should be avoided at this stage, we cannot escape from the implications of the model of man which determines our perspective. A psychodynamic model, for example, may lead us to view hyperactive children in terms of a slow build-up of frustrations which must be vented through aggression; hence we may describe a school room in terms of a series of frustrating situations rather than an exchange relationship. In order to prevent or at least minimize such contamination from models or theories, strict adherence to pure description in as great detail and broad a scope as possible should be the norm.[37]

2. Definition of Goals

Once we know the problems that are to be solved or the situations which are to be changed, we can begin to define the goals of a social program. In our examples we may want to reduce or eliminate the aggressive behavior of children and to improve their academic performance, to eliminate discriminatory activites, and to reduce delinquency. The more specific we have been in the first step, the more detailed we can be in the description of our goals; now we can say, for example, that we want to eliminate pathogenic exchange relations in the class room and in interactions among people of different races and cultures.

We have deliberately chosen small examples in areas which are generally recognized as requiring alleviation, so that the problems of size and a program designer's bias are greatly reduced. Other goals of greater scope, however, such as cultural homogeneity or the fostering of middle-class life

---

[35]Illich (1971). It is a worthwhile exercise to outline and evaluate the model of man which underlies this work.

[36]Postman and Weingartner (1973).

[37]For a good description of what should be done, see Hamblin et al. (1971).

styles, are likely to be subjects of considerable debate. A major problem we encounter especially in larger goals is their lack of specificity. If one is interested in merely describing the future one might speak of a just society characterized by responsive institutions and humane working conditions, with a population of loving, self-actualizing, contented individuals. But while such general description is perhaps a desirable first step in the process of goal definition, it will be of little use unless we go far beyond it. The kind of society we want to live in does not do anyone much good; the kind of society we eventually do live in is of great significance. How can we transform one into the other? Mainly by being as careful as we possibly can about the precise details of that future society and its component parts, which form the end products of our several programs. An emphasis on details may remove much of the romance of our vision, and we will certainly lose some of the inspiring words of our original conception, but there is no other way of laying the foundation for effective designs.

Historical experiences with utopias indicate that many designers have paid insufficient attention to the major components of their communities.[38] They often took great pains in designing living accommodations, dress, and other physical components; but they usually did not think enough about the human components. Their plans in effect told people what to do and regulated life in often rather dreary fashion, but little or no thought was given to individuals' previous experiences, the need for and means of learning and adjustment, and the very real possibility that the designer's image of man might not correspond to reality.[39]

What we have to do, then, is express program goals in terms of the behaviors, relationships among activities, and ideas of individuals. We might say, for example, that our goal is to have people react to one another's behavior rather than to their physical or cultural characteristics. Even when we speak of institutions or large groups—for example, responsive churches—we must refer to those behavior patterns of particular persons which we summarize as being "responsive."

Some program goals will consist of the elimination of presently existing conditions, such as poverty. Here again we must emphasize the empirical referents of what exists and should be eliminated. In the case of poverty, for example, we will be concerned with social and other skills, jobs, wages, and relative deprivation. While it used to be argued that the major barrier for most of the unemployed was the lack of skills, recent experience with unemployed engineers and college graduates has forced us to be much more specific as to what skills are needed in the economy. Furthermore, the existence of structural unemployment and the persis-

---

[38]For such descriptions, see Kanter (1972); Mumford (1962).
[39]Richter (1971).

tence of business cycles shows that not all aspects of poverty involve the behavior of potential workers. Yet an attempt to view poverty in terms of a detailed behavioral survey, showing what activities and relationships should be established or eliminated, is a prerequisite for determining the kind of societal and individual factors which should be modified and the extent of modification that is desirable.

Some goals may not have any clearly related behavioral referents. "Self-actualization," for example, is something which presumably occurs *within* a person. The first question we must ask here is: How do we know whether this process is actually occurring within a person, and how do we know when the process has been completed? No doubt an important part of the answer will refer to the person's behavior: he will say certain things, he will engage in certain activites and not in others; or we may simply notice that his whole demeanor and outlook will be different. The last phrase, however, will not be very useful unless we indicate which activities make up the "demeanor" that is "different," and which words would signify a "different outlook." Unless we can do this, we cannot design a program to accomplish our goal. Even when we think of "self-actualization" in terms of a range of behaviors, we must specify the empirical referents of this range. No matter how we view self-actualization, we must be able to specify the behaviors which should be present, and absent, if the process is to occur. Thus we may hypothesize that basic communication skills are a prerequisite and that the behaviors involved therein should be established. Or we may assume that time for reflection is a crucial element; then we should structure people's social environment in such a way as to provide this. And if discussions with other people are necessary, then we should make arrangement for them. Now we see that the behaviors of both an individual and the people in his context are involved, and that our program will therefore have to deal with both. There no doubt are other aspects of and prerequisites for self-actualization, and these, too, must be translated into behaviors if they are to be part of our program.[40] Even idiosyncratic views—for example, the position that a thorough knowledge of the Bible or a particular philosopher is necessary for true self-actualization—can become part of a program, but only if they are phrased in terms of measurable elements. It is entirely possible, of course, that after we provide the right environment and all the prerequisites, either no "self-actualization" occurs or it takes detrimental and even dangerous forms. When this happens we should go back to the original concept, examine it closely, and perhaps consider the possibility that it is not a useful one. If we judge it to be useful, we may have to view it in terms of different empirical referents and prerequisites, or as subject to additional

[40]For an example, see Progoff (1963).

causal factors and cultural limitations. Or we may even have to conclude that it is a process which simply does not occur in some people.

If the goal of a program is to foster certain ideas, we must dissect each idea into at least two parts: the verbal statement which we take as expressing the idea, and the empirical referents of the idea itself. One can argue that verbal statements are not ideas, and this may well be true. Yet how else are we to know what a person's ideas are? He tells us what he thinks, or he acts in accordance with his ideas.

Let us take as an example the idea that "individuals are important in the scheme of things" or, simply, that "individuals count." We will assume that this idea fits better into the general belief of how people should feel about themselves and their fellow man than the presently popular view that most people are small cogs in a great, impersonal machine. Our goal, then, would be to have people come to believe in the importance of all human beings; and the concrete manifestations of this goal would be expressions of this belief and behavior consistent with such a conviction. To achieve this goal, we will have to either reconstruct the social system in such a way that its operations convince people that individuals count, or we will have to get people to see the present society in a different way. Which method we choose will depend on whether the prevalence of the undesirable notion that individuals do not count stemmed from an actual flaw in the existing social system or from a widespread misapprehension of that system.

An important part of the idea that an individual does or does not count results from the consequences of his various activities, sometimes phrased in terms of control over one's environment. For example, if people hardly listen to what a person says, if no one accepts his suggestions, and if people hardly notice that he is back from a trip, there are, in effect, no consequences to his actions. More specifically, the reactions of the context are the same no matter what he does, even if he does nothing or goes away. It seems as if there is no connection between what he does and other people's behaviors. He would be quite justified in summing up his experiences and the operation of the system in which he lives by saying that "I do not count, I am just a cog." If, however, people do listen to him, if his suggestions are at least considered and sometimes accepted, and if upon his return people comment on his absence, he is likely to get the idea that he does count. In general terms, if a person can affect his environment, if variations in his behavior lead to variable reactions from his environment, if there is, in short, a definite link between his own behavior and others' reactions, the idea that "man is relevant" is likely to arise. And, as we pointed out in a previous chapter, one's behaviors arising from this idea or view of the world are likely to support and thus maintain the idea. The behavioral and structural goals of our program, therefore, would include the establishment of connections between people's behaviors and the reactions of their context, so that variations in the former will result in changes in the latter. Such relationships need not exist in all facets of life, but should be present in many of those which are significant to a person.

The result of our behavioral analysis of goals will be several lists, perhaps quite long, of target activities: those we want to (1) extinguish, (2) maintain, (3) increase in frequency, (4) reduce in frequency, and (5) establish.

Such lists however, will be useful only when we are designing limited programs or dealing with small, simple, and homogeneous communities. When we focus on urban-industrial, dynamic, complex, heterogeneous total societies, the goal design will have to differentiate among the activites of men and women, the various occupations, the young and the old, and other categories which may be relevant in a particular place and time. For each of these groups we will need a different set of our five lists, so that a nation-wide program may well encompass a score of lists and hundreds of activites. We will also have to make careful comparisons, lest we find that the same activities appear on two incompatible lists. For example, we can establish and extinguish the same behaviors only if we are talking about different categories of persons.

In preparing these lists we may be tempted to be quite general and to skip over the detailed analysis which is required for an accurate portrayal of the specific target behaviors which make up the goal. In fact, one may be quite impatient, consider this work somewhat premature or irrelevant, and view both the analysis and its result as trivial, pretentious, or presumptuous. Yet if we are interested in designing a program, we must know as precisely as possible what we want to accomplish. A cursory description of general goals cannot tell us what must be done, and while target behavior lists are based on assumptions as to the nature of discrimination or poverty, for example, any program dealing with, say, poverty must make such assumptions. The behavioral approach to social phenomena leads us naturally to bring our assumptions out into the open, while many existing attempts at analysis and solutions do not. It is only when our analytical assumptions are made explicit that we can examine and evaluate them, and it is only by making lists of specific target behaviors that we can determine what is involved in the nature and solutions of particular social problems.

3. Analysis of Determinants

The next step consists of the study of the major determinants of the several target behaviors. We will not be interested in "ultimate causes," however, because when these lie far in the past, as they usually do, there is nothing we can do about them; we can blame a bigot's parents for his antisocial behavior, for example, but this will tell us very little about what we should do today. As long as we are interested in designing programs of problem solution and social change it is enough simply to ask what factors determine behaviors today, and what might be done about them tomorrow.

As we mentioned in chapter 3, the answers must be given on at least two levels. First we look at *primary determinants, i.e.,* those factors which, according to the best available information, directly affect the existing target behaviors or those we wish to establish. Usually these factors will be the various characteristics of an individual's immediate social environment which serve as discriminative, aversive, and reinforcing stimuli. Class-room operations, family and living arrangments, one's place of work, and conditions in the neighborhood are some of the major sources of primary determinants. As we pointed out in chapter 3, however, it is rare for the total situation—for example, *all* aspects of a school—to affect the target behaviors. Usually we will need to consider only a relatively small number of factors, such as the teachers' methods of handling hyperactive children.

Most primary determinants are elements enmeshed in, and at times even characteristic of, larger units. When we ask what factors affect these primary determinants, the answers provide us with a number of *secondary determinants.* These latter usually require some sociological analysis for their explication, for they are likely to be the larger and more complex elements of a society. For example, if we should find that primary determinants are located in a child's family and school, then the secondary determinants must be sought among societal influences on family structure, community characteristics which affect school operations, and commonly held beliefs which support both.

As in the previous step, we must be as specific as we can: the more we know about the particulars of primary and secondary determinants, the greater the likelihood that we can find a way of altering them—and that, after all, is what a program is designed to accomplish. If we have only a vague notion as to what might be the determinants of a target behavior, we will be able to do very little about it because we will not have a "handle" for action, so to speak. But the behavioral perspective of aggressive children, for example, by focusing on pathogenic exchanges between child, parent and teacher, provides us with a number of quite specific possible actions, which we will describe in the next chapter.

The major difficulty encountered in this step revolves around the fact that we are usually dealing with phenomena we cannot alter simply for purposes of experiment and validation. Only rarely can we test our causal hypotheses in order to assess the validity of a determinant we have inferred. Consequently, we end up with hypotheses which are derived from observation but usually lack rigorous tests and vast empirical support. Yet Hamblin and others[41] have demonstrated that careful observations of a class-room situation, together with a behavioral model of man, can result in valid causal hypotheses, as demonstrated by effective programs based upon them. The same procedures can be used in less structured environments, such as normal family life,[42] but as the situations become larger and more complex we have to rely increasingly on one-time observations, impressions, and inferences.[43] In the analysis of secondary determinants, especially, these problems are aggravated by the researcher's model of society and philosophical preconceptions.

The result of step three, then, is a large number of hypotheses, each linking a behavior on our five lists with one or more characteristics of the immediate context which provide discriminative and contingent stimuli and affect the relevant state variables. Most of these contextual characteristics, in turn, will also be activities, and for each of them we will list the operating S^D, S^r or S^a, and SV. As long as we recognize that we are dealing with hypotheses and not with fully validated propositions, and that we should, therefore, be open to contrary data and ready to change our formulations, there is a good chance that we will eventually come up with an effective program design. But when we are convinced that we already know the true determinants, and that we can safely disregard or reinterpret contrary evidence, it is not likely that we will be able to design effective programs or viable communities.

Since the character of determinants and the method for analyzing them has been described in chapter 3, we will now look at only one type of target behavior—activities to be established—for it is not discussed there. These target behaviors do not yet exist; hence we must design a program for establishing the determinants if we cannot use existing situations and events. Furthermore, we must make sure that there are adequate models of the new behavior, some deprivations and their associated reinforcers, and appropriate discriminative stimuli. In general, it is not necessary to establish new SV and S^r, for most programs can be designed to take advantage of existing reinforcers and state variables as long as these can be tied to the new behavior patterns. The analysis of major determinants of new activities, therefore, will concentrate on discovering which existing reinforcers can be attached to which new activities, and how this might be done.

The third step in program design involves considerable sociological knowledge as we proceed from individuals' activities and their primary

---

[41]Hamblin *et al.* (1971); Kirby and Shields (1972); Medland and Stachnick (1972).

[42]For example, see Hall *et al.* (1972).

[43]For example, see Kozol (1967).

determinants to the structure and operation of communities and nations. Careful analysis based on detailed observations as well as inferences and imagination are required in order to determine which aspects of a target activity's social context should be modified. One danger here is that we will not go far enough, that we will stop with the definition of primary determinants. If a program design is to be successful, it must pay considerable attention to secondary determinants as well, even if they should involve political controversies and conflicts of various factions in a community.

The information required for the first three steps of a program design is usually gathered through one or another type of policy research—that is, research which addresses itself to action-oriented questions. One might also call this "applied research," as distinct from the more common "pure research," which has as its major purpose simply the addition of knowledge regardless of its action implications. While social scientists have been engaged in pure research for some time, policy (or applied) research is of more recent origin, and the problems it encounters have produced considerable debate.[44] A major difficulty arises from the fact that researchers and subjects, as well as the wider community in which they live, have a stake in the results of the research project, and thus may attempt to influence the gathering, analysis, and interpretation of data. Pure research is usually thought to be quite harmless, while policy research is often seen as a way of "putting something over" on someone or of justifying an alteration in the status quo. The information required by the first three steps in a program design, then, may well be difficult to acquire and be faulty or partial. Yet the first principle governing policy research—that "partial information available at the time an action must be taken is better than complete information after that time"[45]—justifies our working with whatever information we have.

4. Specification of Procedures

The behavior patterns which a program is designed to establish, extinguish, or maintain are usually the results of modifications in the primary and secondary determinants. The range of possible procedures for dealing with primary determinants is rather limited, for the alternatives are largely dictated by learning principles (see chapter 4). When we cannot directly influence primary determinants, we will have to look to the alteration of secondary determinants. While these are often thought to be rather amorphous—for example, schoolboard policies or the "stratification system"—

---

[44]For recent examples, see Coleman (1973); Empey (1973); Etzioni (1971); Gans (1971); Volkart (1973); and the essays in Horowitz (1971).
[45]Coleman (1973), p. 1.

they do have their behavioral manifestations, and it is these which need to be altered. Ideally, we should follow each hierarchy of determinants until we find a way of modifying one of them in a practical, efficient, and effective manner. In some cases we will be able to alter the primary determinants and thus modify the behavior in accordance with our program goals, as Hamblin was able to change the methods his teachers used in dealing with aggressive pupils. Most of the time, however, we will have to be concerned with the secondary determinants, *i.e.,* social factors and their behavioral manifestations.

THE EXTINCTION OF BEHAVIOR. The selection of procedures will be governed by pragmatic considerations involving a combination of psychological principles and political parameters. For example, we could extinguish R by eliminating the S^D for R. A common problem here, however, is that many S^D are complex sets of many elements, subtle and difficult to ascertain, and likely to be so common that their elimination might lead to a significant alteration of a person's context in ways not intended by the program. Hence this procedure may not be feasible.

Another procedure is the elimination of S^r. For example, we can simply cease reinforcing a particular behavior, or we can reduce the associated deprivation and thus reduce the power of the reinforcer. The major difficulty here is that not all deprivations are subject to easy or rapid satiation. Food and drink quickly cease to be reinforcers, and a good meal is all that will be necessary to bring this about; but money and expressions of esteem are difficult to reduce in value. No matter how much money or praise we give a person, he is likely to want still more.

We can also present S^a when the undesirable target activity occurs. As pointed out in chapters 3 and 4, however, emotional reactions and spontaneous recovery reduce the efficacy of punishment; the reinforcing of alternative desirable activities is considerably more effective. In fact, in the case of aggression, Hamblin found that punishment actually increased the number of aggressive acts, in part because the children knew that they had "gotten to the teacher,"[46] and there is evidence that being caught and punished increases the probability of future delinquency.[47] Both experimental and observational data suggest that, in general, punishment is not an effective procedure when used by itself.[48]

All of these procedures imply several perhaps fundamental alterations in a person's or group's context, and require that we have considerable control over the social environment. But it is also possible in some

[46]Hamblin *et al.* (1971), pp. 104ff.
[47]Gold and Williams (1969).
[48]Bandura (1969), pp. 293–354.

cases that institutions and communities are operating in largely "correct" fashion, but that individuals, not knowing these operations, are unable to take advantage of them. In this case behavior modification of individuals should be attempted by an expansion of their perspective. For example, there may be several significant S^a in the future, but unless a person can see that far ahead the S^a will not exist for him (see chapter 5). By extending a person's time horizon, perhaps through education, the perceived total contingency of the target behavior may be significantly altered and brought into correspondence with reality. Lateral extensions, perhaps through the realization of the complexity and interrelations of social systems, will also bring additional elements into one's total contingency, thus modifying behavior. When we tell a high school student that he should not drop out, that college graduates have better jobs and higher lifetime earnings, we attempt to extend his time horizon and to alter the total contingency related to staying in school. And when we say that racial strife will continue and get worse unless discrimination ceases, we attempt to bring additional elements into the total contingency of White middle-class citizens.

THE MAINTENANCE OF BEHAVIOR. Alterations required for the extinction and establishment of target behaviors may inadvertently affect those activities which we want to maintain. The best procedures, of course, would entail a continuation of the old S^D, SV, and the contingencies and their schedules. But when these have to be altered in connection with another part of our program, we may be forced to find new reinforcers for old activities, to establish new schedules, or to define new S^D. Instructions and gradual transitions will be the most effective means for maintaining old activities within changed environments.

THE MODIFICATION OF RATES. If we want to maintain activities but change the frequency with which they occur we have a choice of two major procedures. First, we can simply change the schedule of reinforcement. For example, fixed-interval schedules are characterized by low rates of activity, while variable-ratio schedules are associated with high rates. While we can easily create pure schedules in the laboratory, however, daily life presents us with a mixture of schedules; hence it is not likely that we will be able to modify behavior frequencies by the alteration of schedules alone.

Second, we can treat the frequency of a target activity as another characteristic of the activity which is to be established and maintained in ways outlined above. For example, we might reinforce an activity only if it occurs during a particular time span, or only when a certain time has elapsed since the activity last occurred.

THE ESTABLISHMENT OF BEHAVIOR.   The best procedure is to provide models and/or instruction, along with frequent reinforcement of the new target activities. As we pointed out in chapter 4, observation is most effective when combined with actual practice; hence we should provide not only models but also opportunities to engage in the observed target actions and to be reinforced for them.

In the laboratory and in relatively structured and controlled environments, such as schools and hospitals, these procedures are quite effective. But in the free and relatively unstructured situations of daily life these procedures cannot be followed for any length of time, and extraneous factors, such as inadvertent modeling, frequently interfere with our efforts. Furthermore, many of a nation's most conspicuous models do not present consistent pictures of word and deed, or do not present the behaviors needed for our program. Politicians, especially holders of high office, serve as models not so much by their words as by their deeds, and while their words may concern ideals and the long-term future, their behavior is likely to be governed by short-term, pragmatic considerations.

Since most social programs involve the modification of several activities, we will have to employ a number of procedures. This does not mean, however, that the total program will have to be as diverse as the number of activities might imply. If we indicate the specific procedures which could be used for each behavior on our five lists, allowing for alternative procedures, we will see that the same procedure will be required several times. By altering some characteristics of an institution's or community's operations we may be able to modify several target activities in the desired direction. As in the earlier steps, however, specificity and careful analysis are the fundamental requirements for the selection and description of appropriate modification procedures.

5. Implementation of Procedures

As we have just seen, the variety of effective procedures is rather limited, centering on the alteration of S^D, SV, contingencies, and their schedules. It matters little whether we are looking at the target behaviors which form the goal of our program, the activities of individuals in the social context (primary determinants), or the actions of people which affect these individuals (secondary determinants). No matter on which level we operate, we will always have to ask what the activity's contingencies are, and how they can be changed.

Yet the variety of ways in which procedures of behavior modification can be implemented is great indeed; in fact, the only limitations are set by practical feasibility and by standards of political, philosophical, economic, and ethical acceptability. In the course of evaluating the several alternative ways of implementing our program we must keep in mind two additional points. First, behavior modification is a slow process which demands our best efforts for a considerable period of time. We have to continue reinforcing new behavior patterns for a while, and schedules of reinforcement must be changed slowly. Second, we cannot expect new or modified activities to persist on their own. It is erroneous to assume that some activities have no contingencies; when this appears to be the case we simply have to look harder for them. For example, we may hear that people are moved by duty, loyalty, or perhaps a sense of calling or accomplishment. Yet these concepts do refer to rewards, though they may be difficult ones for an outsider to recognize. Group members reward loyalty by acceptance and esteem, and when a goal is achieved both the achiever and others are likely to provide some form of approval.

Because of the great variety of means by which behavior modification procedures can be implemented and the many different types of social situations in which this occurs, we will devote the following chapter to this topic.

6. Monitoring the Program

The final step in any program design consists of making provisions for the periodic assessment of procedures and their effectiveness. Since most social programs affect large numbers of people and involve efforts spread over a considerable period of time, it is imperative that we know where we stand, not only at the end of the program but also at various times between initiation and completion.

Most social programs are of necessity based on incomplete information, causal hypotheses of uncertain validity, educated guesses, inferences, and, at least to some extent, trial-and-error procedures. A designer does the best he can, but within the complex dynamics of social life in an urban-industrial, heterogeneous society he cannot afford the luxury of assuming that everything he needs to know for the designing of a program is in fact known. Consequently, periodic corrections in the design, involving the modification of procedures or their implementation, are likely to be necessary. Yet, while we should be prepared to make adjustments, both the need for them and their nature can be determined only when we know what the goal is and what has been accomplished up to a particular moment.

It may be difficult to assess a procedure's overall efficacy, especially in terms of its final consequences, which may well involve a rather long time scale; hence we must seek more immediate indicators. For example, if a procedure is designed to modify some specific activities of a particular group of individuals, we should build into the program a means of assessing the beginning and direction of such change. While most alterations in behavior are gradual, there will always be some indications of movement, and it is these which our program must enable us to measure. By the employment of a behavioral model of man we are provided with at least a theoretical basis for such interim measurements; activities we observe at any one time are useful in assessing the efficiency of procedures and foreshadow the character of the ultimate target activity.[49]

The monitoring of a program during its operation involves a number of problems which are not always easy to solve. The necessary measurements are often difficult to ascertain and interpret, and sometimes they are collected so infrequently (*e.g.,* the decennial census) that a program has run much of its course by the time they become available. At times we are not sure what measures to collect: those of phenomena onto which our procedures impinge directly (*e.g.,* actual discrimination), or those of events and characteristics somewhat removed but essential to the goals of our program (*e.g.,* the reduction of Black-White income differentials). Our procedures may be quite effective and meet our expectations in regard to secondary characteristics, but the wider repercussions, which may well be the very goal of the program, may not be of the kind or magnitude we predicted, perhaps because our model of the particular social system was invalid.

Another problem is that of time scales. Especially if we are interested in the alteration of social phenomena—for example, the distribution of income within a nation—the time scales of changes in the appropriate system components may be much longer than our program or the limitations of political expediency.

Problems related to measurement, social indicators, and statistics and their interpretations have occupied the attention of many sociologists over the years and are far from being solved today.[50] If we concentrate on behavior or its products we will at least have a chance of making regular and rapid assessments of a program's progress, because these are measurable and we can build our indicators upon them. For example, we can count the number of aggressive or discriminatory acts during sample periods. When we have established a base line and defined our goal—a much lower rate of these activities—we will be able to judge whether, over time and as a result of our program, behaviors are actually being altered. The school children in Hamblin's studies, for example, began with a rate of about 140

---

[49]For good examples of the use of baseline data and measurements over time once a program has started, see Bandura (1969) and Hamblin *et al.* (1971). Miller and Feallock (1973) describe some of the ways in which various aspects of normal life can be measured, especially when programs occur in the free environment.

[50]See Barton (1971); Blalock and Blalock (1968); Lehman (1971). Social indicators are discussed in Bauer (1966); Klages (1973); Sheldon and Land (1972).

aggressive acts per day. During a month and a half of new teaching methods, this rate was reduced to about 15 a day, which was thought to be normal.[51]

The last component of a program design, then, is based largely on the second, because only when we know the specifics of the goal can we determine what should be expected during the various stages of a program. A vague goal not only leaves us in the dark as to where we are going but also tells us very little about where we are at any one moment. When programs fail because they cannot be improved in time, the lack of effective monitoring is largely responsible.[52]

IMPLICATIONS

As we confront social problems which appear to be insoluble, and as we face social changes which appear to be uncontrollable, we ask with increasing desperation, Is there really nothing that can be done? During the last twenty years, official views and unofficial statements concerning problems in economic development both at home and abroad have undergone subtle and significant changes. In general, the optimism and enthusiasm of the 1950s, which crested in the ambitious conception of a war on poverty at home and a peace corps abroad, have been replaced by ever stronger expressions of failure and hopelessness.[53] Criticism of programs, expenditures, and the social scientists who promoted them has mounted, for poverty, discrimination, ignorance, inequality, hunger, and injustice are still with us, and indeed it is difficult to say whether they have been substantially reduced. Worse yet, no thoughtful studies provide us with palatable and easy solutions,[54] and it is becoming increasingly evident that billions of dollars and the efforts of thousands of dedicated people have been of little help—because it is said, we have no solutions and do not know what to do.[55]

A somewhat more optimistic position has been voiced by some engineers and others impressed by the success of America's space program.

[51]Hamblin *et al.* (1971), p. 104.

[52]For examples of program evaluations and their problems, see Carter (1971); Ferman (1969), Weiss and Rein (1969); Williams and Evans (1969).

[53]Berger *et al.* (1973).

[54]For examples of difficult and unpalatable solutions, see Banfield (1970); Forrester (1968).

[55]See, for example, Erasmus (1961); Paddock and Paddock (1973).

They have suggested that a NASA-type agency and program be set up to solve some of the knotty and persistent social problems the way space problems have been solved. The major assumptions which underly such a proposal are (1) that the major difficulties which must be overcome in the solution of social problems, the design of better social systems, and the guidance of social change are those of expertise and technique; (2) that the task is mainly one of developing these techniques and applying them; and (3) that social phenomena and processes are not very different from those we meet in the world of physics and mathematical formulas. The question we need to ask, however, is whether these assumptions are valid and whether the engineering perspective makes sense.

As we saw in chapter 4, psychologists have a rather good though not as yet complete understanding of learning principles and the procedures of behavior modification. Sociologists and others specializing in the analysis of various social problems have proposed a number of solutions which are at least worth trying out. What holds us back, then, is not ignorance of causes, limited expertise, and lack of knowledge of techniques. Neither has the lack of funds been a significant obstacle, for during the last two decades billions have been spent on a great variety of social projects. The barriers to success lie elsewhere.

As we contemplate the experiences of the last quarter century, a number of rather disturbing questions arise:

1. Are there no solutions to social problems, or are there no easy, quick, and painless solutions acceptable to all members of a community or nation?

2. Do we know of no solutions, or do we not know any which are morally acceptable and politically feasible, *i.e.,* which require no major changes in the existing social system and value structure?

3. Do we know of no solutions, or do we not know any which are inexpensive and guaranteed to work no matter how little effort we put into them?

These questions—and their answers—become especially significant when we look at social problems from a behavioral perspective. Many people do not wish to recognize that behavior modification will be necessary—not only of minorities but of Whites, not only of the poor but of the rich, not only of lower-class individuals but of middle-class persons, not only of children but of adults, not later but now. And the best way of not recognizing these necessities is to deny our knowledge of them.

Perhaps, as we read the description of the behavioral model of man in chapter 4 and of social programs in this chapter, we feel uneasy, unable or unwilling to face the ethical and moral implications of both the principles and their application. Yet we must examine the implications of our own ethical and moral assumptions as carefully as the implications of the learning principles themselves. The moral, political, and financial restrictions under which the designers of social programs are forced to operate today are equivalent to our saying to a physician, "Heal this man, but do not give him any medicine unless it tastes good and he is willing to take it; do nothing unless it is painless to both the patient and observers; forget about any cure which takes longer than a very few days; require no changes in food, shelter, dress, and life style; prescribe nothing that costs more than a bottle of good gin; and embark on no program unless you have permission from the patient, his immediate family, and their spiritual advisers." These limitations would exclude most drugs and perhaps even aspirin, most injections and operations, and result in taking medical practice and its success rate back into the eighteenth century.

The engineering perspective of social phenomena and processes, conversely, leads to the designing of social programs which disregard nontechnical restrictions and assume that problem solutions operate in what amounts to an ideological vacuum. Techniques that work with metal are thought to work with men as well. Engineers build the components of a technological masterpiece separately, to precise specifications, and without regard to what the metals and wires might have to say about being bent and cut. When the components are joined, the result is often magnificent. But in designing communities, or even in more limited programs, we cannot make such assumptions of independence, precision, insensitivity, and additivity. Learning principles and the procedures of behavior modification, even though they are only parts of a program design, cannot be applied in an ideological vacuum; from the very beginning of their employment, and in the face of considerable and continuing success, questions of morality have been raised. Social planning has always encountered the problem of having to convince citizens and politicians that a rationally designed program should be tried out in its pure form for a sufficiently long time. Less rigorous components of partial solutions, such as those discussed by Banfield,[56] run into similar problems of morality, ethics, and political feasibility.

As long as a psychodynamic model of man dominates our thinking about social problems and the design of programs, as long as we subscribe to a general view of "situational analysis" without specifying the link between context and activity, and as long as we know little about behavior modification, we can escape from moral questions and historical and political considerations by saying that our methods of conceptualizing and solving social problems are so primitive that we simply cannot do much in any case. But with the development of behavioral principles and their

[56]Banfield (1970).

increasingly effective application in all kinds of settings, the excuse of inadequate concepts and primitive methods evaporates.[57] Now we are faced with the fact that we *can* do something, and if we still want to do nothing, we must look elsewhere for support. Ethical and moral considerations, it seems, will do very nicely.

The rather gross components of program designs outlined in this chapter—the specification of problems and goals, the procedures of behavior modification, their implementation, and ways of monitoring—are only a small part of any rigorous effort to solve social problems or guide social change; they stop short of indicating the detailed procedures and large-scale policies which are implied by them. For example, the behavioral model does not tell us whether poverty can be solved best by policies leading to full employment or by increased transfer payments, or indeed whether there are other—or any—effective methods. Behavioral principles tell us only the general outlines of alternatives in social analysis and program designs, and what a policy's effects are likely to be. A more fully developed statement of our model's implications for social programs requires that we take a careful look at the implementation of behavior modification procedures within the cultural and social realities of real communities. This we will now attempt to do.

[57]Homme *et al.* (1968).

7
Models and the Implementation of Programs

In this chapter we will investigate the roles which models of man play in the implementation of programs for the solution of social problems and the guidance of social change. Design and implementation go hand in hand and sometimes are difficult to separate; yet we must try to keep them apart because they focus on fundamentally different aspects of a program. Designs usually have a theoretical basis, are concerned with what *should* be done and *why* it should be done, and thus are likely to have some abstract and idealistic features. Implementation, conversely, emphasizes practical questions of what *can* be done and *how* it is to be done, taking into account the requirements of the design, the characteristics of both the present social situation and its history, and the limitations arising from political necessities and ethical and other values. By themselves, designs of social programs are rather useless and are open to accusations of being utopian; yet action by itself, without the guidance of some design, however vague and amorphous, makes no sense. Thus, while in the previous chapter an important question looming in the background was, "How can this design be implemented?" we now have to face the question, "How well do acceptable procedures fit into our original design?"

PROCEDURES AND POLITICS

The procedures involved in program implementation vary greatly in their scope and generality. They are not independent, and in fact the probability of a program's success is greatly influenced by the degree to which the several procedures are combined to support one another.

Our behavioral model of man—or any model of man, for that matter —presents the change agent with a small set of general procedures which any particular program must incorporate (see chapter 4). The general procedures involved in the modification of target behaviors are small in number and focus mainly on the behaviors' contingencies: a consistent presentation or removal of S^r and S^a, directly or by means of changes in deprivations and time horizons.

The number of specific procedures, however, is large indeed. Not only are there many ways in which S^r and S^a can be presented, and several different means for modifying people's deprivations, but the means to be employed will also depend on the particular target behavior, its context, and the position of the planner. In fact, the number and kinds of specific procedures is so great and so closely tied to social and physical conditions that no description or even categorization is possible. Hence we will have to be content with providing a number of examples of effective programs to illustrate the range of possible procedures. If the planner knows the general procedures which can be employed, he will simply have to use his ingenuity and knowledge of case studies to select the appropriate specific procedures. In short, there is no cookbook method to successful behavior modification—an important factor, by the way, in protecting society from incompetent planners. As in the case of medicine or law, a knowledge of general principles must be combined with insight or "feeling," the use of inferences and imagination, and considerable practice in both the selection and use of the right procedures.

So far we have focused on the target behaviors and their immediate contingencies. Now we turn to the context and its modification. This often provides the planner with problems, for it involves changes in the primary and secondary determinants which make up a target behavior's wider social context. For example, we may come up with a list of changes that should be made in a school's operations, based on general and specific procedures of behavior modification. But knowing what alterations in the context should occur raises the question of how they are to be brought about. If we conclude, for example, that some new legislation should be passed and that some existing laws should be better enforced, we then must ask how this can be done.

If we say that the behavior patterns of legislators and enforcement officials must be changed, we are led back to the modification of contingencies discussed above. Lobbying, publicity, and threats to withdraw electoral support are attempts to alter the contingencies that influence the behavior of public functionaries. But we must also recognize conflicting interests, community cleavages, differences in power among contending groups, obligations to clients and friends, and perceived necessities for compromise. Hence the changes in primary and secondary determinants required by our general and specific procedures associated with the target behaviors may be quite difficult to implement, especially on the level of states and nations, where time is an important factor. As the perceived threat of "long, hot summers" declines, so does the probability of effective legislation to change the behaviors of secondary determinants, such as governmental agencies. While it is true that the principles of behavior modification apply on the level of community and national politics, for even here we are dealing with individuals and their activities, it is useful to accept the terms and concepts of political scientists, sociologists, planners, and others who study social life on this level. Behavioral principles will tell us why a politician acted as he did and whether he will change his mind, but the factors which enter into his total contingency (see Chapter 5) and its alteration can be viewed more efficiently from the standpoint of community and national structures and operations. We will not be concerned with procedures on this level, however, because the literature on planning is replete with theoretical statements and case histories in this area,[1] and there is little need to repeat the complex points made, even if it could be done in one chapter.

Procedures for the implementation of programs often are justified in terms of general policies. National policies to assure civil rights or eliminate poverty, and even such specific policies as tax reform or national health insurance, in effect provide planners with some authority to modify the behaviors of individuals who constitute the secondary determinants of the target behaviors.

Again we find an immense literature on policy formation and implementation,[2] and it is therefore not necessary to present the details and problems here, even if justice could be done to it in a chapter. Our behavioral perspective leads us to ask: how does any particular policy actually affect the target behaviors it is designed to influence? As the policy literature shows all too clearly, by the time a policy reaches the grass roots level its effects are likely to be quite different, and may indeed be opposite, from those intended.[3] A behavioral perspective enables us to predict the likely consequences of any policy, for we will be concerned with the behavior

[1]For examples, see Bennis *et al.* (1969).
[2]Heidt and Etzioni (1969); Kahn (1970b); Rein (1970); Stein and Miller (1973).
[3]Kahn (1970a); Zurcher and Bonjean (1970).

modifications it will actually bring about—or fail to produce—on all levels. Interestingly enough, the mere statement of a policy can have great effects when it is repeated often enough to be believed. Then, if it is not implemented or if for other reasons the results do not match expectations, there will be many frustrated individuals who had hoped for much and received little. As we saw in chapter 3, an actual S^r which is much smaller than what was expected is equivalent to an S^a and is likely to result in anger and aggression. Many expressions of popular discontent in recent times, both in the United States and in developing countries, are in large part due to the high expectations aroused by the war on poverty, the Alliance for Progress, and other programs designed to increase the quality of life everywhere, which were successful only in rare instances and for small numbers of people. The outlining of behavioral consequences of policies, and even of mere policy statements, therefore, is a significant part of social analysis. Even today, our knowledge of behavioral principles is adequate for the task of designing programs and implementing them on the level of individuals, groups, and communities. The more ambitious the design and the larger the program, however, the narrower will be the parameters set by the cultural and historical context, and the more severe will be the limitations exerted by conceptions of political acceptability, the conflicts of interests, and compromises required by the heterogeneous character of most nations.

Unfortunately, political and social realities do not necessarily coincide with behavioral realities. All too often the compromises which have to be made for the mere acceptance of a program design, let alone its implementation, greatly impede the employment of the necessary procedures for the required length of time. Thus, even when the moral issues discussed in the previous chapter have been resolved, a program might not be implemented in terms of the necessary applications of adequate procedures.

We will now take a look at some successful programs of varying size and complexity. In each case it will be instructive to consider what would happen if the program were expanded, what political and other issues would arise, and what the likely outcome would be.

EXAMPLES OF IMPLEMENTATION

We will begin with a clinical case, *i.e.,* a program designed to deal with a relatively simple, individual problem, and proceed from there to a discussion of more complex programs of greater size and designed for increasingly large groups. In every example, we will highlight the implementation of procedures and point to difficulties and their solutions. These thumbnail sketches cannot do justice to the often rather complex programs, of course, but enough will be presented to give an overall impression of the procedures and problems involved.

Anorexia Nervosa

Individual case histories of behavior modification have been common effective means for describing procedures and for comparing the efficacy of various treatments. The literature covers a large variety of symptoms, individuals, and diagnoses and includes both light and severe forms of problems and illness. Snake phobias have been reduced through modeling and gradual desensitization, for example, eating problems have been solved through differential reinforcement, and one hospital patient who had been hoarding towels for nine years was treated by freely giving her all the towels she wanted until she was "satiated" and began to return towels to the supply room; she did not hoard towels thereafter, and no other symptoms appeared.[4]

Today it is widely known that procedures based on learning principles have been successfully employed to reduce behavior difficulties and neurotic symptoms. But what about severe problems which threaten the individual's life? We will illustrate the application of behavioral procedures by describing such a case of anorexia nervosa (the rejection of food). Methods vary from one problem and situation to another and must be adjusted to fit the goal and circumstances; hence one should not suppose that the specific measures described below are typical and will be needed —or effective—in other instances.

Bachrach and his associates[5] have reported the remarkable case of a patient whose normal weight of about 110 pounds over several years had decreased to only 47 pounds, necessitating hospitalization. Exhaustive tests had failed to indicate physical causes, and psychiatric examinations had proved equally fruitless. Eventually she was diagnosed as suffering from "anorexia nervosa" and several different treatments were instituted. When none of these proved to be effective, she was practically given up as hopeless; while seemingly close to death, no further treatments were being contemplated. As a last resort, procedures based on a behavioral model of man were instituted, without the patient's awareness but with the support of physicians, nurses, and her family.

The goals were quite obvious, simple, and measurable—an increase in the patient's weight brought about by increased and systematic food intake—and the empirical referents were clear: ounces and eating. A careful examination of the total situation revealed that the patient's physical deterioration, as well as the behavior patterns leading to it, were followed

---

[4]Bandura (1969), pp. 182ff. Krasner and Ullmann (1965), pp. 80–82.
[5]Bachrach *et al.* (1965).

by a number of rather positive events. For example, she was thought by the hospital administration to deserve a pleasant room with a beautiful view, along with books, records, a radio, TV set, and unlimited visiting privileges. Since she could stand only with assistance and was generally quite weak, nurses and visitors frequently had to hold her book, read to her, and play records for her. She greatly enjoyed visitors, and her precarious condition, which had made her a center of considerable attention, brought a steady stream of the curious and concerned, of physicians, psychiatrists, interns, students, and visiting VIP's to her bedside. The tentative causal hypothesis, therefore, was that her present behavior— eating little—were being maintained by strong rewards. Hence the solution to the problem would be twofold: cease reinforcing poor eating and begin rewarding normal eating. Accordingly, the patient was moved to a bare room with a dismal view, the books, records, and TV sets were removed, and social interactions were kept to a minimum. Nurses had to enter the room, of course, but were instructed to be as brief and professional as possible. Since this was contrary to the nurses' sense of duty, some time had to be spent convincing the nurses that these new methods were best for the patient.

Bachrach and his two associates each ate one meal a day with her and, since the patient's social life now was quite limited, presumably served as reinforcers for her eating. More specifically, they only talked with her while she made attempts to eat. When she did not eat, the physicians remained quiet and the food was simply taken away. Additional reinforcers, such as a radio or TV set, were brought into the room for a specified period after she had consumed some food. For much of the time she was left alone. Gradually, she was required to eat more and more of the food on her plate, the portions themselves were increased, and eventually she had to finish her food before she could use the radio or TV set.

During the first month of treatment her weight increased to 60 pounds, but then stabilized. This was partly due to physiological factors, such as the build-up of tissue, but later she was suspected of vomiting the food into the sink in her room. Instead of turning the sink's water off, an immediate and attractive idea, reinforcers were now attached to weight gain rather than to eating. At her daily weighing in the afternoon there had to be some evidence of gain before she was allowed access to radio, TV set, books, visitors, and, later on when she was able, walks on the hospital grounds. She continued to gain weight and eventually was discharged as an outpatient, about three months after treatments had begun.

At this time her family and friends were given instructions concerning the importance of reinforcing eating with pleasant conversation during meals, dining out with people she enjoyed, and comments on her improving figure. In addition, some natural reinforcers began to operate, such as the reappearance of healthy hair, the pleasures of setting it, and various people's favorable comments. Eventually she could again wear attractive clothes, which resulted in further compliments. During the 18 months after discharge she gained 23 pounds, and two years later she was doing well, had enrolled in a practical nursing program, and weighed around 83 pounds.

This type of case, in which solid success was achieved in a rather short period of time and without recourse to normal psychotherapeutic procedures, might well be expected to arouse scepticism. One could argue, for example, that while one kind of symptom disappeared, the underlying problem was not touched and would reappear in some other form. Yet no new symptoms appeared, and ten years after the program the individual was doing well. In any case, the general hypothesis of symptom substitution seems to have little empirical support,[6] and reported instances of it should be carefully investigated. It is quite reasonable, for example, that a person should try out another activity in an attempt to gain the rewards, such as attention or sympathy, which he previously received with other behaviors; but this is an instance of the operation of behavioral rather than psychodynamic principles. Second, one might suggest that the rapid success of the treatment was due mainly to luck or some unreported factors rather than the employment of behavior modification procedures. The probability of this, however, is reduced by a replication of the above procedures on four cases of severe anorexia nervosa, reported by other investigators.[7] Patients were treated with a program based on the same principles but adapted to the hospital's particular situation, and similar improvements were observed.

Aggressive Children

Hyperactivity is the bane of many a school room, and its most disturbing variant, hyperaggression, has often led to chaos in the class, poor academic performance, and despair among teachers. As we mentioned in the previous chapter, only about half the cases are helped by drugs, and it is especially among normally developed children that neither chemotherapy nor psychotherapy is likely to be effective. In the present study no effort was made to discover the original causes of this behavior, and the explanations given by social workers, school psychologists, and psychiatrists— such as genetic defects, character disorders, or simply being a "sociopath" —were ignored.

Hamblin and his associates[8] began their studies by bringing together

[6]For a discussion of this important point, see Bandura (1969), pp. 48ff.
[7]Blinder *et al.* (1970).
[8]Hamblin *et al.* (1971), pp. 96–135.

the worst problem children in a grade school: those who had been expelled or were on the verge of being expelled, those who had been given up as hopeless cases, and those who were about to be committed to a mental institution. The children, all boys, were placed into two special classes, one of first graders and the other of fifth graders. Descriptions of their behaviors in these classes provided a base line of the relatively low percentage of time spent on school work (approximately 60 percent) and the high rate of disruptive activities (about 60 instances per 45 minute period). The goal, derived from these observations, was simple, clear, and measurable: increase the time spent in studies, presumably leading to improved academic performance, and decrease the amount of aggression.

A careful analysis of the ways in which teachers dealt with the children led to the conclusion that they inadvertently reinforced aggressive acts and thereby maintained them. For example, the teachers generally ignored boys who were quiet and working well, but paid considerable attention to those who were loud and unruly. The boys "would continue to disrupt aggressively as long as the teacher reciprocated with some kind of attention; only when she gave up did they stop. The teacher thought she was punishing the boys, that she was inhibiting their disruptions, but she was actually reinforcing them. The sequence, disruption-attention, disruption-attention, continued until she finally walked away."[9] The fact that these exchanges pleased the boys was indicated by the frequent smiles behind the teacher's back. A program was therefore set up to change the contingencies of both relevant behaviors; the boys who were quiet and studied received attention, support, praise, and tokens, while those who were disruptive were ignored. Punishment was not used, for earlier studies had shown that harsh words and fines actually increased the rate of disruptions.[10] Tokens, which amounted to about 20 cents a day, could be exchanged for snacks.

Careful records of the boys' activities were kept, and by the 29th day it was evident that significant changes had occurred. More than 90 percent of the time was now spent on studies, and the rate of disruptive events had been reduced to less than ten per period. By the end of the year, achievement tests revealed that all the hyperaggressive children had made great strides in catching up with their peers in regular classes.

Difficulties which are frequently encountered in programs such as these, involving the implementation of procedures which are too weak, are illustrated in the case histories of the two "worst" boys. One had been diagnosed as suffering from brain damage; yet he improved markedly between October and February. Then he regressed, and after several weeks

[9]Hamblin *et al.* (1971), p. 111.
[10]Hamblin *et al.* (1971), p. 105.

of attempting to determine the causes, it was hypothesized that the reinforcers available in the school situation were insufficient. Since he liked to work in his father's print shop, where he earned 3 dollars an hour, new procedures were instituted at the father's suggestion. The boy was not allowed to work in the shop unless he behaved well in school and improved in his studies. In addition, he was not permitted to work on a printing job until he could read it well enough to meet his father's standards, which were gradually raised. In October his reading had been at the first grade level; by April he was reading fourth grade books well. In mathematics he improved from the third to the sixth grade level and his relationships with peers became such that at the end of the program he was a leader in his class.

Another boy was added to the program just before he was scheduled to be committed to a mental institution; he had been diagnosed as being a sociopath with a probable physiological or even genetic defect. Hamblin's system worked for only a few days, because his aggressive acts were so violent that they simply could not be ignored. Hence a new strategy was developed: "When he attacked another boy in this vicious fashion, his teachers were to avoid entering into his aggressive games or contests with him, as had his former teachers; they would restrain him, give the other boy attention, then time John out[11] either in the hall or in the cloak room. If he left the time-out room to roam through the school, they would not chase him; they would merely inform him that his time-out had to be served before he could rejoin the group. The longer he spent roaming the school, the longer he would have to wait."[12]

The boy must have liked the class, for this procedure worked very well, at least for a while, and his aggressive acts diminished markedly. After about nine weeks, however, he began to regress. Again it was hypothesized that the reinforcers available in the school were too weak. The dollar a week he could receive for being good was nothing compared to his 5 dollar weekly allowance and the material comforts available to him at home: a personal TV set, pool table, unlimited pop and candy, snacks, etc. Arrangements were made with his parents that these items would be used as back-up reinforcers for those available in school. A daily note from the teacher determined the privileges available to him that evening; after a bad day there would be none and he was restricted to his bedroom. On Fridays the daily points were added up and weekend privileges were

---

[11]"Time-out" refers to a period (in this case usually rather short) in which there are no opportunities to engage in what the subject regards as pleasant activities or in behaviors which are reinforced. Time-out is most effective when it occurs quickly, without explanation, and without the showing of emotion on the part of the parent, teacher, or program manager, so that it takes on the character of a natural event.

[12]Hamblin *et al.* (1971), p. 120.

assigned accordingly, ranging from all privileges to being grounded without TV, records, or friends. His behavior changed abruptly, violent aggressions diminished from nine a week to fewer than one, and he became quite friendly with students, teachers, and his family. This, of course, produced additional reinforcement in natural social settings, and the idea of committing him to an institution was dropped.

As we read these two short case histories and others in the recent literature, we might be tempted to say that the procedures are not new, that much of what was done was self-evident, and that any understanding grandmother would have suggested the same methods. Perhaps. But the point is that professionals—school psychologists, counselors, and psychiatrists—were confounded by these children and did not know what should be done; after all, expelling a student or sending someone to a mental institution simply removes him from one's jurisdiction. Hamblin purposely asked for the worst cases and showed that successful and rapid behavior modification is possible even there. One lesson for the implementation of programs, then, is to be aware of how one's model of man can blind one to the roots and solutions of a problem. When attempts to manipulate the internal state of hyperaggressive boys failed, the children were defined as practically hopeless and no attempt to use different procedures was made; in fact no such attempts *could* be made until Hamblin with his new model of man came along. The problem of model-derived myopia in the analysis of behavior affects learning theorists as well, of course, and the solution is equally applicable to them: to be on the lookout for better and more appropriate models when procedures fail and when one cannot detect any errors in the implementation of a program.

Hamblin cautions us not to conclude that procedures such as his work only in extreme situations. Rather, it "turns out that the procedures which are effective in handling the extreme cases of hyperaggression are also the best ones for handling the disruptive, aggressive behavior of less bothersome children."[13] As Thomas has so eloquently demonstrated, normal classes can be turned into veritable chaos by the frequent use of punishment, such as scolding and other forms of disapproval, in conjunction with a low rate of reinforcement.[14] In fact, the rate of reinforcement seems to be the crucial element, not only in the examples presented in this chapter, and in others cited by Bandura,[15] but also in many societal processes.[16]

[13]Hamblin *et al.* (1971), p. 134.
[14]Thomas *et al.* (1968).
[15]Bandura (1969).
[16]For example, see Hamblin and Crosbie (1972).

Achievement Place

When much of a group's life and activities are artificially structured around the frequent provision of differential reinforcement in the form of points which can be exchanged for other rewards, we usually speak of a "token economy."[17] One example of such a system, called "Achievement Place," is a community-based, family-style rehabilitation center established by citizens of a Midwestern city for pre-delinquent boys. At any one time six to eight boys aged 11 to 15 years live in a home with a house father and mother who are trained psychologists. All of the boys have been referred to the home by the courts, most have personality and school problems, and some have committed the equivalents of felonies. Boys usually remain in the home for a year or more and attend public schools. Life in the home is carefully structured and closely supervised; boys have to "buy" most of their privileges, such as watching TV, having snacks, or going out, with tokens they receive for doing chores around the house, doing well in school, and performing the various tasks usually associated with life in a normal, middle-class home.[18]

When the home was first established, about 1000 points a day were necessary for a comfortable life, but with the increasing number of programs, and the associated reinforcers, the cost slowly increased to about 2000 points. Each boy carried a card with him on which points were added and subtracted whenever necessary; normal behavior and good academic performance usually resulted in his obtaining the number of points required for the purchase, on Fridays, of the following week's privileges. In order to engage in these privileges on any particular day, however, a boy had to earn at least 1500 points the previous day, though he would not have to spend those points to enjoy what he had already bought. While such a combination of weekly schedule and daily prerequisites for privilege purchases worked well for the experienced boys, newcomers initially lived on a daily schedule until they had adjusted to life in Achievement Place.

All privileges had set prices, and points could be earned and lost in many different ways, depending on the programs, only a few of which are sketched below. Thus a loss of points did not necessarily mean a loss of privileges, but rather that some additional "appropriate behaviors" had to be performed to earn points in another way. Hence points served as S^r but the loss of points (S^a) was never so serious as to make the situation aversive. As a result, the boys seldom suffered the loss of their privileges but sometimes had to work rather hard for them.

[17]Ayllon and Azrin (1968).
[18]Phillips (1968).

Over the years, a large number of programs were designed and implemented, each with its specific behavioral goal. For example, promptness at dinner time was quickly established when each minute of tardiness resulted in a loss of points, and being late in returning from school and errands was greatly reduced by fines. The frequency of aggressive statements was similarly reduced. Boys were responsible for cleaning up their rooms but did not do a good job until contingencies were attached to the relevant behaviors. Rooms were well kept as soon as it was established that a room "80 percent or more clean," as defined by specific criteria, would bring in points, while a room "less that 80 percent clean" would lead to a loss of points. When, as part of this program, there was a period when no points were given or taken, the cleaning of rooms decreased markedly. Later on, an intermittent schedule was successfully established, in which reinforcement was gradually reduced to only 8 percent of the days; yet this was enough to maintain clean rooms.[19]

Another program revolved around the kinds of activities usually associated with good academic performance, such as studying, obeying rules, and not disturbing others in school. These behaviors were established and maintained by having the teachers send daily report cards to the home. Boys were told that a "yes" in each of several categories would result in 1000 points and the consequent purchase of privileges, while even one "no" (*e.g.,* the boy did not study the whole period) would result in the loss of points. In one experiment, these contingencies were systematically altered, with interesting results. In the "yes only" condition, when the report cards were invariably positive regardless of classroom behavior, studying declined rapidly from 90 to 25 percent of the time while rule violations increased greatly. In the "yes and no" condition, when the report card accurately reflected class-room behavior, studying quickly increased to the previous level and rule violations declined to 5 percent during a period. When report cards were sent but there were no back-ups, *i.e.,* no associated privileges or their loss, studying again declined, from 95 to 25 percent of the time in only six days. This program was repeated for several of the new boys when they entered the home, and similar changes in behavior resulted from the various situations just described. After two months the time between report cards was gradually lengthened to several days without disturbing the previously established normal class-room behavior.[20]

Finally, speech articulation errors were greatly reduced through the corrective actions of a boy's peers. When the other boys noticed mispronounced words, corrected them, and approved a boy's successful attempts at correct pronunciation, they received a few points, while failure

---

[19]Phillips *et al* (1971).
[20]Bailey *et al.* (1970).

to do so resulted in fines. For each treatment session the problem boy received some points, but he lost a few for each mispronounced word, as judged by his peers. By the end of a month most of the target words were correctly pronounced in the ordinary speech of daily life, and some generalization to similar problem words had occurred.[21]

The programs of Achievement Place illustrate the importance of back-up reinforcers outside the school, as we also saw in Hamblin's study. It also appears that some schools can remain largely as they are and still take care of problem children as long as there are back-ups at home and good communication between home and school—or, as we would say, a definite link between behavior and its consequences. When contingencies have no relation to preceding behavior, as in the "yes only" condition and while the report card was irrelevant, it is just about impossible for schools to shape and maintain behavior. Yet modern schools and many parents approach precisely this condition. The lack of systematic and predictable consequences, and especially a low frequency of significant rewards, are the hallmark of what sociologists have called "anomie" [22] and what the young mean when they speak of "being lost."

The case studies also show that it is quite possible gradually to change the schedule of reinforcement, from continuous rewards to a low-frequency schedule in which behavior could be maintained when S^r occurred only 8 percent of the time. Finally, while the operations of Achievement Place at first glance might appear to be overly materialistic, one should not forget that symbolic and self-reinforcement must be learned and that few of the children had the necessary experiences outside their new home. The boys had severe behavior problems and came from families that used few symbolic rewards. Once new activities had been established, they could be maintained in much the same way that parents employ when they raise their children: not only differential reinforcement and the giving of privileges and symbolic rewards, but also the opportunity either to avoid losing points or to make up points so that no privileges need be lost.

An important criterion of any program's success is the degree to which it is self-administered. Initially, program managers perform three tasks: they set the behavioral goals, observe the activities which occur, and provide the relevant contingencies. Eventually, however, the program should run by itself, without continual external supervision; the behavior-consequence links should operate in terms of natural relationships.

Achievement Place has been operated to an increasing degree on the basis of rules made and enforced by the boys themselves, and peer "man-

[21]Bailey *et al.* (1971).
[22]Hamblin and Crosbie (1972).

agers" now are responsible for the performance and evaluation of routine household and maintenance tasks. During a three-year period a variety of different systems were tried out and evaluated, such as "managers" who were selected at random, who were elected by their fellows, or who bought their positions (for up to 5000 points). Their authority varied; under one plan they had the power to give and deduct points, under another they could do only one of these, and under a third they were not able to provide any contingencies. The most preferred and effective system consisted of elected managers who had power to give and deduct points. Group assignments and group consequences were the least preferred system and the least effective as well.[23]

At the National Training School in Washington, D.C., a similar program achieved considerable success in teaching and maintaining behavior patterns and cognitive skills essential for normal life.[24] Boys aged 14 to 18 with various felony records made remarkable progress in the acquisition of basic academic and social skills and the learning of self-reliance and responsibility. A cottage was set aside from the rest of the institution and its operations were designed to approximate the conditions of daily existence in the normal society. For example, boys were responsible for the routine household and maintenance tasks required for cottage life. Only the bare necessities, such as institutional food and a dormitory bed, were provided free, while conveniences and luxuries such as cafeteria-style food and private rooms, had to be purchased. The necessary tokens could be acquired through study, academic course work, and a variety of tasks. During the year that the project lasted, performance on achievement tests increased greatly, up to 2.5 grade levels, and I.Q. scores rose as well (as much as 27 points, with a 12.5 point average gain).[25] Competence in social skills increased, and many graduates were judged to be ready for life outside.

Follow-up studies of Achievement Place "graduates," and a comparison of these youths with former inmates of a nearby reformatory, showed that two years later the graduates had a much lower rate of recidivism (19 percent versus 54 percent), a higher rate of school attendance (90 percent versus 9 percent), and were receiving better grades.

A second home which replicated the token economy was not as sucessful initially as the first, although the same procedures were employed. Careful comparisons of the two sets of teaching-parents led to the conclusion that success depends not only on the use of behavior modification techniques but also on the manner in which they are used and the

[23]Phillips *et al.* (1973).
[24]Cohen and Filipczak (1971).
[25]Cohen and Filipczak (1971), chapter 6.

personal overtones perceived by the youths. A good, *i.e.,* successful teaching-parent behaves in a nonthreatening and enthusiastic fashion, which gives the house a positive atmosphere; provides encouragement and social reinforcers rather than mere points; makes constructive criticisms and gives specific instructions, so that the youths know precisely what to do and what they did wrong; and involves the youths in decisions affecting the program.[26]

Vicos

The Vicos hacienda in the Peruvian Andes 250 miles northeast of Lima was the locale of the Cornell-Peru Project, the best-known program of successful large-scale behavior modification in recent years. While the procedures which were used are congruent with the behavioral model of man outlined in chapters 3 and 4, however, they have not been explicitly labeled as being derived from learning theory.[27]

The hacienda used to be leased for 10-year periods, at a rent which was quite low because the enterprise was not very productive. The 1850 Indians living in the village belonging to the hacienda were poor, illiterate, apathetic, and not wont to work hard. Only 5000 of the 35,000 acres of the property were suitable for grazing, and only 2500 for growing crops; 90 percent of the arable land was used for subsistence agriculture to support the population, while the remainder, the best land, was used for the production of cash crops, mainly potatoes, for the benefit of the patrón. During the 400 years prior to 1952 the lot of the Indians had changed little; in return for the use of a plot of land, each family owed the patrón the labor of one adult for three days a week, the free use of its animals, and additional services as cooks, servants, shepherds, etc. Village life was disorganized, there were few cooperative efforts, and apathy and pessimism prevailed among the people.

In 1952 the anthropologist Allan Holmberg leased the hacienda and instituted programs to raise living standards, increase self-reliance, and develop a viable community which could operate on its own. We will take a look at only two programs and their procedures to illustrate the nature and operation of the project.

Two major characteristics of the Indians in Vicos, and in many other parts of Latin America as well, were the behaviors and deficits we usually label "laziness" and "apathy." Part of the project's goal was to eliminate them. An examination of the situation revealed that it was customary not to pay wages and that there were no rewards for hard work, initiative,

[26]Fixsen *et al.* (1973).
[27]Dobyns *et al.* (1971).

independence, and foresight. For example, when an Indian's crop happened to be especially good the patrón took a larger share of it, and when a villager showed some independence he was punished or banished. In short, life held few rewards and much that was aversive, and one of the most common, and eminently logical, reactions was to do very little.

While descriptions of the Vicos Project mention the internal states of the Indians before and after the various programs, the procedures themselves disregarded such matters. Instead, they emphasized alterations in the immediate social environment of the villagers, and success was defined in terms of what the peasants did rather than what they thought or felt. In short, the variables which entered into the programs were observable and measurable. Some of the results, of course, could be, and were, phrased in terms of internal states and community characteristics.

The project's goals of productive labor and self-reliance were achieved within a very short time by simply changing the contingencies of various behaviors. Unpaid services to the patrón were eliminated and a wage system for Indian labor was instituted. The hacienda's potato crop had never been very profitable, largely because of poor seeds, lack of fertilizer, carelessness, and lackadaisical cultivation. Holmberg offered to lend the peasants new seeds and fertilizer, and provided instruction for soil preparation, planting, and cultivation. Repayment was to consist of a specified part of the crop.

In the first year only two or three Indians took up Holmberg's offer. The others were distrustful, suspecting either that the crop would fail or that the new patrón would take more than the agreed-upon share, resulting in no benefit at all. But the crops of those who joined Holmberg's program turned out to be very good, the patrón kept his word, and the result was a substantially larger amount of potatoes for those families. In the next year many more peasants took advantage of the loans and information, with equally positive results. Two years later almost every family had adopted the new methods, yields had increased greatly (up to 400 percent), and potatoes could now be exported, providing cash and a host of other goods. Indians now worked hard, improved their lands and methods of cultivation, and began to make plans for the future—to build a school and roads and to govern themselves and the hacienda.

Education had never been popular, and while a school had existed for several years, few children attended and most youths and adults were illiterate. The major reasons for this state of affairs were that the teacher had been mediocre, had used pupils as servants and gardeners, and had taught very little that was useful to the children or their parents. Fathers thought that if children worked they should help the family rather than the teacher do his chores. Holmberg brought in a good teacher, revised the curriculum, abolished child labor, and instituted a school lunch program.

Attendance gradually increased, performance improved, and when the parents found that their children actually learned useful things they began to speak well of education and to support the school and its plans for expansion. The increased potato crops and their sale now demonstrated the utility of literacy and mathematics, and villagers became enthusiastic enough to build a new school. In fact, within a few years the community was quite proud of its school, which became a model for the surrounding area.

Other programs—for example, those leading to cooperation and self-government—were equally successful. By 1957 the potato crop was so large and the community so well organized that arrangements could be made for the gradual transfer of the hacienda to the Indians themselves—a dream which was realized in 1961.

This thumbnail sketch of some of the characteristics and events cannot do justice to the carefully laid out program, of course. The project is remarkable in a number of respects: many different activities were changed, the villagers' lives were significantly improved, the time required was less than a decade, the program costs were small except for the rental charges, and at any one time there were no more than three outsiders, besides the teacher, living on the hacienda and supervising the programs. The overall success, then, was due largely to a well-designed program, careful implementation of the procedures required for behavior modification, and the gradual and planned withdrawal of the change agents. The Vicos Project is, furthermore, a remarkable illustration of the hypothesis that behavior and indeed much of life can be significantly changed—and on a large scale—by the systematic alteration of external contingencies without attempts to work on men's internal states.

As the descriptions of the project make abundantly clear, the major difficulties encountered were of a political and bureaucratic nature, especially when it came to the transfer of the hacienda to the peasants. Indian ownership and successful operation of a large hacienda not only did not fit well into traditional Peruvian social structure but, insofar as it implied that the traditional image of the "lazy and apathetic" Indian is man-made and self-serving, it also threatened the security of landowners, who depend so greatly on that image.[28] Interestingly enough, criticism also came from other quarters, the argument being that no lessons can be learned from Vicos because it was an imperialist adventure which "succeeded" only because of vast monies poured into it.[29] Yet the total budget of the project, which forms the basis of this criticism, included large sums for graduate student fellowships and for a training program in applied an-

[28]Whyte (1969).
[29]For an example, see MacDonald (1973).

thropology for Peruvian and American students, and without this item the cost was much less than $15,000. Another factor, of course, is that the Vicos Project, if successfully applied in other areas, would be a proven and viable alternative to bloody revolution.

The four cases we have described should sensitize us to two major problems which we are likely to encounter in any behaviorally oriented program. First, the procedures themselves, and especially their successful applications, are likely to undermine many people's essentially psychodynamic models of man; to the extent to which this model is cherished we should expect opposition. Second, apparent success in modifying behavior and in solving social problems is likely to encounter opposition from those who have something to gain by the continued existence of the problem, including not only those who profit by the traditional system, but also those who make a living by analyzing and "working with" the problem and those who need the problems as a foundation for their political beliefs and programs.

REQUIREMENTS FOR
SUCCESSFUL IMPLEMENTATION

The four examples discussed in the previous section are illustrative of the great number and variety of cases which have been described in recent years. It is true that the majority of behavior modification programs so far have been concerned with individuals and small groups rather than with larger units, such as communities. Nevertheless, the factors responsible for success and failure appear to be much the same throughout the range of size and complexity and do not depend on the program's purpose. We will now look at these factors in order to determine the requirements which any attempt at program implementation should meet if it is to have a high probability of success. Then we will indicate the practical lessons which might be learned from the above cases and others appearing in the recent sociological, psychological, and anthropological literature.

The major factors and lessons are reflections of learning principles and operate, as far as we can tell today, regardless of a program's goal, target group, or social context. Yet these principles work within a particular social structure, physical environment, and history. It is the combination of all these elements which determine the nature and requirements of the program and the probability of success.

In the above cases, for example, the programs were designed and implemented by those who were powerful for the benefit of those who were weak: physicians treated their patient, teachers helped their students, adults modified the behavior of children, and an anthropologist ran an estate in a humane way. But there are also instances of programs working in the opposite direction. Graubard, for example, describes a successful program in which students modified the discriminating behaviors of their teacher, and Whyte shows how Peruvian peasants were able to take over a hacienda from the patrón; [30] in fact, we are all familiar with children who control their parents quite effectively and with politicians who are "brought around" by their constituents.

Answers to the important question, "Who can modify whose behavior, and when?" which is involved in all programs, large or small, depend on the factors we will now discuss. We should note that what follows is derived entirely from our behavioral model of man rather than from the canons of political science or the insights of sociologists. Interestingly enough, however, all three approaches to planning come to quite similar conclusions; hence one should pay special heed in operating a program of change accordingly.

1. Specificity of the Goal

In each of the four cases the goals of the program were quite specific, had empirical referents, and were of manageable proportions, as defined by available personnel and powers. Even when the overall goal was rather amorphous, such as the Vicos Project's goal of transforming Vicos into a viable, independent community and improving the lives of its citizens, it could be subdivided into smaller units, such as school attendance, agricultural labors, or self-government, which served as endpoints of relatively circumscribed programs. In general we can say that the more specific a goal is, the more specific we can be about the procedures that should be employed and other requirements that must be met, such as control over the environment.

2. Knowledge of the Situation

Both the primary and secondary determinants of the target behaviors were analyzed with considerable care, and causal hypotheses were formulated and incorporated into the programs to serve as foundations for specific procedures. The inadvertent reinforcement of children's aggression by teachers and the lack of rewards in the lives of Vicos Indians, for example, turned out to be significant aspects of the situation which needed to be changed. Procedures could then be instituted to bring about the necessary modifications in the social structure.

Other aspects of the situation which had to be taken into account were the opportunities and limitations within the social environment for

[30]Whyte (1969).

altering the major determinants of behavior. Holmberg was able to change much of the hacienda's operations and encountered few limits; but Hamblin soon found that the reinforcers available in the normal school setting were much too weak and had to be supplemented by back-up reinforcers provided by parents. Here we see that the original limitations provided by the school situation were significantly reduced by knowledge of the boys' home situations and the incorporation of the home into the procedures of the program.

As a general rule, then, we can say that the greater and more accurate the knowledge of the total situation, the greater will be the likelihood that effective procedures can be found and employed.

We should note, however, that the definition of "significant" environmental aspects depends to a large degree on the model of man we employ in our description and analysis of the situation. The school psychologist and even the psychiatrist who had been consulted by the parents of one of the aggressive boys believed that the major cause was genetic or physiological and that the solution, therefore, lay in institutionalization, while Hamblin's learning approach directed his attention to the environmental factors maintaining aggressive behavior. Similarly, a psychodynamic view of the Vicos situation would emphasize authoritarian personalities, low need achievement, or a host of other internal characteristics rather than the hacienda patrón's exploitation of villagers.[31] Furthermore, psychodynamic models would hold the immediate social context to be largely irrelevant and concentrate instead on past and usually inaccessible causal factors, such as childhood experiences and the present internal state. But the past, of course, is immutable, and the internal state is rarely subject to rapid alteration. Thus Bachrach's analysis of the situation in which the woman with anorexia nervosa found herself led to a definite set of procedures, while the official view, that the cause of her condition was fear of oral impregnation, could lead only to psychotherapy, which had already been tried and found wanting. It is essential, therefore, that one be aware of how one's model of man influences one's view of the situation and employ a different model if the procedures arising from one situational analysis turn out to be ineffective.

3. Deprivation

Procedures revolving around differential reinforcement—be it to establish new activities or to maintain old ones—cannot be successful unless there are sufficient deprivations to make the reinforcers effective. This usually does not require the creation of new deprivations or an increase in those which already exist, because even in affluent societies few individuals are

[31]If one employed, for example, the theories of Hagen (1962) and McClelland (1961).

content with all aspects of their lives. What needs to be done in most programs is to tie existing reinforcers for existing deprivations to new behavior patterns. When parents or teachers begin to ignore "deviant" behavior and reward prosocial activities or studies instead, children usually end up receiving more positive attention than they did before the program started. Both the program design and its implementation should employ incentives that people value, within the existing level and system of deprivations; this is not too difficult a task, for daily life is full of incentives (which at the moment may be attached to the "wrong" behavior patterns).

When we implement a program design, then, we usually make use of pre-existing or natural deprivations, as Holmberg did on the old Vicos hacienda, where the Indians were poor, illiterate, and had insufficient food. Sometimes we may have to look around until we find a way of increasing existing, mild degrees of deprivation, as Hamblin did when he contacted the parents of two aggressive boys and arranged for the withholding of privileges at home. Only in a few cases need we create deprivations in order to make available procedures effective, as Bachrach did when he removed the anorexia patient from social interactions and withheld her books, TV, and radio. Since deprivation and reinforcers are two sides of the same coin, we could also speak of reinforcers which must be available if a program is to succeed.

An essential early part of any program is to make sure that its reinforcers are congruent with the population's deprivations. When there is great divergence we must either use different reinforcers or look for deprivations which fit available reinforcers. The latter method is a dangerous one, however, for there is the temptation to read our own feelings and opinions into other people's characteristics. Anthropologists and others who have been concerned with different cultures, for example, have often spoken of people's "felt needs" and the fact that programs should be geared to a community's "felt needs." [32] Yet as long as a felt need is an inferred internal state it is subject to misinterpretation, especially on the part of outsiders. Thus it has been suggested that the failure of many programs has been due to a disregard or misinterpretation for people's felt needs. [33] Nevertheless, careful observations of people's behavior can tell us what people "like" to do and which behaviors are reinforcing, [34] and knowledge of a culture can tell us much about individuals' probable deprivations. The almost universal acceptance of money makes it a useful token, yet the importance which people attach to dignity, esteem, tranquility, and independence indicates that there are other significant deprivations as well.

[32] As described, for example, by Foster (1973).
[33] Goodenough (1963); Erasmus (1961).
[34] See, for example, Premack (1965).

As we pointed out in chapter 3, human beings can learn to be deprived of a great number and variety of things, and as yet we do not know the range of those which are innate. It seems reasonable to assume, therefore, that no matter how hopeless the situation may appear at the beginning of a study, the analyst will eventually come across existing deprivations and associated reinforcers which can be incorporated into a program, even though the search may be difficult, especially in an affluent society.

Finally, we can now point to one aspect of the problem of "who can modify whom." He who controls reinforcers can modify those individuals and behaviors for which the reinforcers operate, and he who feels deprived is subject to possible modification. The answer to the question depends, then, on the circumstances rather than on particular persons. While parents hold important reinforcers, for example, children at times can have just as much control, and as poets have said many times, he who loves is at the mercy of his beloved.

4. Contingency Management

Any program which relies on differential reinforcement requires that those who are responsible for its operation have sufficient control over the environment to present, withhold, and alter both positive and negative contingencies whenever necessary. This usually implies sufficient information about the behaviors which are occurring to present the "right" contingencies, at least at the beginning of a program. In later stages, the environment's more or less naturally operating contingencies should be sufficient to maintain the behavior, without any interference by program operators. The anorexia nervosa case is an illustration of initially complete and later decreasing control over contingencies. At first the physicians managed the reinforcers, such as books and the radio, but eventually the natural contingencies provided by others, such as people's praise for good grooming, were sufficient to maintain eating and weight.

The initial restructuring of contingencies for the initiation and support of new behaviors often necessitates some changes in the context. In fact, we cannot call a program a success as long as the newly established behaviors depend on artificial reinforcements provided mainly by the program operators. Hamblin exerted considerable control over many contingencies of his aggressive pupils, but eventually good grades and respect from peers and family became the "naturally operating" reinforcers for normal school activities. Thus we can say that the hallmark of success is not only the establishment of the target behaviors but also the program's gradual withdrawal from active involvement in contingency management. Ideally, the new behaviors and their natural consequences emanating from the environment (or self-administered) should form reciprocal, self-sustaining links.

The importance of contingency control in large-scale programs is illustrated by the Vicos Project. As owner of the hacienda, Holmberg could easily change its daily operations, the regulations applying to Indian labor, and the power given to villagers and their representatives. It is not difficult to imagine the course of the program if Holmberg had not been able to institute a system of wages, or if he had not been able to keep his word to take only a prearranged amount of potatoes in repayment for the seed loans.

As several studies in Achievement Place showed, the dispensing of aversive consequences is as important as control over reinforcers. Threats without S^a quickly become worthless, and in fact it may be said that empty threats are the hallmark of insufficient control. When power over the dispensing of contingencies is lacking, the program is bound to fail. After we have completed our program design and are ready for its implementation, therefore, we must assess the degree of control we have over the relevant aspects of the environment. When control is insufficient, and when we can find no way of increasing it, we might well consider abandoning the project altogether, if only to prevent a further waste of effort.

Another aspect of the problem of contingency management is reluctance to make use of the powers that are available; insufficient control may be due to such reluctance as well as to a genuine absence of power. Bachrach and his associates, for example, could have refused to consider the possibility of moving the patient and withholding her privileges, perhaps on superficially humanitarian grounds. In fact, they had some difficulty in persuading the nurses to cooperate in the treatment program precisely because many aspects of it seemed rather drastic, especially since the patient was thought to be close to death. A psychodynamically oriented anthropologist might not have made use of the controls available in Vicos because of the belief that a program such as Holmberg's could not possibly succeed—a belief perhaps based on the hypothesis that the basic problem lay in the Indians' personalities.

We must distinguish, then, between the potential control that one has over the relevant aspects of the social environment and the actual control one is willing to exert. The question of willingness leads us not only to moral considerations, some of which we discussed in the previous chapter, but also reflects one's model of man and one's attitude toward problems and solutions. If our model of man indicates that contingency management is essentially irrelevant, as would be the case with most psychodynamic models, then we will be reluctant to change consequences, and moral considerations are likely to deter as easily and quickly. If we believe that problems have always existed and will persist, that they are too large for us to handle, or that they will disappear on their own, then the amount of control we actually have will matter little. But if we decide to try and help a patient with anorexia nervosa, if we decide that hyperactive children should be treated in other ways than with drugs and confinement in mental institutions, if we believe that children should do well in school and learn basic skills there, and if we believe that poor and illiterate peasants deserve a better life—then we must seriously consider making good use of the control we do have, no matter how little it might be. What is required of program designers and operators is a mixture of idealism— the simple belief that problems *can* be solved by man—and hard-nosed realism—a conviction that behavior can be modified by changing the immediate context, and that this requires procedures which have been proven effective. Thus our discussion of contingency management provides another part of the answer to the question of who can modify whom and when: he who controls the dispensing of reinforcers emanating from the social and physical context can modify the behavior of others whenever he is willing to exert such control.

The final aspect of management concerns two important aspects of the establishment of a target behavior $\longrightarrow$ reinforcement linkage: the independence and versatility of the change agent. If reinforcement is limited in kind or has to be approved by an agent's superiors, too much time is likely to elapse before reinforcement occurs, and if other activities happen between the target R and S^r, another behavior might well be strengthened instead. Furthermore, local variations in definitions, kinds, and degrees of deprivation, as well as corresponding differences in reinforcers, require that change agents have not only considerable training and judgment but insight and autonomy as well. Centrally directed definitions and provisions of discriminative and contingent stimuli may well apply to average persons living in average circumstances, and may even be derived from statistical measures, but any attempt at implementation in the real world must deal with individuals and not average members of a population, and confronts particular situations and not statistical indices. The flexibility provided by local management of programs, especially of the often delicate operations involved in behavior modification, is therefore, essential. Ultimately, the ideal size of a program will be a function of two requirements: adequate flexibility to take into account local variations, and adequate power to control the essential contingencies which operate on the local level.

A factor closely associated with control, and one which can make even relatively weak control sufficient for some programs, is protection from confounding influences, especially during the initial stages. The major reason for some degree of isolation is that it facilitates the consistent presentation of contingencies. Bachrach's patient had a separate room; Vicos was a rather isolated community; and Hamblin's pupils initially studied in special rooms away from the influence of their peers.

Protection from confounding influences is a matter of degree and is useful mainly in facilitating the establishment of those $S^D \longrightarrow R \longrightarrow S^r$ triads which are part of a program. Since the links between any two elements of the triad are sometimes difficult to establish and usually require some time, external influences and confounding factors should be reduced as much as possible. Once the behaviors have been established, isolation is no longer necessary.

5. The Provision of Contingencies

In chapter 4 we outlined the ideal conditions for behavior modification and indicated that the closer a situation approaches these ideals, the greater is the probability that a program will be successful. The above four factors in effect tell us how well the context of our program meets the ideal requirements, *i.e.*, whether we will be able to provide contingencies in the manner which is necessary for the establishment, maintenance, and extinction of the target behaviors which constitute the goals of our program. Environmental control, for example, is necessary for the provision of consistent reinforcement on the kind of schedule best suited for the program —*e.g.*, continuous for the establishment of new activities and intermittent for the maintenance of behavior.

We must recognize, however, that adequate information and control by themselves do not guarantee that appropriate contingencies will be presented consistently, at the right time, and on a correct schedule. The factors discussed above refer largely to characteristics of the situation which form the prerequisities of a program's success, while the actual provision of contingencies—the very heart of implementation—is a matter of concrete human acts. The prerequisites of a successful program may exist, but it is not until we take action that success becomes possible. In our four cases we saw the correct application of principles within situations that met most of the ideal requirements described in chapter 4; yet we also saw the consequences of inadvertent and incorrect provisions of reinforcement in those same situations. For example, the attention given the anorexia nervosa patient had contributed to her final weight problem, and the attention teachers had paid to aggressive children maintained their disturbing activities.

In chapter 4 we pointed out that there are no free-floating contingencies and that people's activities usually serve as contingencies for others' behaviors even when such roles are not intended. The kindness and concern which nurses showed to Bachrach's patient prior to his taking over the case affected her behavior, and when *hacendados* prior to Holmberg's arrival simply followed traditional ways of treating Indians they contributed to the villagers' apathy and "laziness." Thus, when we shy away from the systematic provision of contingencies required by a program, no matter what the reasons might be, this very inaction on our part will have as much of an effect as if we had actually done something. We may not wish to be our brother's keeper, but we cannot help providing him with contingencies.

6. Behavior and Things

As we attempt to modify those determinants of the target behaviors which are embedded in the social context, we must make sure that any modifications of the context actually affect these behaviors. It is not enough to simply change some aspects of the physical or social environment and to forget about the behavioral ramifications; after all, the goals of the program are not environmental changes but rather their beneficial effects on individuals.

    We are often tempted to concentrate our efforts simply on the presumed environmental "causes" of a problem, to modify them, and to forget about the behavioral ramifications. This is especially true when we believe the causes to be of a largely physical nature, or want them to be so, for the visible changes in the supposed causes, which usually can be produced quite easily and quickly, lead to the superficial impression that the problem has been solved. The most common example of such misplaced physical or material emphasis is the program which presumes to solve a problem with money and material, where the implementation begins with the dispensing of funds and ends with the acquisition of goods. For example, vast amounts of money have been spent on modern school buildings, well-equipped laboratories, lunch and breakfast programs, scholarships for teachers, and higher salaries. Yet the crucial factor, the interaction between pupil and teacher, has been largely neglected or treated in an irrelevant manner, as when students are given the freedom to select and plan their curriculum. It is of interest that Hamblin does not tell us anything about the physical aspects of his class rooms and that we know nothing about the laboratories and other facilities in the schools attended by the boys who lived in Achievement Place. As these case studies and those reported in the *Journal of Applied Behavior Analysis* so eloquently demonstrate, what is important is the behavior of the teachers, the linkage between school and parents, and the back-up reinforcers at home.

    When we perform the tasks which make up a program's implementation, we must remember that the frequent failure of programs emphasizing physical causes and solutions of social problems results primarily from the failure to place proper emphasis on the behavioral aspects of such problems. Here the question is, how can one make sure that physical changes result in the desired modification of specific target behaviors? It has often

been said that the "human aspects" of social programs must not be ne-
glected; that is true enough, yet here as elsewhere the definition of "human
aspects" depends on one's model of man. When we employ a behavioral
model it enables us to specify what is all too frequently forgotten in an
emphasis on simple physical changes and more money: the fact that people
learn, that it is *human beings* who influence and modify the target behaviors
of other *human beings*. To be effective, therefore, physical and fiscal programs must include the recognition of social learning, that one cannot
escape from the behavior of human beings in a historically rooted social,
political, and economic context.

7. Time

Another requirement is that we recognize the long time scale built into
most programs, and especially those which are complex and directed at a
large population. The psychological literature shows that behavior therapy
is usually much faster than psychotherapy.[35] On the one hand, Bachrach's
patient was well on the road to recovery after only three months, Hamblin's pupils were ready for normal class rooms after a few months, and
Achievement Place brought about behavior modification in a matter of
weeks. On the other hand, more complex programs of a larger scope, such
as the Vicos Project, require a few years. Yet even here the time scale is
much shorter than that implied by programs and theories with a psychodynamic base.[36] The question arises, then, whether, when long-range
projects are required, the average citizen and the average politician are
ready and willing to embark upon programs with a time scale of five to ten
years. While there are examples of policies with that kind of life span—
for example, the fight against polio or efforts to reach the moon—the
consistency of implementation required by behavioral programs has been
much less common in recent history and is less likely in the future.

8. Programs and Consequences

Finally, a program should lead directly into opportunities and reinforcers
that are part of the real world. The new activities established in a program
will disappear unless individuals have a chance to engage in them and to
be rewarded for them. As part of the program, therefore, we may have to
modify the wider environment so that it will operate according to the new
behaviors' requirements, unless we can be sure that the environment's
natural operations reinforce the new activities. Conversely, if a program is
designed to extinguish certain behaviors, the larger environment must not

[35]Illustrations are found in Bandura (1969); Ullman and Krasner (1965).
[36]For example, Hagen (1962); McClelland (1961).

provide reinforcers for these actions. All too often it is not the program that fails but rather the old environment in which the people continue to live.

These points may appear so obvious as to require no statement; yet the larger society rarely provides the right environment, especially in terms of opportunities and contingencies, for the maintenance of newly acquired skills and views of the world. What is the usual fate of convicts when they are released? What would happen to Hamblin's pupils if they returned to class-room situations where teachers pay attention only to aggressive children? What would happen if Achievement Place graduates encountered prejudiced teachers, as described in the Pygmalion Effect,[37] and found no jobs? What would happen if an old-fashioned patrón took over the Vicos hacienda again?

Many programs simply return the individual to the old environment and pay little attention to his future relations with it. Such indifference is usually a corollary of the proposition that the problem lies within the individual and is only minimally affected by the structure and operation of the social environment. For example, a follow-up of the National Training School program graduates showed that, while the recidivism rate was only one-third of the expected normal rate after one year, the two rates were nearly equal after three years. The beneficial effects of the program had just about disappeared, in large part because the youths had returned to the injurious subcultures from which they had come and not to the type of society whose operations, including many rewards and behavior-consequence links, were reflected in the operation of the cottage where they had stayed.[38]

Clearly, the failure of program graduates to maintain the new behaviors cannot be ascribed to any shortcoming of the program, but instead is due to the fact that individuals returned to the same old environment which had produced the problem-behaviors and deficits in the first place. Before we condemn a program, then, we must take a careful look at what happens to the people at whom it is directed, be they children in a Head Start project, delinquents, or adults in various rehabilitation enterprises. In all too many instances, a person's experiences with a program approach the ABA experimental design. In this well-known research design, the original situation (A) is observed, then the experiment (B) is performed, and finally the original situation (A) is reinstated. If the original behavior is affected by the experimental manipulation, it should recur at the end. In many ways a program of action is equivalent to the experimental (B) stage, but the goal of a program is to modify the behavior permanently. To make sure that change is permanent, people should not be returned to the original (A) context immediately.

[37]Rosenthal and Jacobson (1968).
[38]Cohen and Filipczak (1971), chapter 7.

If the newly acquired behavior patterns make people more competent to deal with their environment, these new skills in effect produce a new environment, in the sense of actualizing many of its potential responses (see chapter 5), and the new activities will be maintained. But when this does not happen to the required degree we will have to help out by restructuring the relevant aspects of the environment outside the program setting, much as the physicians required the temporary assistance of the patient's relatives after she left the hospital in order to maintain her eating habits.

Conclusions

These eight requirements of successful program implementation can be easily derived from our behavioral model of man, and it is obvious that the four cases come rather close to meeting them. Yet it is legitimate to ask whether these requirements also must be met—and indeed *can* be met—by large-scale programs designed to operate in a free and open society rather than in a schoolroom or an isolated Peruvian valley. The answer, unfortunately, is not comforting: as far as we can tell today, these requirements *must* be met if a program is to be successful, and the degree of success will depend, ultimately, on the degree to which they *are* met.

Whenever we confront a problem and formulate appropriate actions we should ask not only, "What policy do we follow?" but also, and primarily, "What will happen when we follow it?" Thus, when we begin to implement a program, we should not so much look up at the policy it represents as down at its consequences; after all, the important question is, "What behaviors of whom does it affect in which way, and when?" One cannot evaluate policies on their own level of generality, especially not those which at first glance appear to be global and humanitarian, for the quality of a policy does not reside in the results it is supposed to have or which we might desire, but rather in its actual behavioral consequences.

DOING GOOD

Much of what is presently done to ameliorate social and individual problems is classified as "doing good." The rarity of success and the frequency of ineffective and even thoughtless action have contributed to making "do-gooder" a pejorative term, and the question arises whether it is possible for a program designer to escape such a label.

Ideally, attempts to "do good" are designed to ameliorate people's temporary and long-terms difficulties, either by helping them to help themselves or, less frequently, by changing the circumstances in which they find themselves. Thus, according to the arguments presented in the preceding three chapters, one would prescribe a program for modifying the behaviors and deficits which constitute the problem, the behavioral determinants within the social context, or both.

But what do we see when we look at past and present efforts to "do good"? In general, the procedures employed are those which are commonly called "humanitarian." All too often, however, we find that the core of the program consists of the indiscriminate distribution of what the designers view as essential for "the good life," regardless of the recipients' actual needs and behaviors. That is, the donor operates in terms of his own perception of other people's deprivations and his own view of reinforcing, neutral, and aversive events. Furthermore, material goods are usually presented on the basis of the donor's conception of what normal people (*i.e.,* those like him) need now or have a right to, again as defined by what he himself believes. We will not go into the moral implications of such actions, and pass over the outrage which often is directed toward recipients who fail to do what is expected of them—*i.e.,* behave in ways roughly similar to those of him who does good. Our concern, rather, is the relation of such a program's goals with the procedures used to achieve them.

He who wishes to "do good" would probably attempt to comfort the anorexia patient by continuing the old system of providing her with all the pathetic amenities which a hospital can offer. He would shower the hyperactive pupils with care and attention, for he would see them as being sick, too. He might give the pre-delinquents one more chance and, upon their failure, send them to a psychiatrist, reform school, or mental institution (to which he would have also sent at least one of Hamblin's students). And he would send care packages to Vicos, containing food, medicine, and tools. But such procedures, as we have seen, can lead to slight improvement at best, and in many cases might actually aggravate the problem.

Programs of "doing good" are usually predicated on psychodynamic models which view most problems as being due to individualistic internal factors. This leads to a definition of "humanitarian" efforts in terms of custodial care and the satisfaction of presumed needs, to the exclusion of considering what people actually do and what their context does to them. Hence the emphasis on amelioration rather than solution, on helping individuals live in their context rather than on changing the context itself and, thereby, the lives of individuals.

In reality, then, "doing good" usually has opposite effects of those intended, and a behavioral model of man tells us why this is so. Through the indiscriminate distribution of material goods one in effect provides reinforcers; but since there are no free-floating S^r, as we showed in chapter 4, one usually reinforces precisely those activites or behavior deficits which made the "doing good" necessary in the first place. In short, by "doing good" one often maintains the wrong behavior patterns, and thus in effect "does evil."

If one really wanted to do good, in the sense of helping people to help themselves now and in the future, one would make a careful, hard-nosed analysis of the behavioral referents and determinants of the problem. Thus we should ask, "What do these people do, or what are their characteristics, that make us come to their assistance?" Then we would ask, "What maintains these activities, or what are the environmental consequences of their characteristics?" The answers would lead us to design a program of behavior modification—of target activities and their determinants in the social context—as described in preceding chapters. The essence of helping others help themselves is twofold: to assist people in acquiring those behavior patterns which will enable them to receive the normal amount of reinforcement from their context; and/or to modify their context so that existing behaviors will be more rewarding. Which aspect is necessary, or what combination of them, will depend on the behaviors, people, and situations, and cannot be determined in an *a priori* fashion.

The cases described in this chapter indicate that even methods which at first glance appear questionable in the short run often are precisely those which in the long run are humanitarian. To be truly humanitarian requires not so much that one give a person something, but that one analyze a situation and then engage in a course of action based on principles which have been derived from a valid model of man. To truly do good requires not so much that our heart speak as that our brain work and our vision not be obscured by tears.

CONCLUSION

The requirements and characteristics of implementation described in this chapter provide little more than the essential skeleton of successful program implementation. Additional factors, such as the nature of the population, the kind of target activity toward which a program is directed, and the character of the social context with its political, cultural, and historical values, are equally important ingredients in determining a course of action and its overall effectiveness. Thus, while we have attempted to indicate some requirements of implementation in general, we could only illustrate the variety of people, problems, and contexts one might encounter. No one book can reflect the rich variety of social life, and especially when we are interested in the implementation of procedures, we can do little more than give general descriptions, guidelines, and sketches of the "usual" methods.

Once we understand basic learning principles, once we know the factors and processes involved in the establishment, maintenance, modification, and extinction of behavior, once we know the general procedures which have proven effective in the past, then we must apply them to the problems which vex us within the particular situations surrounding us. We can learn much from examples, but in the end we must somehow, on our own, combine the principles with the real world and do what is necessary to modify the behaviors of groups of people. The word "somehow" is used advisedly, to indicate that there is no specific set of detailed directions we can follow. The general rules are quite clear: "look for the deprivations," "reinforce immediately," and so forth, but to act accordingly requires considerable insight into particular situations and empathy for individuals. Unfortunately, no guide can show us exactly where to find the reinforcers or precisely how to gain an understanding of the myriad situations which make up a complex, dynamic society, any more than books can show a physician all he needs to know.[39]

The psychological literature of the last two decades demonstrates an increasing interest in behavioral models of man, and during the past few years we have learned much about the principles and limitations of behavior modification. Yet much remains to be learned and understood. At the moment only a handful of social scientists are using behavioral models in their work, and the number of policy makers, program designers, and change agents with an explicit behavioral perspective is small. But if past experience is any guide the fact that it generally takes several years for knowledge in one field to be accepted and employed in another indicates that the future will bring widespread social applications of the behavioral perspective.

While this may please those who know of unfortunate human beings and situations similar to the ones we saw in the four cases described in this chapter, one might also ask what kind of society we will then live in. During the last two thousand years the dominant models of man have been largely theological and psychodynamic, each with important ramifications for both the structure and operation of social systems. What does the future hold if behavioral models should become dominant? In the next chapter we will take a look at this question.

[39]For a discussion of procedures and problems one is likely to encounter in any attempt to modify behavior in the natural environment, see Tharp and Wetzel (1969).

8
Prospects

What will the future be like? Will ours be a society without freedom and dignity, designed by behavioral engineers and supervised by big brothers? Will there be room for poets and dreamers, for laughter and tears? Will there be a place for creativity and conflict, for progress and change? What will happen to deviants, the Rilke and Beethoven to come, the Van Gogh and Rodin of the future? These and similar questions are being asked with increasing urgency as behavioral principles are applied to an ever widening array of individual and social problems and become known to and accepted by the general public. Many who ask are fearful and foresee little good.[1] In this chapter we will provide some answers, on the basis of both psychological principles and knowledge of social structures and processes.

Any attempt to seek objective answers must take into account the several fundamentals of the behavioral perspective outlined in previous chapters: (a) learning principles describe relationships, constitute a *formal* model of man, and have little content; (b) an individual's context, and the social structure as such, are significant aspects of any analysis of social life; (c) learning principles by themselves are not sufficient to define the major goals and purposes of a social program; and (d) procedures derived from

[1] For a discussion of these topics, see the essays in Wheeler (1973).

learning principles are ethically neutral. These elements, when they are combined with a nation's cultural characteristics and historical trends, allow us to sketch at least the parameters of its future.

THE CHARACTER OF
THE MODEL

A behavioral model of man can tell us little about the specific content of a culture or the ideal characteristics of a society; it does not indicate what the class structure should be, whether governments should support the performing arts, or what the style of clothing should be. Rather, the model describes many of the essential principles which underlie the structure and operation of a viable social system, such as behavior-consequence linkages and the absence of free-floating reinforcers. From these principles we can derive conclusions about the way judicial systems should be structured or the way schools should operate, but the specific content of these institutions—*e.g.,* what is to be punished or taught—cannot be specified.

A behavioral model of man can tell us little about human ideals, the way men should behave, what people should strive for, believe in, or disparage; it does not indicate whether one should be oriented toward achievement or self-knowledge, whether one should prefer Beethoven over Mozart, El Greco over Rembrandt. The model simply describes how people learn, how behavior is maintained, and what can be done to modify activities. By emphasizing the social context, though not to the exclusion of internal states, the model focuses attention on the environment and what might be done to produce a more humane social structure—one which is more likely to achieve the goals defined and accepted by a culture.

Finally, a behavioral model of man can tell us little about the goals of social designs, the purposes a program should have, or the ends toward which we should direct our efforts; it does not require that men be literate, that there be music appreciation programs, or that we attempt to make people politically sophisticated. Instead, the model describes the structure of potentially successful designs, the best methods for achieving a goal, and the principles involved in effective implementation.

We must conclude, therefore, that it is up to citizens and politicians, artists and authors, to define the goals, purposes, and ends of social systems and programs. In both social analysis and the design of programs we find that learning principles lend themselves to many uses, that they may be employed by anyone for almost any purpose, although not necessarily with success. Thus, behavioral models of man provide us with tools, though not the only ones, that are necessary for building a world that can be better, or worse, than the one we live in today. Will we use these tools? Will we use them wisely? And toward what ends will we use them?

Much of what we read today about behavior and its modification, and most critical discussions of this area, are concerned with three major topics: (1) learning principles, (2) their individual and social implications, and (3) behavioral philosophy. The basic learning principles, summarized into one or another behavioral model of man, are supported by considerable and largely unchallenged empirical evidence. At present there is much uncertainty, however, about the models' implications for the daily lives of individuals and the character of society. All too often inferences are drawn from inappropriate societal extensions of individualistic principles or exclude social and cultural elements altogether. Furthermore, many of the consequences for individuals and society which one perceives and dreads, such as a world approaching Orwell's *1984,* are greatly influenced by one's predilections, hopes and fears, and general conception of man and view of history.

Behavioral philosophy, finally, attempts to describe and reconstruct all of man and much of society on the basis of operant principles, instead of viewing these principles as describing only one aspect of individuals.[2] Many of these attempts are idiosyncratic and repel or appeal on bases which have little to do with the learning principles themselves. Here we find debates about such issues as individuals' freedom and responsibility, the mind-body problem, the reality and role of emotions, the kinds of factors necessary for the explanation of "love" and "altruism," and the question of whether these topics and others associated with a complete image of man can be answered in terms of learning principles alone. As the neurophysiologist Pribam points out, the extreme "realist" position of Skinner is difficult to reconcile with recent studies that demonstrate the importance of "cognitive organization" in behavior and processes occurring within individuals.[3]

Unfortunately, these three initially separate topics have become so indistinct that one is often uncertain about the basis of a particular statement or prediction. All too often principles, implications, and philosophy are fused into one amorphous position that is difficult to reconcile with available evidence. For example, many people, including Skinner himself, think that the widely discussed social implications of "operant conditioning" follow from learning principles; in fact, most of the implications, especially the more dramatic visions of a new societal order based solely on the operant conditioning paradigm, have been derived not so much

[2]For examples, see Skinner (1971; 1972).
[3]Pribam (1973).

from behavioral principles developed in the course of work with humans in a free environment as from an expressly "realist" or behavioral philosophy which denies the existence of anything that appears to be mental or internal or that is derived from introspection. It may well be that Skinner has done a disservice with his later publications, for they have led to a confusion of behavioral principles with behavioral philosophy, to an erasing of the line between logical extension and mere speculation about the future.[4] Consequently, many people today think of, evaluate, and reject the principles when their actual target is the philosophy. Unfortunately, such a rejection of behavioral philosophy and its presumed societal implications, perhaps justified, may well lead to a disregard of learning principles, depriving social analysts and program designers of valuable and effective tools.

"INDIVIDUALISTIC" AND "STRUCTURAL" APPROACHES

As we pointed out in chapters 3 and 4, the behavioral perspective inevitably leads from an initial concern with individuals to the study of their social context, and from there to an analysis of the structure and operation of neighborhoods, cities, institutions, and nations. Thus we move from psychological principles governing behavior to sociological propositions about organizations and larger systems, and especially to the examination of social change, of human intervention and guidance. In chapters 5 and 6 we showed how the behavioral perspective indicates in both general and specific terms which characteristics of society must be changed in what way. Since most of these characteristics upon careful dissection turn out to consist of behaviors, and since we know how these can be modified, there is at least a theoretical possibility of bringing about and guiding social change in benevolent directions. As we showed in chapter 5, the individualistic and structural approaches to the analysis of societal phenomena, and thus social problems and change, are complementary; each has virtues and limitations and both are necessary for the designing and implementation of social programs.

The possibility and methods of behavior modification, as illustrated by the several cases described in chapter 7, and the recognition of social structures and processes as complex systems of behaving, interrelated individuals, together provide a firm basis for an optimistic appraisal of future possibilities. Man does make himself—he always has, he cannot help doing so. The difference between the present and the past is that now we

---

[4]Pribam (1973).

know how. Not perfectly yet, to be sure, but reasonably well. Some sociologists are optimistic about the future and others are pessimistic, depending on their image of society and their beliefs about the course of change.[5] An important source of these views, however, is one's model of man. Freud's model, for example, cannot help but instill pessimism because man is forever tied to infantile wishes and subject to societal repression, whereas the largely contentless behavioral model we have described says little about human imperatives and leaves the shape of the future to man's ingenuity. Indeed, the malleable character of behavior and the possibility of altering existing patterns provide solid grounds for considerable optimism. Once we know the social learning basis and the situational character of human aggression,[6] for example, we can propose and implement programs to reduce debilitating aggression and design social systems in which there will be much less.

While such a social design will have individualistic components—derived from answers to such questions as, "Under what conditions will aggression be minimal?"—its structure will have to conform to basic societal requirements. A behavioral analysis, in short, cannot remain psychological but naturally becomes sociological. A nation's stratification system, its educational and economic institutions, and religious and governmental organizations are all part of the analysis of social behavior.

PROGRAMS AND GOALS

The path from principles and theories to successful applications in the real world is a long and arduous one. We usually find that there is a gulf between propositions and effective designs, and often it is difficult within the constraints that are part of the world to bridge the gap between procedures derived from principles and actual implementation. Principles, propositions, and even procedures rarely tell us in minute detail what must be done, when, and under what circumstances. The history of rocketry, for example, shows that knowledge of principles of combustion and propulsion was of little importance until the gradual development of techniques enabled engineers to transform propositions and formulas into modules and engines. Both in the early days and in later large-scale efforts to reach the moon and probe the planets, engineering problems presented the major barriers to successful missions.[7]

Psychological and sociological propositions can be easily enough incorporated into a social design. The problems of implementation, of what

[5]Killian (1971); Kunkel (1966).
[6]Bandura (1973).
[7]Von Braun and Ordway (1969).

to do when, however, are matters to be decided by human ingenuity, limitations, and caprice. He who would implement a program must combine knowledge of learning principles with an understanding of the population, its cultural and historical context, and the relevant economic, ethical, and political considerations. No proposition can tell us how to combine these elements or how to act accordingly.

A more significant problem than that of program implementation revolves around the question of goals. Most behavior modification programs can be viewed from several different perspectives. On the one hand, for example, class-room projects have been accused of being designed largely to create docile children who sit quietly in their seats, look only at their teachers or workbooks, and have few interactions with their peers, until they become unimaginative robots.[8] Thus the application of learning principles can be viewed as a defense of the status quo and as an instrument to perpetuate the kinds of ineffective schools criticized by Silberman.[9] On the other hand, it has been pointed out that basic intellectual skills are necessary to express imagination, and that little learning will occur in disorganized class rooms where children talk to each other, run around, and pay little attention to teachers or books; thus behavior modification programs generally have been designed to produce environments that are conducive to learning and a child's education.[10] A careful reading of program descriptions shows that the goal is not the production of perfectly silent children who stay glued to their seats all day, pay attention continuously, and never let their eyes wander. Rather, most programs have been designed to reduce problem behaviors or to establish activities conducive to higher rates of learning.[11]

Evidently it is quite easy to read positive or negative motives and goals, or even both, into the same design, even when the results of the program indicate simply that there was an increase or decrease in rates. While it is true that the designer must wrestle with the ethical question of whether the target behaviors should be changed and how much, there is little he can do about the interpretations others will attach to the program, its goals and procedures.

The goals of programs in the recent psychological literature involve mainly the development of basic skills necessary for normal existence, and the elimination of detrimental behavior which interferes with a normal, productive life. Modern urban-industrial society usually serves as the major frame of reference. The more general goals implied by these studies

[8]Winett and Winkler (1972).
[9]Silberman (1970).
[10]O'Leary (1972).
[11]Hamblin *et al.* (1971); O'Leary and O'Leary (1972).

revolve around an increase in people's various capabilities: their capacity to take advantage of the opportunities provided by society, to make the best choice of alternatives, and to develop their potential to the fullest. It would be difficult to find fault in these goals.

At the same time, however, the procedures of social programs have been questioned on grounds of legal principles and efficacy. For example, questions have been raised about the legality of producing "therapeutic behaviors" and the definition of "rights to contingencies." For the moment, these questions are centered mainly on the rights of individuals in mental institutions and the legality of procedures used in token economies, but they are equally relevant to other populations and other types of programs, especially when these are on a larger scale.

While some target behaviors, such as personal hygiene, are difficult to criticize on legal grounds, the performance of many other activities which form part of daily life, such as housework, may be viewed as exploitation on the part of an institution. For example, recent court cases indicate "that the law will not tolerate forced patient labor that is devoid of therapeutic purpose and which is required solely as a labor saving technique."[12] Yet it is often difficult to distinguish between therapeutic and nontherapeutic activities, for the label will depend largely on the nature of the individual case. Household tasks may be viewed as part of normal life (hence the learning of them would have therapeutic value) or simply as chores (with little or no therapeutic value). In the end, the line one draws will in part reflect one's model of man and one's assessment of behavioral procedures. A psychodynamic approach to mental illness, which emphasizes the provision of a warm and tender environment conducive to the healing of the patient's internal state, for example, would not define work in the institution as therapeutic unless it were completely voluntary.

A major aspect of any solution is a detailed specification of the behaviors to be shaped, maintained, or modified within a program, and a clearly stated rationale for the several target behaviors, their role in normal life, their effects on individuals, possible long-range repercussions, and societal implications. In most studies the rationale for target behaviors has not been made explicit, largely because the goals were "obviously beneficial" for the individuals concerned. The very real possibility of divergent assessments, however, leads to the conclusion that we can no longer rely on implied justifications.

Many of the contingencies which are altered in the course of behavior modification may be viewed as rights and, therefore, not subject to the more or less arbitrary removal and manipulation sometimes found in social

---

[12]Wexler (1973), p. 10.

programs. It has been correctly argued, for example, that the work performed by mental patients should be voluntary and subject to minimum
wage laws. Furthermore, many of the amenities provided by hospitals may
be defined as patients' rights, such as decent furniture, comfortable quarters, visiting privileges, an open ward, TV in day rooms, a decent quantity
and quality of food, opportunities for exercise, and access to the grounds.
In fact, one court has ruled that "patients have a right to the least restrictive
conditions necessary to achieve the purposes of commitment."[13] Again we
see the importance of models of man, for what is considered to be "necessary" for the achievement of the purpose, presumably rehabilitation, will
depend on the procedures one intends to use, and these are derived from
propositions about human characteristics and the nature of mental illness.

ETHICAL CONSIDERATIONS

The existence and increasing ac eptance of effective procedures
which can be employed to modify behavior within the purview of social
programs raise important ethical questions. As we pointed out in the last
two chapters, these questions arise when one attempts to define criteria for
selecting and defending the purposes of an overall social design, the more
immediate goals of a social program, the choice of procedures to be used,
and the roles of the individuals involved. As the number, scope, and size
of programs increases, the problem of ethics will become ever more significant.[14]

Governments have always attempted to influence people, and sanctions such as the threat or possibility of avoiding punishment have been
used for thousands of years. Effective programs of deliberate behavior
modification based on social learning theories emphasizing rewards, however, have been theoretically possible for only a short time. The ethical
debates engendered by the employment of procedures derived from behavioral models of man, therefore, have a short history, and few of the
answers that have been suggested enjoy widespread acceptance.

Those engaged in programs of social amelioration are not alone today
in facing questions about the ethics of their activities. Even in the field of
medicine, where no one seriously opposes the general attempt to prolong
life and relieve human suffering, the recent development of more effective
procedures, for example in keeping terminal patients alive through the
miracles of modern medicine, has raised new ethical questions, such as

[13]Wexler (1973), p. 12.
[14]For discussions of ethical issues, see Bandura (1969), pp. 81–89, 234–240; Kittrie
(1971); and London (1971), chapter 8.

when it is appropriate to cease administering these miracles, and who should make this decision. But while these particular questions are new, debate on the ethical aspects of medical practice and research has been going on for some time. In this case, resolution of the issue will be aided by the availability of measurable criteria, such as those which provide clear definitions of brain death. But discussions of ethical aspects of social program designs and their implementation have just begun. So far, we can only sketch the problems and indicate the basis of possible solutions. Although a program designer might want to wait until all ethical issues are settled, the imperatives of life in urban-industrial societies require him to begin the planning process immediately, regardless of ethical uncertainties. Even a sketch of the issues, then, should be helpful.

The problem of ethics cannot be avoided or even postponed, because it will become increasingly evident that to "do nothing" is indeed to "do something." As we pointed out in chapters 3 and 4, there are no free-floating contingencies and every behavior eventually has some conse-quence. Thus inaction on anyone's part cannot help but affect the behavior of others. As the citizens of a country become more sophisticated in their understanding of behavioral principles, the need for guiding principles will become more urgent; everyone will face the dilemma of having to make a choice in reacting to people's activities on some basis or other. The traditional norms and values of a society are likely to be of limited use as long as the ethical problems are new, the population is heterogeneous, and variations in beliefs among subcultures are quite common.

How, then, is one to determine whether the design of a social system or the goals of a program are ethically acceptable? There are four possible criteria.

Two of them are based on the concept of competence levels, as described in an extensive literature that has accumulated during the last few years.[15] First, as described in the previous section, most projects di-rected by psychologists have been designed to develop people's basic social and instrumental skills to the point where they satisfy at least minimal requirements for effective communication with peers and officials, for getting and keeping a job, and for dealing with the normal problems that arise in the course of daily life. There is little doubt that such skills benefit both individuals and society while harming neither, and that normal life in the urban-industrial world demands considerable competence in these skills.

Second, if one assumes that human beings have a variety of potential abilities to be developed, talents to be utilized, and creative powers to be

---

[15] As described, for example, in Hunt (1968) and Smith (1968). For specific applications, see Cohen and Roper (1972) and Kohn (1972).

set free, then it would benefit both the individual and society to provide people with the behavior patterns that are necessary for the development of their potentialities. Such requirements vary from one person to another, of course, and cannot be determined until there are some tangible signs of what potentials are involved. The relevant behaviors may be more highly developed basic skills, or they may be special or even esoteric skills. For example, one cannot be much of a poet if one has a limited vocabulary, a composer must know how to write music, and a philosopher must be able to express his thoughts.

We assume that both individuals and groups cannot help but live within a social context, a cultural heritage, and a system of values, to which there is at least minimal adherence. A third criterion, then, is that a program should reflect the consensus of values which operate in the larger social environment.

Finally and most important, a program is ethically acceptable if it produces those alterations in the social structure which are required to maintain the new behaviors of the target population. There is no point in continually "adjusting" individuals so that they will be able to live in a nonsane society; rather, one should attempt to restructure the social system itself. For example, it makes no sense to teach job skills to minorities until structural changes are made to provide opportunities for the exercise and reinforcement of those skills.

We conclude that a social program is ethically acceptable when it meets either the first or second criterion and both of the last two. That is, it must be designed to increase the population's basic skills or to further the development of individuals' potentialities as long as these are consistent with the society's general value system, and it must provide a social context in which these behaviors can be maintained without continued external intervention. To be sure, all criteria, and especially the third, must be interpreted quite broadly and should not reflect the narrow views of only one segment of a nation's citizens. Basic instrumental skills usually are prerequisites for a person's ability to develop his potential, and the latter may include a large variety of endeavors. Creative acts, such as developing new styles of painting, new forms of music, or new ways of literary expression, for example, would be quite possible and even encouraged under the third criterion, for artistic experimentation is an old tradition within the dominant value system of our society. The development of new types of murder or rape, however, is not.

Ethical questions arise not only in connection with a program itself but also regarding the people who design and implement it; "Who controls the controllers?" and "Who watches the big brothers?" are significant questions today, just as they have always been. Questions regarding the extent to which individual characteristics affect a program are yet to be answered, but the nature of behavioral principles and the parameters which they impose on procedures indicate that the roles of designers and implementors is more restricted than many people believe.[16]

Programs in a free environment are likely to fail when behavioral principles are applied in a merely mechanical fashion. It is usually not enough to simply "present an S^r," especially in the early stages of a program and in the case of really novel activities. The selection of effective reinforcers requires considerable insight into the character, history, and present life of a person, and the very process of rewarding often involves subtle factors such as friendliness and a helpful attitude. Yet there are exceptions, and some programs depend for their success on a matter-of-fact atmosphere, where S^r and especially S^a are presented in a neutral fashion.[17] An appreciation of other people, an understanding of the subtleties of the total situation, an awareness of one's own behavior, and an ability to meld all of these into one smooth operation are important aspects of empathy. One might also say that "emotional involvement" is required, not in the sense that one is blind to facts but in the sense that one's eyes are open to all the nuances of another person's view of the world and his position in it.

These aspects of empathy involve relationships among people and dealings with individuals. But what of social life, what of our attempts to plan and implement social programs, to design a humane culture? Here we need an understanding not of one or a few persons, which we could acquire simply by getting to know them, but of large groups and of *man in general.* There are no commonly accepted means for acquiring such an understanding; hence we will mention only two possible ways. One is to live within a group or neighborhood for some time, to experience all of the realities of daily existence which confront the members of the group. The other is to consider the wisdom of great writers, philosophers, and historians. One need not agree with them, by any means, but merely understand what they say and why they say it. When one understands Unamuno's *Tragic Sense of Life,* Burckhardt's works on the Renaissance, and Goethe's *Faust,* for example, one will also have a better understanding of the nonmaterial characteristics and necessities of human existence, of the requirements of social life that lie beyond behavior.

According to an old Chinese proverb, "If the wrong man uses the right means, the right means work in the wrong way."[18] The four ethical criteria described above offer some protection, in the sense that the character of the teacher, for example, matters little as long as the program indeed

[16]Bandura (1969), chapter 3.
[17]Bandura (1969), chapter 5.
[18]Quoted by Jung (1967), p. 7.

increases the basic instrumental skills of pupils. More significant protection against "unscrupulous manipulators," however, is provided by the
character of the behavioral principles themselves. These principles lead to
very complex procedures which, to be effective, must be applied with great
care and skill, with considerable insight, wisdom, and humanity. While
these requirements are no guarantee that "the wrong man" will not employ
the behavioral method, they do reduce the likelihood that "the wrong
man" will be able to make effective use of it; for "the wrong man" is wrong
not only because of his goals but also because he usually lacks the insight,
wisdom, and empathy for human desires and failings necessary for being
the "right man." Furthermore, any attempt to shape behaviors that conflict
with a population's basic values would require more environmental control, especially a much longer time horizon, than historical dictatorships
have had available. From this we should not conclude, of course, that
behavioral principles cannot or will not be used for selfish purposes or by
mean-spirited men, but only that such endeavors are not likely to be
successful when they are performed on a large scale and are directed
toward people with a long history of contrary values.

THE LIMITATIONS OF SCALE

Large social programs are not simply the sums of smaller ones. Typically we find that the populations are greater, that the sets of target behaviors are more complex, and that the relevant social contexts are a more
significant part of the society and thus more difficult to restructure. Yet we
rarely find that those who design and implement large programs have
sufficiently increased control over contingencies and a better understanding of people's deprivations and perceptions. Furthermore, with an
increase in the scale of a program, its targets and societal aspects, new
problems arise. Large populations are generally quite heterogeneous, and
both behaviors and environmental operations are often tied to important
components of diverse ethnic or subcultural value systems and heritages.
    Finally, the increasing number of legal questions which have been
raised about procedures in general, together with the recent development
of judicial guidelines concerning acceptable methods, will limit the conditions in which procedures of behavior modification can be employed.
    There are two major solutions to the problem of scale: first, whenever
possible we should use individualistic reinforcers; and second, a program
should be based on a broad view of the procedures and circumstances that
affect learning and behavior maintenance. Instead of using the relatively
crude and simplistic measures which would be required if one were to
operate with the general cultural definitions of deprivations and rein-

forcers applicable to large populations—for example, money or the threat of fines—one should attempt to work with the specific deprivations and reinforcers that operate in particular smaller groups, such as neighborhoods and perhaps even families. This has been done with considerable success whenever the individuals were well understood and the program, particularly with respect to reinforcers, could be tailored to their special characteristics.

The problem of such specialized programs, however, is that they are rarely feasible when the population is large, heterogeneous, or not well known to those who design and implement the procedures. Material reinforcers are often necessary at the beginning of a program, and only in later stages of behavior modification and maintenance are social, intrinsic, or symbolic reinforcers likely to be effective.[19] Whenever possible, programs should eventually utilize natural social reinforcers, such as pleasure in accomplishment, pride in group membership, and acceptance of the amenities of normal life. Again it remains to be seen, however, whether such procedures, which have been shown to be effective in small groups, can be employed on a larger scale.[20] Pride in one's city's accomplishments, for example, requires a broad perspective and long time horizon, which may be difficult to establish in a highly mobile population that has lost its sense of community.

We should expect, therefore, that in the foreseeable future social designs and programs will be of limited scope. Large-scale programs cannot help but be unwieldy or rely on tenuous assumptions of population homogeneity; both characteristics are likely to reduce the probability of success. If, as a last alternative, a program should come to rely on aversive contingencies or even the use of force as planners and agencies lose their patience, both experimental and historical experience indicate that failure is practically guaranteed.[21]

In short, the kind of grey, robotlike society imagined by alarmed readers of Skinner's books is quite unlikely to come into being.[22] Those who do not understand behavioral principles, and those who know little about the learning and maintenance of behavior, tend to ascribe more power to these principles and imagine a much easier implementation than is warranted. As described in the last chapter, for example, the second "Achievement Place" got off to a poor start because the procedures, while correct in the textbook sense, were not being applied in the right—and we should add "humane"—way. Those who simply read books on behavioral

---

[19]Bandura (1969), chapter 4.

[20]Bandura (1969), pp. 269–278.

[21]See, for example, Bandura (1969), chapter 5.

[22]For a good debate on this issue, see Wheeler (1973).

procedures and know nothing else about human beings will not be able to apply those procedures effectively, for the critical elements for success will be lacking: what one might call an almost intuitive understanding of man, of people and their problems, and a feeling for people's self-conceptions and hopes for the future.

CULTURE AND TRENDS

Any assessment of the social implications which behavioral principles might have, and any conclusions one might reach about the kind of society they are likely to produce must incorporate the constraints inherent in essentially individualistic principles and the general historical trends within a society. It is these trends and the general cultural milieu, rather than learning principles, which will shape the future. Behavioral principles are invariant and have operated for thousands of years, while trends and cultural characteristics fluctuate and vary from one epoch to another.

To be sure, behavioral principles shed considerable light on the operation of large systems, and thus are necessary for sociological analysis and the designing of social programs. Large aggregates, however, and especially self-adjusting social systems, include characteristics and processes beyond those found in individualistic learning. For example, various types of feedback loops, inconsistencies and even conflicts among them, and the conditions for and consequences of mutual causal processes, are typical of social systems and affect their operations and future states.[23] Thus one cannot simply extend behavioral principles to social systems; one cannot simply "add up" individuals to arrive at a society; and it is inappropriate to view learning principles as the only basis of social life.

When we attempt to describe the future we must consider not so much the behavioral principles as the larger trends of social change described by historians, sociologists, and economists. Those who dread a society based on "operant conditioning" and those who fear life in a national Walden II assume that learning principles are modern creations which operate in a cultural vacuum, and that social systems and their histories are largely irrelevant in shaping the future. But those assumptions are false.

Learning principles are as old as mankind, and they have always operated within a culture, within a system of values, and within a historical setting. It is in these other factors that we must seek the roots of a civilization's character and future, for they are responsible for the rise and fall of nations. Individuals have always learned and behavior has always

---

[23]For a discussion of these topics, see Buckley (1967).

been affected by its perceived consequences based on past experiences; but these are not the most important characteristics of a society. *What* people learn, *which* behaviors are followed by *which* consequences—these are the significant elements, and these variables are a function of particular cultures, societies, and historical epochs.

What is new today, then, and the only aspect of behavioral principles that is new, is that man has begun to formulate these principles, to derive procedures from them, to apply these techniques in a deliberate fashion, and to make this knowledge available to all who would design and implement individual and social programs.

The probability of application, the goals to be desired and the methods to be used will depend on the characteristics of the particular society, the parameters defined by its culture and value system. These are by no means static, but vary as a consequence of ongoing trends within the society. Changes in parameters, in turn, will affect these trends. The fabric of the future, therefore, will arise from the interaction of ever-changing trends and limits, of past and present events, and of any one nation and the rest of the world.

The complexity of existing trends, as well as the diversity of directions and rates that have been observed, are illustrated by the variety of views put forward in the last few years. Daniel Bell's vision of post-industrial society, Kenneth Galbraith's description of the new industrial state, Barrington Moore's reflections on past and present human misery, and Amitai Etzioni's concept of an active society all present significant components of the social fabric we are likely to see in coming decades.[24] The diffusion and application of behavioral technology are only two strands, meaningless without the others.

PROSPECTS

Today behavioral principles are as much a part of social life as they have always been. What differentiates the present, and the future especially, from the past is that we now have a better understanding of the conditions and processes of learning and are therefore able to make better use of them. Behavioral principles, which heretofore were known only in rather general and vague forms, such as in proverbial and conventional wisdom, now have been formulated as specific propositions and given an empirical basis. Now we have the technology to build a better world or one that is worse, to create more humane social structures or keep the ones we have.

[24]Bell (1973); Galbraith (1967); Moore (1973); Etzioni (1968a).

And what are "humane" social structures? If we assume that a major purpose of social life is to enable individuals to develop their potentialities to the fullest, given the ideals of a society and the constraints of its cultural heritage, social structures will be "humane" to the extent to which they not only allow but foster and encourage such development for all of a society's members. In concrete terms, this means at the very least that social structures will be open and operate in such a way that individuals are able to acquire the behavior patterns necessary for both adequate role performance in normal daily life and the development of their special talents. Humane social structures would also operate so as to maintain these activities by providing reinforcement for an individual's performance rather than on the basis of extraneous social and physical characteristics, such as class and sex. Equal opportunities and encouragement to gain social and individualistic competence, open and equal exposure to the contingencies available within a nation, and strong behavior-consequence linkages throughout the social system are the hallmarks of life in a humane society.

Those who would go out and design whole cultures on the basis of learning principles, those who would solve social problems by instituting large-scale programs of social reform based on a behavioral model of man, as well as those who dread both of these prospects must never lose sight of the fact that learning occurs *within* a social system. Once we have decided to use a particular model of man we must be careful not to overlook the constraints imposed by cultural definitions of deprivations and contingencies, not to overestimate the efficacy and range of applicability of the procedures derived from our model, and not to underrate the difficulties of actual implementation within a social environment that has a long history. It is all too easy for eager and confident designers to underestimate the degree and extent of environmental control that will be needed to modify behavior and restructure the social environment, and to underestimate the time required for the establishment and modification of behavior in people and their context. Any program design or attempt at implementation which includes an unrealistic view of these factors is bound to fail. During the last thirty years, developing countries have experienced a staggering number of efforts that have failed, programs that were discontinued, and hopes and dreams that have come to naught.

What, then, can we say about behavioral models and the future of man? Quite clearly, learning principles and their implications for social analysis and action do not provide a panacea for the world's ills. Such models provide us with empirically founded principles for study and design, a solid foundation for implementation, but no blueprint for a perfect state or individual happiness. Behavioral principles provide us with a theoretical and practical basis for action directed toward some specific problem, but only if that problem has some measurable dimensions. The model we have described in this book focuses our analysis, channels our actions, describes the requirements for effective implementations of social efforts, and gives us hope for the future. The rest is up to us.

The conscious and widespread recognition of learning principles, both as components of social life and as the basis of deliberate social action, neither constrains nor encourages dreamers, artists, or plodders. We can design a social system with room for painters and philosophers, or we can implement programs that have no place for composers and poets. Creative efforts are honored in most societies and many nations pay homage to those who were once viewed as deviants; hence there is every reason to believe that the future in which we participate, with or without the conscious recognition of a behavioral model of man, will continue to encourage new expressions of the human spirit. In fact, we can now design humane social structures which not only encourage individuals to acquire the basic social and instrumental skills needed for normal life and creativity, but which also provide opportunities and rewards for their expression. The future, then, depends not so much on psychological principles as on what we actually do. True enough, the doing must be based on careful analysis and will require considerable time, much effort, and some sacrifice. Yet a behavioral model of man provides us with a firm basis for effective programs and a reason for optimism, as long as we remember that the designing of a humane culture must aspire to goals that lie far beyond behavior.

References

ABRAHAMSSON, BENGT
 1970 "Homans on Exchange: Hedonism Revived," *American Journal of Sociology,* 76:273–285.
AKERS, RONALD L.
 1973 *Deviant Behavior: A Social Learning Approach.* Belmont: Wadsworth.
ARONSON, ELLIOTT
 1968 "Dissonance Theory: Progress and Problems," in Robert P. Abelson, Elliott Aronson, William J. McGuire, Theodore M. Newcomb, Milton J. Rosenberg, and Percy H. Tannenbaum (eds.), *Theories of Cognitive Consistency: A Sourcebook.* Chicago: Rand McNally, pp. 5–27.
AYLLON, TEODORO, AND NATHAN AZRIN
 1968 *The Token Economy: A Motivational System for Therapy and Rehabilitation.* Englewood Cliffs: Prentice-Hall.
BACHRACH, ARTHUR J. (ED.)
 1962 *Experimental Foundations of Clinical Psychology.* New York: Basic Books.
BACHRACH, ARTHUR J., WILLIAM J. ERWIN, AND JAY P. MOHR
 1965 "The Control of Eating Behavior in an Anorexic by Operant Conditioning Techniques," in Leonard P. Ullmann and Leonard Krasner (eds.), *Case Studies in Behavior Modification.* New York: Holt, Rinehart and Winston, pp. 153–163.
BAILEY, JON S., MONTROSE M. WOLF, AND ELERY L. PHILLIPS
 1970 "Home-based Reinforcement and the Modification of Pre-delin-

quents' Classroom Behavior," *Journal of Applied Behavior Analysis*, 3:223–233.

BAILEY, JON S., GARY T. TIMBERS, ELERY L. PHILLIPS, AND MONTROSE M. WOLF

1971 "Modification of Articulation Errors of Pre-delinquents by their Peers," *Journal of Applied Behavior Analysis*, 4:265–281.

BANDURA, ALBERT

1969 *Principles of Behavior Modification*. New York: Holt, Rinehart and Winston.

1971 "Vicarious and Self-reinforcement Processes," in Robert Glaser (ed.), *The Nature of Reinforcement*. New York: Academic Press.

1973 *Aggression: A Social Learning Analysis*. Englewood Cliffs: Prentice-Hall.

BANFIELD, EDWARD C.

1958 *The Moral Basis of a Backward Society*. Glencoe: Free Press.

1970 *The Unheavenly City: The Nature and the Future of Our Urban Crisis*. Boston: Little, Brown.

BARON, ROBERT A., AND ROBERT M. LIEBERT (EDS.)

1971 *Human Social Behavior: A Contemporary View of Experimental Research*. Homewood: Dorsey.

BARTON, ALLEN H.

1971 "The Use of Surveys in the Study of Social Problems," in Erwin O. Smigel (ed.), *Handbook on the Study of Social Problems*. Chicago: Rand McNally, pp. 85–148.

BAUER, RAYMOND A. (ED.)

1966 *Social Indicators*. Cambridge: MIT Press.

BAUER, RAYMOND A., AND KENNETH J. GERGEN (EDS.)

1968 *The Study of Policy Formation*. New York: Free Press.

BECKER, HOWARD S.

1964 "Personal Change in Adult Life," *Sociometry*, 27:40–53.

1968 "The Self and Adult Socialization," in Edward Norbeck, Douglas Price-Williams, and William M. McCord (eds.), *The Study of Personality: An Interdisciplinary Appraisal*. New York: Holt, Rinehart and Winston.

1970 *Sociological Work: Method and Substance*. Chicago: Aldine.

BELL, DANIEL

1973 *The Coming of Post-industrial Society: A Venture in Social Forecasting*. New York: Basic Books.

BEM, DARYL J.

1970 *Beliefs, Attitudes, and Human Affairs*. Belmont: Brooks/Cole.

BENDIX, REINHARD

1970 *Embattled Reason: Essays on Social Knowledge*. New York: Oxford University Press.

BENNIS, WARREN G., KENNETH D. BENNE, AND ROBERT CHIN (EDS.)

1969 *The Planning of Change* (second edition). New York: Holt, Rinehart and Winston.

BERGER, PETER, BRIGITTE BERGER, AND HANSFRIED KELLNER

1973 *The Homeless Mind: Modernization and Consciousness*. New York: Random House.

BERKOVITZ, LEONARD
1973 "The Case for Bottling Up Rage," *Psychology Today*, 7:24–31.

BERNSTEIN, B.
1964 "Aspects of Language and Learning in the Genesis of Social Process," in Dell Hymes (ed.), *Language in Culture and Society*. New York: Harper and Row, pp. 251–263.

BERTHOFF, ROWLAND
1971 *An Unsettled People: Social Order and Disorder in American History*. New York: Harper and Row.

BETTELHEIM, BRUNO
1943 "Individual and Mass Behavior in Extreme Situations," *Journal of Abnormal and Social Psychology*, 38:417–452.

BLAKE, JUDITH, AND KINGSLEY DAVIS
1964 "Norms, Values, and Sanctions," in Robert E. L. Faris (ed.), *Handbook of Modern Sociology*. Chicago: Rand McNally, pp. 456–484.

BLALOCK, HUBERT M., AND ANN B. BLALOCK (EDS.)
1968 *Methodology in Social Research*. New York: McGraw-Hill.

BLAU, PETER M.
1964 *Exchange and Power in Social Life*. New York: Wiley.
1968 "Interaction: Social Exchange," in *International Encyclopaedia of the Social Sciences*, vol. 7. New York: MacMillan, pp. 452–457.

BLINDER, BARTON J., DANIEL M. FREEMAN, AND ALBERT J. STUNKARD
1970 "Behavior Therapy of Anorexia Nervosa: Effectiveness of Activity as a Reinforcer of Weight Gain," *American Journal of Psychiatry*, 126:1093–1098.

BLUM, ALAN F.
1971 "Methods for Recognizing, Formulating, and Describing Social Problems," in Erwin O. Smigel (ed.), *Handbook on the Study of Social Problems*. Chicago: Rand McNally, pp. 177–208.

BOGUSLAW, ROBERT
1965 *The New Utopians: A Study of System Design and Social Change*. Englewood Cliffs: Prentice-Hall.
1971 "The Design Perspective in Sociology," in Wendell Bell and James A. Mau (eds), *The Sociology of the Future*. New York: Russell Sage Foundation.

BRAUN, WERNHER VON, AND FREDERICK I. ORDWAY III
1969 *History of Rocketry and Space Travel* (second edition). New York: Thomas Y. Crowell.

BROOM, LEONARD, AND PHILIP SELZNICK
1968 *Sociology* (fourth edition). New York: Harper and Row.

BUCKLEY, WALTER
1967 *Sociology and Modern Systems Theory*. Englewood Cliffs: Prentice-Hall.

BURGESS, ROBERT L., AND RONALD L. AKERS
1966a "A Differential Reinforcement Theory of Criminal Behavior," *Social Problems*, 14:128–147.
1966b "Are Operant Principles Tautological?" *The Psychological Record*, 16:305–312.

CAREY, ALEX
1967 "The Hawthorne Studies: A Radical Criticism," *American Sociological Review*, 32:403–416.

CARTER, REGINALD K.
1971   "Clients' Resistance to Negative Findings and the Latent Conserva-
tive Function of Evaluation Studies," *American Sociologist,* 6:118–124.

CASSIRER, ERNST
1944   *An Essay on Man: An Introduction to a Philosophy of Culture.* New
Haven: Yale University Press.

CHEIN, ISIDOR
1972   *The Science of Behavior and the Image of Man.* New York: Basic Books.

CLOWARD, RICHARD A., AND LLOYD E. OHLIN
1960   *Delinquency and Opportunity.* New York: Free Press.

COHEN, ALBERT
1955   *Delinquent Boys.* Glencoe: Free Press.

COHEN, ELIZABETH G., AND SUSAN S. ROPER
1972   "Modification of Interracial Interaction Disability: An Application of
Status Characteristic Theory," *American Sociological Review,* 37:643–657.

COHEN, HAROLD L., AND JAMES FILIPCZAK
1971   *A New Learning Environment.* San Francisco: Jossey-Bass.

COLE, STEPHEN, AND ROBERT LEJEUNE
1972   "Illness and the Legitimation of Failure," *American Sociological Review,*
37:347–356.

COLEMAN, JAMES S.
1964   "Implications of the Findings on Alienation," *American Journal of Sociology,* 70:76–78.
1973   "Ten Principles Governing Policy Research," *Footnotes,* 1:3:1.

COLEMAN, JAMES S., ERNEST Q. CAMPBELL, CAROL J. HOBSON, JAMES MCPARTLAND,
ALEXANDER M. MOOD, FREDERICK D. WEINFELD, AND ROBERT L. YORK
1966   *Equality of Educational Opportunity.* Washington: U.S. Government
Printing Office.

DAHRENDORF, RALF
1958   "Out of Utopia: Toward a Reorientation of Sociological Analysis,"
American Journal of Sociology, 64:115–127.
1968   "Sociology and Human Nature: A Postscript to Homo Sociologicus,"
in his *Essays in the Theory of Society.* Standford: Stanford University Press.

DEFLEUR, MELVIN L., AND FRANK R. WESTIE
1963   "Attitude as a Scientific Concept," *Social Forces,* 42:17–31.

DELAMATER, JOHN
1968   "On the Nature of Deviance," *Social Forces,* 46:445–455.

DOBYNS, HENRY F., PAUL L. DOUGHTY, AND HAROLD D. LASSWELL (EDS.)
1971   *Peasants, Power, and Applied Social Change: Vicos as a Model.* Beverly
Hills: Sage Publications.

DOBZHANSKY, THEODOSIUS
1959   "Human Nature as a Product of Evolution," in Abraham H. Maslow
(ed.), *New Knowledge in Human Values.* New York: Harper and Row, pp.
75–85.

DOLLARD, JOHN
1937   *Caste and Class in a Southern Town.* New Haven: Yale University
Press.

DOLLARD, JOHN, AND NEIL E. MILLER
1950   *Personality and Psychotherapy.* New York: McGraw-Hill.

DONIGER, S. (ED.)
1962   *The Nature of Man.* New York: Harper and Row.

DRUCKER, PETER F.
1974   *Management: Tasks, Responsibilities, Practices.* New York: Harper and Row.

DUMONT, RICHARD G., AND WILLIAM J. WILSON
1967   "Aspects of Concept Formation, Explication, and Theory Construction in Sociology," *American Sociological Review,* 32:985–995.

EMERSON, RICHARD M.
1969   "Operant Psychology and Exchange Theory," in Robert L. Burgess and Don Bushell, Jr. (eds.), *Behavioral Sociology.* New York: Columbia University Press.
1972   "Exchange Theory," in Joseph Berger, Morris Zelditsch Jr., and Bo Anderson (eds.), *Sociological Theories in Progress,* vol. 2. Boston: Houghton Mifflin, pp. 38–87.

EMPEY, LAMAR T.
1973   "Reactions to Coleman on Policy Research," *Footnotes,* 1:6:4.

ERASMUS, CHARLES J.
1961   *Man Takes Control: Cultural Development and American Aid.* Indianapolis: Bobbs-Merrill.

ETZIONI, AMITAI
1968a   *The Active Society: A Theory of Societal and Political Processes.* New York: Free Press.
1968b   "Basic Human Needs, Alienation, and Inauthenticity," *American Sociological Review,* 33:870–885.
1971   "Policy Research," *American Sociologist,* 6:8–12.

FEAGIN, JOE R.
1972   "God Helps Those Who Help Themselves," *Psychology Today,* 6:6:101–110.

FERMAN, LOUIS A.
1969   "Some Perspectives on Evaluating Social Welfare Programs," *Annals,* 385:143–156.

FISCHER, CLAUDE S.
1973   "On Urban Alienation and Anomie: Powerlessness and Social Isolation," *American Sociological Review,* 38:311–326.

FISHBEIN, M.
1966   "The Relationship Between Beliefs, Attitudes, and Behavior," in S. Feldman (ed.), *Cognitive Consistency.* New York: Academic.

FIXSEN, DEAN L., ELERY L. PHILLIPS, AND MONTROSE M. WOLF
1973   "Achievement Place: Experiments in Self-government with Predelinquents," *Journal of Applied Behavior Analysis,* 6:31–48.

FORRESTER, JAY W.
1969   *Urban Dynamics.* Cambridge: MIT Press.

FOSTER, GEORGE M.
1965   "Peasant Society and the Image of Limited Good," *American Anthropologist,* 67:293–315.

1967   *Tzintzuntzan: Mexican Peasants in a Changing World.* Boston: Little, Brown.
1973   *Traditional Societies and Technological Change* (second edition). New York: Harper and Row.

FREUD, SIGMUND
1930   *Civilization and Its Discontents.* London: Hogarth Press.

FRIEDAN, BETTY
1963   *The Feminine Mystique.* New York: W. W. Norton.

FROMM, ERICH
1955   *The Sane Society.* New York: Rinehart.
1959   "Value, Psychology, and Human Existence," in Abraham H. Maslow (ed.), *New Knowledge in Human Values.* New York: Harper and Row, pp. 151–164.

GALBRAITH, JOHN KENNETH
1967   *The New Industrial State.* Boston: Houghton Mifflin.

GANS, HERBERT J.
1968.   *People and Plans: Essays on Urban Problems and Solutions.* New York: Basic Books.
1971   "Social Science for Social Policy," in Irving I. Horowitz (ed.), *The Use and Abuse of Social Science.* New Brunswick: Transaction Books, pp. 13–33.

GEERTZ, CLIFFORD
1965   "The Impact of the Concept of Culture on the Concept of Man," in John R. Platt (ed.), *New Views of the Nature of Man.* Chicago: University of Chicago Press, pp. 93–118.

GERTH, HANS AND C. WRIGHT MILLS
1953   *Character and Social Structure: The Psychology of Social Institutions.* New York: Harcourt Brace Jovanovich.

GIBBS, JACK P.
1965   "Norms: The Problem of Definition and Classification," *American Journal of Sociology,* 70:586–594.
1968   "The Study of Norms," in *International Encyclopaedia of the Social Sciences,* vol. 2. New York: MacMillan, pp. 208–213.
1972   *Sociological Theory Construction.* New York: Dryden Press.

GLADWIN, T.
1967   "Social Competence and Clinical Practice," *Psychiatry,* 30:30–43.

GOLD, MARTIN
1970   *Delinquent Behavior in an American City.* Belmont: Brooks-Cole.

GOLD, MARTIN, AND JAY R. WILLIAMS
1969   "The Effect of 'Getting Caught': Apprehension of the Juvenile Offender as a Cause of Subsequent Delinquencies," *Prospectus,* 3:1:1–38.

GOODENOUGH, WARD H.
1963   *Cooperation in Change.* New York: Russell Sage Foundation.

GOODMAN, PAUL
1960   *Growing Up Absurd: Problems of Youth in the Organized Society.* New York: Random House.

GOULDNER, ALVIN
1970   *The Coming Crisis of Western Sociology.* New York: Basic Books.

GUITERAS-HOLMES, CALIXTA
1961   *Perils of the Soul: The World View of a Tzotzil Indian.* New York: Free Press.

HAGEN, EVERETT E.
1962   *On the Theory of Social Change.* Homewood: Dorsey.

HALL, CALVIN S., AND GARDNER LINDZEY
1970   *Theories of Personality* (second edition). New York: Wiley.

HALL, R. VANCE, SAUL AXELROD, LUCILLE TYLER, ELLEN GRIEF, FOWLER C. JONES, AND ROBERTA ROBERTSON
1972   "Modification of Behavior Problems in the Home with a Parent as Observer and Experimenter," *Journal of Applied Behavior Analysis,* 5:53–64.

HAMBLIN, ROBERT L., DAVID BUCKHOLDT, DANIEL FERRITOR, MARTIN KOZLOFF, AND LOIS BLACKWELL
1971   *The Humanization Processes: A Social, Behavioral Analysis of Children's Problems.* New York: Wiley.

HAMBLIN, ROBERT L., AND PAUL V. CROSBIE
1972   "Remediating Anomie." Paper presented at the Denver meeting of the American Sociological Association.

HANEY, BILL, AND MARTIN GOLD
1973   "The Delinquent Nobody Knows," *Psychology Today,* 7:4:49–55.

HEIDT, SARAJANE, AND AMITAI ETZIONI (EDS.)
1969   *Societal Guidance: A New Approach to Social Problems.* New York: Thomas Y. Crowell.

HEMPEL, CARL G.
1966   "Recent Problems of Induction," in Robert G. Colodny (ed.), *Mind and Cosmos: Essays in Contemporary Science and Philosophy.* Pittsburgh: University of Pittsburgh Press, pp. 112–134.

HEWITT, JOHN P., AND PETER M. HALL
1973   "Social Problems, Problematic Situations, and Quasi-Theories," *American Sociological Review,* 38:367–374.

HILGARD, ERNEST R., AND GORDON H. BOWER
1966   *Theories of Learning* (third edition). Englewood Cliffs: Prentice-Hall.

HITT, WILLIAM D.
1969   "Two Models of Man," *American Psychologist,* 24:651–658.

HOLLAND, JAMES G., AND B. F. SKINNER
1961   *The Analysis of Behavior.* New York: McGraw-Hill.

HOLLINGSHEAD, AUGUST B.
1949   *Elmtown's Youth.* New York: Wiley.

HOLMBERG, ALLAN R.
1969   *Nomads of the Long Bow: The Siriono of Eastern Bolivia.* Garden City: Natural History Press.

HOMANS, GEORGE C.
1961   *Social Behavior: Its Elementary Forms.* New York: Harcourt Brace Jovanovich.

1964a "Bringing Men Back In," *American Sociological Review*, 29:809–818.

1964b "Contemporary Theory in Sociology," in Robert E. L. Faris (ed.), *Handbook of Modern Sociology*. Chicago: Rand McNally, pp. 951–977.

1974 *Social Behavior: Its Elementary Forms* (revised edition). New York: Harcourt Brace Jovanovich.

HOMME, LLOYD, POLO C'DE BACA, LON COTTINGHAM, AND ANGELA HOMME

1968 "What Behavioral Engineering Is," *Psychological Record*, 18:425–434.

HORNEY, KAREN

1950 *Neurosis and Human Growth*. New York: Norton.

HOROWITZ, IRVING LOUIS (ED.)

1971 *The Use and Abuse of Social Science: Behavioral Science and National Policy-Making*. New Brunswick: Transaction Books.

HUNT, J. McV.

1968 "Toward the Prevention of Incompetence," in Jerry W. Carter (ed.), *Research Contributions to Community Mental Health*. New York: Behavioral Publications, pp. 19–45.

ILLICH, IVAN

1971 *Deschooling Society*. New York: Harper and Row.

INKELES, ALEX

1959 "Personality and Social Structure," in Robert K. Merton, Leonard Broom, and Leonard S. Cottrell (eds.), *Sociology Today: Problems and Prospects*. New York: Basic Books, pp. 249–276.

JUNG, CARL GUSTAV

1961 "Freud and Jung: Contrasts," in his *Collected Works*, vol. 4. Princeton: Princeton University Press.

1963 *Memories, Dreams, Reflections*. New York: Random House.

1966 "Sigmund Freud in His Historical Setting," in his *Collected Works*, vol. 15. Princeton: Princeton University Press.

1967 "Commentary on 'The Secret of the Golden Flower,' " in his *Collected Works*, vol. 13. Princeton: Princeton University Press.

1969 "Analytical Psychology and Weltanschauung," in his *Collected Works*, vol. 8 (second edition). Princeton: Princeton University Press.

KAHN, ALFRED J.

1970a *Studies in Social Policy and Planning*. New York: Russell Sage Foundation.

1970b *The Theory and Practice of Social Planning*. New York: Russell Sage Foundation.

KANTER, ROSABETH M.

1972 *Commitment and Community: Communes and Utopias in Sociological Perspective*. Cambridge: Harvard University Press.

KAZDIN, ALAN E., AND RICHARD R. BOOTZIN

1972 "The Token Economy: An Evaluative Review," *Journal of Applied Behavior Analysis*, 5:343–372.

KELMAN, HERBERT C.

1965 "Manipulation of Human Behavior: An Ethical Dilemma for the Social Scientist," *Journal of Social Issues*, 21:31–46.

KILLIAN, LEWIS M.
1971 "Optimism and Pessimism in Sociological Analysis," *American Sociologist*, 6:281–286.

KINKADE, KATHLEEN
1972 *A Walden Two Experiment: The First Five Years of Twin Oaks Community*. New York: William Morrow.

KIRBY, FRANK D., AND FRANK SHIELDS
1972 "Modification of Arithmetic Response Rate and Attending Behavior in a Seventh-Grade Student," *Journal of Applied Behavior Analysis*, 5:79–84.

KITTRIE, NICHOLAS
1971 *The Right to Be Different: Deviance and Enforced Therapy*. Baltimore: Johns Hopkins Press.

KLAGES, HELMUT
1973 "Assessment of an Attempt at a System of Social Indicators," *Policy Sciences*, 4:249–261.

KOHN, MELVIN L.
1972 "Class, Family, and Schizophrenia: A Reformulation," *Social Forces*, 50:295–304.

KOZOL, JONATHAN
1967 *Death at an Early Age*. New York: Houghton Mifflin.

KUNKEL, JOHN H.
1966 "Individuals, Behavior, and Social Change," *Pacific Sociological Review*, 9:48–56.
1967 "Some Behavioral Aspects of the Ecological Approach to Social Organization," *American Journal of Sociology*, 73:12–29.
1970 *Society and Economic Growth: A Behavioral Perspective of Social Change*. New York: Oxford University Press.

KUNKEL, JOHN H., AND MICHAEL A. GARRICK
1969 "Models of Man in Sociological Analysis," *Social Science Quarterly*, 50:136–152.

KUNKEL, JOHN H., AND RICHARD H. NAGASAWA
1973 "A Behavioral Model of Man: Propositions and Implications," *American Sociological Review*, 38:530–543.

LANGER, JONAS
1969 *Theories of Development*. New York: Holt, Rinehart and Winston.

LEHMAN, EDWARD P.
1971 "Social Indicators and Social Problems," in Erwin O. Smigel (ed.), *Handbook on the Study of Social Problems*. Chicago: Rand McNally, pp. 149–176.

LERNER, DANIEL, AND HAROLD D. LASSWELL (EDS.)
1951 *The Policy Sciences: Present Developments in Scope and Method*. Stanford: Stanford University Press.

LEVY, MARION J.
1952 *The Structure of Society*. Princeton: Princeton University Press.

LEWIS, OSCAR
1964 *Pedro Martinez*. New York: Random House.
1966 *La Vida*. New York: Random House.

LIEBOW, ELLIOTT
    1967   *Tally's Corner.* Boston: Little, Brown.
LIPSET, SEYMOUR M.
    1963   *The First New Nation.* New York: Basic Books.
LONDON, PERRY
    1971   *Behavior Control.* New York: Harper and Row.
LOVAAS, O. IVAR, B. SCHAEFFER, AND J. A. SIMMONS
    1965   "Experimental Studies in Childhood Schizophrenia." *Journal of Experimental Studies in Personality,* 1:99–109.
LOVAAS, O. IVAR, ROBERT KOEGEL, JAMES Q. SIMMONS, AND JUDITH S. LONG
    1973   "Some Generalizations and Follow-up Measures on Autistic Children in Behavior Therapy," *Journal of Applied Behavior Analysis,* 6:131–165.
LOWENTHAL, LEO
    1957   *Literature and the Image of Man.* Boston: Beacon Press.
LYND, ROBERT S.
    1939   *Knowledge for What? The Place of Social Science in American Culture.* Princeton: Princeton University Press.
MACCOBY, ELEANOR E. (ED.)
    1966   *The Development of Sex Differences.* Stanford: Stanford University Press.
MACDONALD, JOHN S.
    1973   "Review" of Dobyns *et al.: Peasants, Power, and Applied Social Change. Contemporary Sociology,* 2:508–510.
MALINOWSKI, BRONISLAW
    1927   *Sex and Repression in Savage Society.* Cleveland: World.
MANIS, JEROME G.
    1974   "The Concept of Social Problem: Vox Populi and Sociological Analysis," *Social Problems,* 21:305–315.
MARX, MELVIN H. (ED.)
    1963   *Theories in Contemporary Psychology.* New York: MacMillan.
MASLOW, ABRAHAM H.
    1954   *Motivation and Personality.* New York: Harper and Row.
    1959   "Psychological Data and Value Theory," in his *New Knowledge in Human Values.* New York: Harper and Row, pp. 119–136.
    1968   *Toward a Psychology of Being* (second edition). Princeton: Van Nostrand.
MATZA, DAVID
    1964   *Delinquency and Drift.* New York: Wiley.
MCCLELLAND, DAVID C.
    1961   *The Achieving Society.* Princeton: Van Nostrand.
MCGINNIES, ELLIOTT
    1970   *Social Behavior: A Functional Analysis.* Boston: Houghton Mifflin.
MCGINNIES, ELLIOTT, AND CHARLES B. FERSTER (EDS.)
    1971   *The Reinforcement of Social Behavior.* Boston: Houghton Mifflin.
MCGREGOR, DOUGLAS
    1960   *The Human Side of Enterprise.* New York: McGraw-Hill.
MCGUIRE, WILLIAM J.
    1969   "The Nature of Attitudes and Attitude Change," in Gardner Lindzey

and Elliott Aronson (eds.), *Handbook of Social Psychology* (second edition), vol. 3. Reading: Addison-Wesley, pp. 136–314.

MEAD, GEORGE HERBERT
1934   *Mind, Self, and Society: From the Standpoint of a Social Behaviorist.* Chicago: University of Chicago Press.

MEDLAND, MICHAEL B., AND THOMAS J. STACHNICK
1972   "Good-Behavior Game: A Replication and Systematic Analysis," *Journal of Applied Behavior Analysis,* 5:45–51.

MEEKER, B. F.
1971   "Decisions and Exchange," *American Sociological Review,* 36:485–495.

MERTON, ROBERT K.
1957   "Social Structure and Anomie," in his *Social Theory and Social Structure.* Glencoe: Free Press, pp. 131–160.
1971   "Social Problems and Sociological Theory," in Robert K. Merton and Robert Nisbet (eds.), *Contemporary Social Problems* (third edition). New York: Harcourt Brace Jovanovich, pp. 793–845.

MEYERSON, MARTIN, AND EDWARD C. BANFIELD
1955   *Politics, Planning, and the Public Interest.* Glencoe: Free Press.

MICHALOS, ALEC C.
1973   "Rationality Between Maximizers and Satisficers," *Policy Sciences,* 4:229–244.

MICHELS, ROBERT
1949   *Political Parties: A Sociological Study of the Oligarchical Tendencies of Modern Democracies.* Glencoe: Free Press.

MILLER, GEORGE A., EUGENE GALANTER, AND KARL H. PRIBAM
1960   *Plans and the Structure of Behavior.* New York: Holt, Rinehart and Winston.

MILLER, L. KEITH, AND RICHARD FEALLOCK
1973   "A Behavioral System for Group Living," in E. Ramp and G. Semb (eds.), *Behavior Analysis and Education.* Englewood Cliffs: Prentice-Hall.

MILLER, NEIL, AND JOHN DOLLARD
1941   *Social Learning and Imitation.* New Haven. Yale University Press.

MILLS, C. WRIGHT
1959   *The Sociological Imagination.* New York: Oxford University Press.

MONTAGU, ASHLEY
1955   *The Direction of Human Development.* New York: Harper.

MOORE, BARRINGTON, JR.
1973   *Reflections on the Causes of Human Misery.* Boston: Beacon.

MUMFORD, LEWIS
1962   *The Story of Utopias.* New York: Viking Press.

MYRDAL, GUNNAR
1962   *An American Dilemma: The Negro Problem and Modern Democracy* (twentieth anniversary edition). New York: Harper and Row.

NEWCOMB, THEODORE M.
1968   "Interpersonal Balance," in Robert P. Abelson, Elliott Aronson, William J. McGuire, Theodore M. Newcomb, Milton J. Rosenberg, and Percy H.

Tannenbaum (eds.), *Theories of Cognitive Consistency: A Sourcebook.* Chicago: Rand McNally, pp. 28–51.

OFSHE, LYNNE, AND RICHARD OFSHE

1970 *Utility and Choice in Social Interaction.* Englewood Cliffs: Prentice-Hall.

O'LEARY, K. DANIEL

1972 "Behavior Modification in the Classroom," *Journal of Applied Behavior Analysis,* 5:505–511.

O'LEARY, K. DANIEL, AND SUSAN G. O'LEARY

1972 *Classroom Management: The Successful Use of Behavior Modification.* New York: Pergamon Press.

OLSON, MANCUR, JR.

1971 *The Logic of Collective Action* (revised edition). New York: Schocken Books.

PADDOCK, WILLIAM, AND ELIZABETH PADDOCK

1973 *We Don't Know How.* Ames: Iowa State University Press.

PAPANEK, GUSTAV F.

1967 *Pakistan's Development: Social Goals and Private Incentives.* Cambridge: Harvard University Press.

PARSONS, TALCOTT

1951 *The Social System.* Glencoe: Free Press.

1958 "Definitions of Health and Illness in the Light of American Values and Social Structure," in E. Gartly Jaco (ed.), *Patients, Physicians, and Illness.* Glencoe: Free Press.

PHILLIPS, ELERY L.

1968 "Achievement Place: Token Reinforcement Procedures in a Home-style Rehabilitation Setting for 'Pre-delinquent' Boys," *Journal of Applied Behavior Analysis,* 3:213–223.

PHILLIPS, ELERY L., ELAINE A. PHILLIPS, DEAN L. FIXSEN, AND MONTROSE M. WOLF

1971 "Achievement Place: Modification of the Behaviors of Pre-delinquent Boys within a Token Economy," *Journal of Applied Behavior Analysis,* 4:45–59.

1973 "Behavior Shaping Works for Delinquents," *Psychology Today,* 7:1:75–79.

PHILLIPS, ELERY, ELAINE A. PHILLIPS, MONTROSE M. WOLF, AND DEAN L. FIXSEN

1973 "Achievement Place: Development of the Elected Manager System," *Journal of Applied Behavior Analysis,* 6:541–561.

POPPER, KARL R.

1959 *The Logic of Scientific Discovery.* New York: Basic Books.

POSTMAN, NEIL, AND CHARLES WEINGARTNER

1973 *The School Book.* New York: Delacorte Press.

PREMACK, DAVID

1965 "Reinforcement Theory," in David Levine (ed.), *Nebraska Symposium on Motivation 1965.* Lincoln: University of Nebraska Press, pp. 123–180.

PRESIDENT'S COMMISSION

1967 *Criminal Victimization in the United States: A Report of a National Survey.* Washington: U.S. Government Printing Office.

PRIBAM, KARL H.
1973 "Operant Behaviorism: Fad, Fact-ory, and Fantasy?" in Harvey Wheeler (ed.), *Beyond the Punitive Society.* San Francisco: W. H. Freeman, pp. 101–112.

PROGOFF, IRA
1956 *The Death and Rebirth of Psychology.* New York: Julian.
1963 *The Symbolic and the Real.* New York: Julian.

RAINWATER, LEE
1968 "The Problem of Lower-Class Culture and Poverty-War Strategy," in Daniel P. Moynihan (ed.), *On Understanding Poverty: Perspectives from the Social Sciences.* New York: Basic Books, pp. 229–259.

RAPOPORT, ANATOL
1966 *Two-Person Game Theory: The Essential Ideas.* Ann Arbor: University of Michigan Press.

REIN, MARTIN
1970 *Social Policy: Issues of Choice and Change.* New York: Random House.

RICHTER, PEYTON E. (ED.)
1971 *Utopias: Social Ideals and Communal Experiments.* Boston: Holbrook Press.

RISCHIN, MOSES (ED.)
1968 *The American Gospel of Success: Individualism and Beyond.* New York: Quadrangle Books.

ROBERTS, RON E.
1971 *The New Communes: Coming Together in America.* Englewood Cliffs: Prentice-Hall.

ROSE, ARNOLD M.
1962 "A Systematic Summary of Symbolic Interaction Theory," in Arnold M. Rose (ed.), *Human Behavior and Social Processes.* Boston: Houghton Mifflin.

ROSENTHAL, ROBERT, AND LENORE JACOBSON
1968 *Pygmalion in the Classroom.* New York: Holt, Rinehart and Winston.

ROTTER, JULIAN B.
1966 "Generalized Expectancies for Internal versus External Control of Reinforcement," *Psychological Monographs,* vol. 80, no. 1.

RUSHING, WILLIAM A. (ED.)
1968 *Deviant Behavior and Social Process.* Chicago: Rand McNally.

RYAN, WILLIAM
1971 *Blaming the Victim.* New York: Pantheon Books.

SAMUELSON, KURT
1961 *Religion and Economic Action: A Critique of Max Weber.* New York: Basic Books.

SARBIN, THEODORE R., AND VERNON L. ALLEN
1968 "Role Theory," in Gardner Lindzey and Elliott Aronson (eds.), *The Handbook of Social Psychology* (second edition), vol. 1. Reading: Addison-Wesley, pp. 488–567.

SCHORR, ALVIN L.
1971 "Public Policy and Private Interest," in Irving L. Horowitz (ed.), *The*

Use and Abuse of Social Science. New Brunswick: Transaction Books, pp. 155–169.

SCHUR, EDWIN M.
1971 *Labeling Deviant Behavior: Its Sociological Implications.* New York. Harper and Row.

SCOTT, JOHN F.
1971 *Internalization of Norms: A Sociological Theory of Moral Commitment.* Englewood Cliffs: Prentice-Hall.

SEEMAN, MELVIN
1959 "On the Meaning of Alienation," *American Sociological Review,* 24:783–791.
1963 "Alienation and Social Learning in a Reformatory," *American Journal of Sociology,* 69:270–284.

SELIGMAN, MARTIN E. P.
1970 "On the Generality of the Laws of Learning," *Psychological Review,* 77:406–418.
1973 "Fall into Helplessness," *Psychology Today,* 7:1:43–48.
1975 *Helplessness.* San Francisco: W. H. Freeman.

SELIGMAN, MARTIN E. P., AND JOANNE L. HAGER (EDS.)
1972 *The Biological Boundaries of Learning.* Englewood Cliffs: Prentice-Hall.

SELIGMAN, MARTIN E. P., S. F. MAIER, AND R. L. SOLOMON
1971 "Unpredictable and Uncontrollable Aversive Events," in Robert Brush (ed.), *Aversive Conditioning and Learning.* New York: Academic Press.

SHELDON, ELEANOR B. AND KENNETH C. LAND
1972 "Social Reporting for the 1970's: A Review and Programmatic Statement," *Policy Sciences,* 3:137–151.

SHORT, JAMES F., AND IVAN NYE
1957 "Reported Behavior as a Criterion of Deviant Behavior," *Social Problems,* 5:207–213.

SHOSTAK, ARTHUR B. (ED.)
1966 *Sociology in Action: Case Studies in Social Problems and Directed Social Change.* Homewood: Dorsey Press.

SILBERMAN, CHARLES E.
1970 *Crisis in the Classroom: The Remaking of American Education.* New York: Random House.

SIMON, HERBERT
1957 *Models of Man.* New York: Wiley.

SKINNER, B. F.
1971 *Beyond Freedom and Dignity.* New York: Knopf.
1972 *Cumulative Record: A Selection of Papers* (third edition). Englewood Cliffs: Prentice-Hall.

SMITH, M. BREWSTER
1968 "Competence and Socialization," in John A. Clausen (ed.), *Socialization and Society.* Boston: Little, Brown, pp. 270–320.

SOLOMON, ROBERT W., AND ROBERT G. WAHLER
1973 "Peer Reinforcement Control of Classroom Problem Behavior," *Journal of Applied Behavior Analysis,* 6:49–56.

SPILERMAN, SEYMOUR, AND DAVID ELESH

1971 "Alternative Conceptions of Poverty and Their Implications for Income Maintenance," *Social Problems*, 18:358–373.

STAATS, ARTHUR W., AND CAROLYN K. STAATS

1963 *Complex Human Behavior: A Systematic Extension of Learning Principles.* New York: Holt, Rinehart and Winston.

STEIN, BRUNO, AND S. M. MILLER

1973 *Incentives and Planning in Social Policy.* Chicago: Aldine.

STEWART, M. A., F. N. PITTS, JR., A. G. CRAIG, AND W. DIERUF

1966 "The Hyperactive Child Syndrome," *American Journal of Orthopsychiatry*, 36:861–867.

STRODTBECK, FRED L., AND JAMES F. SHORT, JR.

1964 "Aleatory Risks versus Short-run Hedonism in the Explanation of Gang Action," *Social Problems*, 12:127–140.

TALLMAN, IRVING, AND REECE McGEE

1971 "Definition of a Social Problem," in Erwin O. Smigel (ed.), *Handbook on the Study of Social Problems.* Chicago: Rand McNally, pp. 19–58.

TARTER, DONALD E.

1970 "Attitude—the Mental Myth," *American Sociologist*, 5:276–278.

1973 "Heeding Skinner's Call: Toward the Development of a Social Technology," *American Sociologist*, 8:153–158.

THARP, ROLAND G., AND RALPH J. WETZEL

1969 *Behavior Modification in the Natural Environment.* New York: Academic Press.

THIBAUT, JOHN W., AND HAROLD H. KELLEY

1959 *The Social Psychology of Groups.* New York: Wiley.

THOMAS, DON R., WESLEY C. BECKER, AND MARIANNE ARMSTRONG

1968 "Production and Elimination of Disruptive Classroom Behavior by Systematically Varying Teachers' Behavior," *Journal of Applied Behavior Analysis*, 1:35–45.

THORNTON, JERRY W., AND PAUL D. JACOBS

1971 "Learned Helplessness in Human Subjects," *Journal of Experimental Psychology*, 87:367–372.

TITTLE, CHARLES R.

1969 "Crime Rates and Legal Sanctions," *Social Problems*, 16:409–423.

TURK, HERMAN, AND RICHARD L. SIMPSON (EDS.)

1971 *Institutions and Social Exchange: The Sociologies of Talcott Parsons and George C. Homans.* Indianapolis: Bobbs-Merrill.

TURNER, RALPH H.

1962 "Role-Taking: Process versus Conformity," in Arnold M. Rose (ed.), *Human Behavior and Social Processes.* Boston: Houghton Mifflin, pp. 20–40.

ULLMANN, LEONARD P., AND LEONARD KRASNER (EDS.)

1965 *Case Studies in Behavior Modification.* New York: Holt, Rinehart and Winston.

VAZ, EDMOND

1966 "Self-reported Juvenile Delinquency and Socio-economic Status," *Canadian Journal of Corrections*, 8:20–27.

VEYSEY, LAURENCE
   1973   *The Communal Experience.* New York: Harper & Row.
VOLKART, EDMUND
   1973   "The Problem of 'Policy,' " *Footnotes* 1:6:4–5.
WARREN, ROLAND L.
   1971   *Truth, Love, and Social Change.* Chicago: Rand McNally.
   1973   "Comprehensive Planning and Coordination: Some Functional Aspects," *Social Problems,* 20:355–364.
WARSHAY, LEON H.
   1971   "The Current State of Sociological Theory," *Sociological Quarterly,* 12:23–45.
WEISS, ROBERT S., AND MARTIN REIN
   1969   "The Evaluation of Broad-Aim Programs: A Cautionary Case and a Moral," *Annals,* 385:133–142.
WEXLER, DAVID B.
   1973   "Token and Taboo: Behavior Modification, Token Economies, and the Law," *Behaviorism,* 1:2:1–24.
WHEELER, HARVEY (ED.)
   1973   *Beyond the Punitive Society: Operant Conditioning: Social and Political Aspects.* San Francisco: W. H. Freeman.
WHITING, BEATRICE B. (ED.)
   1963   *Six Cultures: Studies in Childrearing.* New York: Wiley.
WHITING, JOHN W. M., AND IRVING L. CHILD
   1953   *Child Training and Personality.* New Haven: Yale University Press.
WHYTE, WILLIAM F.
   1969   "Rural Peru—Peasants as Activists," *Trans-Action,* 7:1:37–47.
WICKER, A. W.
   1969   "Attitudes versus Action: The Relationship of Verbal and Overt Behavioral Responses to Attitude Objects," *Journal of Social Issues,* 25:4:41–78.
WILLIAMS, JAY R., AND MARTIN GOLD
   1972   "From Delinquent Behavior to Official Delinquency," *Social Problems,* 20:209–229.
WILLIAMS, ROBIN M.
   1968   "The Concept of Norms," in *International Encyclopaedia of the Social Sciences,* vol. 2, pp. 204–208.
WILLIAMS, WALTER, AND JOHN W. EVANS
   1969   "The Politics of Evaluation: The Case of Head Start," *Annals,* 385:118–132.
WINKLER, WINNETT, AND ROBIN C. WINKLER
   1972   "Current Behavior Modification in the Classroom: Be Still, Be Quiet, Be Docile," *Journal of Applied Behavior Analysis,* 5:499–504.
WINSLOW, ROBERT W., AND VIRGINIA WINSLOW
   1974   *Deviant Reality: Alternative World Views.* Boston: Allyn and Bacon.
WOLPE, JOSEPH, AND ARNOLD A. LAZARUS
   1967   *Behavior Therapy Techniques: A Guide to the Treatment of Neuroses.* New York: Pergamon Press.

WOLPE, JOSEPH, ANDREW SALTER, AND L. J. REYNA (EDS.)

   1964   *The Conditioning Therapies.* New York: Holt, Rinehart and Winston.

WRONG, DENNIS H.

   1961   "The Oversocialized Conception of Man in Modern Sociology," *American Sociological Review*, 26:183–193.

ZALTMAN, GERALD

   1972   *Creating Social Change.* New York: Holt, Rinehart and Winston.

ZURCHER, LOUIS A., AND CHARLES M. BONJEAN (EDS.)

   1970   *Planned Social Intervention: An Interdisciplinary Anthology.* Scranton: Chandler.

Index